DECODING DANIEL

Verse-by-Verse Commentary

BOB CONWAY

DECODING DANIEL

ISBN-13: 978-1499276480
ISBN-10: 1499276486

CONTENTS

CHARTS AND MAPS

Charts

Maps

ACKNOWLEDGEMENTS AND COVER

Acknowledgements

The author wishes to express special appreciation to his sister, Judy A. Weaver, and his loving wife, Lois, for assisting in the preparation of the first manuscript for this commentary.

I am indebted to the members of the Orrstown Church of the United Brethren in Christ, who encouraged my teaching and provided me with the opportunity to teach numerous in-depth Bible studies, including this one, to laity and pastors for continuing education units.

I give thanks to the Most High God for insights into His Word and the ability to synthesize it. If this commentary proves valuable to its readers, to Yahweh be the glory!

The Front Cover

On the front cover, is a winged-lion photo taken by the author at the Louvre, Paris, France. This relief of the winged-lion on enameled brick comes from the Ishtar Gate at Babylon. In the book of Daniel, the winged-lion is a symbol for the Babylonian Empire as well as King Nebuchadnezzar.

PREFACE

The Book of Daniel reveals God's sovereign control of history from 605 B.C. to the Second Advent of Christ. This prophetic writing contains hundreds of predictions that revolve around five overall themes.

1. The Rise and Fall of Four Empires
2. The Coming of the Everlasting Kingdom
3. The Coming Princes
4. The Time of Israel's Distress
5. The End Times

My objective in *Decoding Daniel* is to show history revealing prophecy and prophecy revealing history. Yahweh is the Lord of time and history. He is sovereign over the world, though considerable power and freedom of will have been given to human and angelic beings. Because of this freedom, a great conflict within the physical and spiritual realms is revealed in the Book of Daniel as humans, angels, Satan and God strive to control the future.

God elects to relate to humanity in such a way that humans become a factor in His life and He becomes part of their lives. Because of this interaction, prayers, dreams and visions play a significant role in the events of this book as God reveals the rise and fall of future empires and princes.

Although biblical history shows that God changes in the way He feels, plans, and acts in response to our response to Him, there are boundaries to His change. The LORD responds to human actions without compromising His revealed, unconditional plans and purposes. In addition, He never violates His veracity, righteousness and holiness. Hence, the future God has mapped out in the Book of Daniel will occur.

From the beginning, man's history has been the story of rebellion against God. Instead of developing morally, humanity continues to head down the slippery slope of decadence, declension and destruction. For this reason, God is able to forecast the future with absolute accuracy as He overrules evil for His plans and purposes. Although in some of Daniel's prophecies evil may appear to be victorious, God is working behind the scenes for good. Joseph characterized God's sovereign rule over evil for good in this same way in Genesis 50:20:

> You intended to harm me, but God intended it for good to accomplish what is now being done, the saving of many lives.

Prophetically, the Book of Daniel is the key that unlocks eschatology, the study of the last days. It is indispensable for understanding Christ's predictions and the Book of Revelation. Many of its symbols are employed in diverse ways in the Apocalypse of Jesus Christ.

God's plan for the world is unfolded in amazing detail in Daniel. Nebuchadnezzar's *Dream of the Great Image*, Daniel's dream and visions of *the Four Beasts,* and *the Ram and Goat,* along with Gabriel's unveiling of *the Seventy Sevens* provide the framework for prophetic history from 605 B.C. to the second coming of Christ.

Daniel is written in prose and it differs from other prophetic books of the Bible, which often have their oracles written in poetry. Consequently, it appears in the Hebrew Scriptures among "the writings" and not "the prophets." Nevertheless, Daniel cannot be read like a narrative or novel since it contains images and symbols that need to be decoded before God's plan for the future can be understood. One cannot decode its predictions without first knowing a great deal about the rest of the Bible and history.

The kinds of predictions in the Book of Daniel are twofold. There are "types" or "foreshadowings" concealed within the narratives, and there are revealed dreams and visions of future events, people and places. The prophet has deciphered the dreams and visions with the help of the Spirit of God, the Second Person of the Trinity, and angelic beings. Herein a significant part of the outline of God's plan for "the times of the Gentiles" has been decoded by the prophet. However, decoding the details of this period is left to the readers. I have endeavored to aid in this task by:

1. Connecting the symbolism decoded by Daniel to historical events, people and places.

2. Interpreting and connecting the symbolism that belongs to yet future events, people and places based on other prophecies contained in the Scriptures.

3. Discovering and interpreting the "types" in the narrative sections.

4. Explaining the words that have been closed up and sealed until the time of the end.

Practically, the Book of Daniel abounds with personal applications. Daniel himself models a godly life, blessed by God from teenage years through old age. Hence, a section appears at the end of each chapter, containing a few applications gleaned from Daniel and others mentioned within that chapter. The first six chapters include types also.

With the exception of chapter twelve, which is a continuation of the two previous chapters, each chapter begins with a time line and background material. Chronological dating of Old Testament events varies slightly among scholars. Many variations arise from the Biblical writers themselves. Some count the ascension year as the first year of a king's reign, others do not. Earlier scholars date the fall of Jerusalem in 587 B.C. and Artaxerxes' decree to rebuild Jerusalem in 445 B.C. I have followed the scholars who date these events as 586 B.C. and 444 B.C.

The Book of Daniel has been a battleground of "higher criticism." For instance, liberals view this book as Pseudepigrapha, written to inspire the hopes of the Jewish victims during the Seleucid persecution of 170-165 B.C. I believe it was written by a historical Daniel at the time of the Babylonian exile. One's beliefs and interpretation of Daniel can be a litmus test of conservative or liberal orthodoxy.

The interpretations of Daniel's prophecies sharply divide premillennial views from amillennial outlooks. The reader should find that the exposition in this commentary is conservative and premillennial.

The bibliography, listed at the end of this book, contain the principal works that I utilized in the preparation of *Decoding Daniel*. I recommend that these sources be consulted concerning the hotly debated issues of the authorship, composition and dating of the Book of Daniel.

These sources represent a mix of liberal and conservative scholarship from theologians who hold diverse views.

In this commentary, I have attempted to blend the prophetic and practical teachings of the Book of Daniel, while showing that God ultimately controls every nation, having determined the times set for them and the exact places where they should live. For that reason, I have structured *Decoding Daniel* upon God's Sovereignty in the Rise of Four Hebrews, Five World Empires, and their Princes.

The outline for the chapter headings of this commentary was modified and expanded from an outline constructed by John C. Whitcomb (*Daniel*, 18-19).

May God add His blessing to your study of the Book of Daniel.

Robert P. Conway

INTRODUCTION

Why Study the Book of Daniel?

The importance of the book of Daniel cannot be overstated.

1. It is an indispensable introduction to New Testament prophecy.

2. It bridges the gap between Israel's historical books and the New Testament.

3. It reveals details about the comings of the Anointed One, the Antichrist and other princes.

4. It tells of the Tribulation, followed by the Lord's return.

5. It speaks about the resurrections and the judgments of God.

6. It covers "the Times of the Gentiles."

7. It shows that God is sovereign in the affairs of man.

8. It proves there is a God in heaven who rules history.

9. It uncovers a great spiritual warfare among the angelic and demonic forces.

10. It illustrates what true dedication to God means, and what God is willing to do through, and for, those who are committed to Him.

11. It provides a solid basis for comfort in the midst of adversity.

12. It discloses godly principles for politicians and officials.

13. It offers hope for God's people so they will not fall away.

14. It challenges God's people to faithfulness.

15. It contains an unusual amount of practical truth that is applicable to Christians today.

16. It predicts an everlasting kingdom ruled by the Son of Man.

Daniel reveals:

1. The time of the Messiah's two advents

2. God's interest in, care for, and chastisement of His chosen people

3. Reasons for the Jews to take comfort during the exile

4. There is a God in heaven

5. God hates and judges sin

6. Pride goes before a fall

7. The appropriate responses to crises

8. History in advance

9. God sets the times and boundaries of nations

10. God is faithful to His covenant promises and to His people Israel

11. Israel's deliverance and blessings in the coming Millennial Age

12. God's interest in and care for His chosen people, even when they sin

13. God's infinite superiority over the gods of Mesopotamia

14. God plans for His people from the time of the Babylonian exile until eternity

15. Israel's time of distress

16. The mighty power of prayer

17. The coming of five kingdoms

18. The triumph of the Son of Man

19. The absolute sovereignty of Yahweh

Purpose of the Book

One can discover a multitude of purposes for this book from the lists above. I believe the primary purpose of the book of Daniel is to reveal God's sovereign rule over five kingdoms and their princes. In doing so, it provides God's blueprint of history from the fall of Jerusalem until the establishment of the everlasting kingdom of the Messiah, who is unveiled as "one like a Son of Man."

With the fall of Jerusalem and the exile of Judah, questions arose as to Yahweh's power and place among the so-called deities of this world. This book vindicates Yahweh's power, honor and glory, which is summed up best by King Nebuchadnezzar.

> Then I praised the Most High; I honored and glorified him who lives forever. His dominion is an eternal dominion; his kingdom endures from generation to generation. All the peoples of the earth are regarded as nothing. He does as he pleases with the powers of heaven and the peoples of the earth. No one can hold back his hand or say to him: "What have you done?" At the same time that my sanity was restored, my honor and splendor were returned to me for the glory of my kingdom. My advisers and nobles sought me out, and I was restored to my throne and became even greater than before. Now I, Nebuchadnezzar, praise and exalt and glorify the King of heaven, because everything he does is right and all his ways are just. And those who walk in pride he is able to humble (Daniel 4:34-37).

Historically, the knowledge that Yahweh is sovereign over the nations has been beneficial for Israel. In the second century B.C., it was this knowledge gleaned from Daniel that bolstered the confidence of the Jews. It provided them with a breath of hope while under the persecutions of Antiochus IV Epiphanes. One can anticipate that it will have a similar affect in the last days when the Wilful King attempts to destroy the nation of Israel and the Tribulation saints. Today, this book challenges us to look beyond our own present circumstances and to rely upon the Most High.

Great Conflicts Unveiled

The book of Daniel maps out world history in amazing detail from the time of Nebuchadnezzar's kingdom to the coming of Christ's kingdom. It tells the reader about God's plans for this period, describing it from both man's perspective and God's perspective. The rise and fall of empires are marked by war. There are not only visible wars to be fought by men on the earth, but also invisible battles being waged between the angelic forces of good and evil. The invisible war spills over into the visible realm. In no other book of the Bible is Ephesians 6:12 so apparent:

> For our struggle is not against flesh and blood, but against the rulers, against the authorities, against the powers of this dark world and against the spiritual forces of evil in the heavenly realms.

> Therefore, let us be strong in the Lord and His mighty power by putting on the whole armor of God and by praying (Ephesians 6:12-18).

As the future is disclosed, the events of each chapter manifest great conflicts that take place in the physical and spiritual realms.

Great Conflicts in the Physical and the Spiritual Realms

Indulgence vs. God's Law, 1
Human Wisdom vs. Divine Wisdom, 2
Idolatry vs. True Wisdom, 3
Pride vs. Humility, 4
Sacrilege vs. Sacredness, 5
Human Scheming vs. Providence, 6
Satan's Dominion vs. The Son of Man's Dominion, 7
The Coming Prince vs. The Prince of Princes, 8
Prayer vs. Unbelief, 9
Demons vs. Angels, 10
King of the South vs. King of the North, 11
Mystery vs. Understanding, 12

Daniel the Prophet

The book of Daniel is named for its main character and author. Daniel (דָּנִיֵּאל) means either "God is my Judge" or "God is Judge." The meaning depends on whether the Hebrew *Yod* (י "*i*"), in the middle of the word, is taken as a first person suffix or merely as a connective.

Daniel is called a prophet by our Lord Jesus Christ (Matthew 24:15). However, he does not fit the typical mold of the biblical prophets since his recorded prophecies were not delivered to Israel until after the exile. He did not hold the office of prophet among the Israelites and it appears he had little contact with his own people during the seventy years of exile.

The lineage, appearance, character, and ability of Daniel are exceptional. Daniel's parents are not mentioned, but we know he was "of the king's seed" and "of princes" (פַּרְתְּמִים *partam*) (1:3), a circumstance itself remarkably foretold by the eighth century B.C. prophet Isaiah.

> And some of your descendants, your own flesh and blood who will be born to you, will be taken away, and they will become eunuchs in the palace of the king of Babylon (Isaiah 39:7).

"Eunuch" (סָרִיס *saris*) denotes an official, officer or chamberlain and it comes from the word castrate, since many eunuchs suffered such a fate. In view of the fact that Daniel is described as a "young man without any physical defect" (Daniel 1:4), Isaiah's use of "eunuch" simply indicates an official.

From the testimony of a contemporary, Daniel was known for his righteousness (Ezekiel 14:14, 20) and known by Yahweh for his wisdom (Ezekiel 28:3). He is mentioned in those passages with Noah and Job, who were historical people, so Daniel was also a historical person, not a fictional character.

Nebuchadnezzar, one of the most capable of ancient rulers, expected to have in his regime the best talent his new empire could provide. He found none equal to Daniel the statesman. Daniel was a man of perception, purpose, principle, prayer, purity and power. He was touched (נגע *naga`*) five times by heavenly beings: (1) to make him see (8:18-19); (2) to give him skill (9:21-22); (3) to make him stand (10:10-11); (4) to make him speak (10:16); and (5) to make him strong (10:18).

What God thought of Daniel is revealed when he is addressed as "highly esteemed" by heavenly beings (Daniel 9:23; 10:11, 19). Daniel stands as one of the most admirable of God's servants in the OT. From boyhood through old age, Daniel never compromised his faith in God. He was a man of conviction and courage to the end. He dared to be a Daniel!

Structure and Themes

The general structure of the book is twofold, with the book being written in two languages, Hebrew (chapters 1, 8-12) and Aramaic (chapters 2-7). Chapters 1-6 set forth events in the life of Daniel, especially during his role as an interpreter of dreams under the reigns of Nebuchadnezzar, Belshazzar, Darius and Cyrus. Chapters 7-12 consist of prophetic visions that Daniel received during the reigns of Belshazzar, Darius and Cyrus.

The book is not in chronological order. Chapters 1-6 are characterized by backward reflections. Chapters 5-6 form a transition from story narrative to the apocalyptic section of chapters 7-12.

There are ten individual stories and visions in the book. The first nine follow the chapter breaks; the tenth is covered in chapters 10-12. The visions have the common goal of showing God's rule in the world.

Daniel has two distinct, although related messages to deliver. One is a message of judgment and concerns the defeat and final overthrow of the Gentile world powers, of which Nebuchadnezzar, Belshazzar, Darius and Cyrus were the chief representatives. The other is a message of consolation and hope concerning the future deliverance for God's people, the nation of Israel. The first message is written in *Imperial Aramaic*, an official dialect known in all parts of the Near East during the sixth century B.C. The use of Aramaic is appropriate for the prophet's message as it concerns the future history of the Gentile kingdoms. The second message, which is exclusively directed to Hebrew people, is appropriately written in Hebrew.

The major themes are that God reveals the future and He rules the kingdoms of men. These themes are summarized by three key verses.

> But there is a God in heaven who reveals mysteries. He has shown King Nebuchadnezzar what will happen in days to come (Daniel 2:28).

> The king said to Daniel, "Surely your God is the God of gods and the Lord of kings and a revealer of mysteries, for you were able to reveal this mystery" (Daniel 2:47).

> The Most High is sovereign over the kingdoms of men and gives them to anyone he wishes (Daniel 4:32).

Style and Interpretation

As a whole, the book of Daniel cannot be assigned to any one genre of ancient literature. It contains narratives, biographical writings, dreams, visions, predictions, prayers, letters, and apocalyptic literature. Yet, Daniel, along with the NT book of Revelation and the Apocrypha's book of 2 Esdras, is usually classified as apocalyptic literature.

Apocalyptic is derived from the Greek αποκαλυψις (*apokalypis*), which means "unveiling, uncovering, or revelation." Apocalyptic genre tells history in advance using symbolic terms. Often these symbols are complex, bizarre and strange. Occasionally, the symbols are interpreted by Daniel. His interpretations help identify other symbols.

Decoding Daniel is a matter of interpretation. This study decodes Daniel from a premillennial perspective. Since all the prophecies fulfilled to date were fulfilled literally, this study anticipates the literal fulfillment of the remaining predictions. True to apocalyptic genre, the prophet is told:

> But you, Daniel, close up and seal the words of the scroll until the time of the end. Many will go here and there to increase knowledge (Daniel 12:4).

Interpreting Daniel is complex; it can be likened to interpreting our own

16

historical situation in light of the past and future. This complexity is multiplied by the symbolism in Daniel. The great statue in chapter four, the four beasts in chapter eight, and the ram and goat in chapter nine are perceived to represent future empires. However, the identification of these empires varies, based on four major views: *Traditional, Maccabean, Dispensational* and *Alexandrian*. The dispensational view is held in this commentary.

Apocalyptic genre is employed by the OT prophets, especially Isaiah, Ezekiel, Daniel and Zechariah. No special rules apply in interpreting apocalyptic writings. Therefore, care must be exercised when interpreting apocalyptic genre, especially when employing symbolism from nonbiblical apocalypses.

The Index of Allusions and Verbal Parallels in *The Greek New Testament*, United Bible Societies, third edition, lists more than 125 references to the book of Daniel in the NT. As a result, the NT casts light on the meaning of Daniel's numbers, symbols and vague language. When these meanings are unraveled and decoded, the prophecy is understood. The practical and typical applications of this book abound. Some interesting comparisons can be made between Joseph and Daniel as well as Daniel and Jesus. All three lived an exceptional, impeccable, and uncompromising life, the kind that we should emulate.

Ancient Translations

In the third century B.C., the entire OT as well as the deuterocanonical books were translated into Greek and often were revised by later Greek translators. This Greek translation is known as the *Septuagint* (LXX). It differs radically from the Masoretic text in the Aramaic section of the book of Daniel. The *Septuagint* is plainly based on another line of textual tradition, one that we now sometimes find supported by the Hebrew manuscripts of Daniel discovered at Qumran.

In the *Septuagint*, several additions to Daniel are considered apocryphal. The first set of additions in the LXX is 3:23-90; verse 91 is verse 24 in the Hebrew text. The first twenty-two verses consist of Azariah's prayer in the fiery furnace. Azariah praises God and requests deliverance from

Israel's enemies and for their punishment. The next six verses tell of the special heating of the furnace and the descent of the Angel of the Lord, who put out the fire. The final forty verses are a prayer and praise offered by the three Hebrews for deliverance by the Angel of the Lord. The prayer and praise takes place within the fiery furnace.

The second set is usually counted as three additions, but five different compositions actually are involved. Easily the most popular of these additions is the story of Susanna. It is appended to the book as chapter 13 in the *Vulgate*, a translation of the Bible into Latin, by Jerome, around the turn of the fifth century A.D. Conversely, *Susanna* appears at the beginning of the book in *Theodotion*, a later Greek translation of the OT published under Emperor Commodus (A.D. 180-182). The translations contain somewhat different versions of this story. In addition, the *Vulgate* adds as chapter 14, "Bel and the Dragon," which is really two separate stories as the title suggests. The apocryphal additions are not covered in this commentary.

Peshitta, the Syriac or Aramaic version of the Bible, was translated by Christians in Syria in the second century A.D. Its readings sometimes support the Hebrew text and sometimes support the *Septuagint*.

In the Critics' Den

Daniel has suffered more in the critics' den than in the lions' den. His book has been the object of more negative criticism than any other book of the OT. In the third century A.D, its authenticity was first challenged by the Neo-Platonic philosopher Porphyry. He alleged that the book was a forgery written during the Maccabean period inasmuch as the history of this period is so clearly detailed in the book. Modern criticism follows this rationalistic conclusion.

Perhaps nowhere has the impact of "higher criticism" been so great or so startling as with the book of Daniel. German criticism under the likes of Wellhausen, Holscher, von Rad, Gunkel, and Schweitzer did not regard the "apocalyptic" language in Daniel as genuine but as later additions. These critics held that "apocalyptic" and "eschatological" genre were optimistic, postexilic developments.

Chapter 11 of Daniel is one of the most amazing chapters in the Bible. It exactly details nearly one hundred thirty-five historically verified events more than two hundred years before they occurred. Therefore, critics deny the historicity of the book of Daniel itself. They believe the book is a pseudepigraph written to buoy the hopes of the victims of Seleucid persecution, somewhere between the beginning of Seleucid persecution in 167 B.C. and Judas Maccabeus' rededication of the Temple in 164 B.C.

In 1947, the discovery of the Dead Sea Scrolls disproves this theory. The documents themselves date from the mid-third century B.C. to A.D. 68; the majority was composed during the first century B.C. and first century A.D., with the oldest manuscripts being biblical ("Dead Sea Scrolls," *1999 Encyclopedia Britannica*).

The range of criticism of this book is wide. Critics found "bones to pick" with virtually every early chronological reference in the book. They also criticized the existence of Darius the Mede, Daniel's use of "Chaldean," Nebuchadnezzar's madness, Nabonidus' extended absences at the oasis in Tema, Greek terms used in Daniel, etc. The critics have been proven wrong by archeology. In fact, archeological finds indicate that only a person living in Babylon during the time of the exile could have written the book. Linguistic studies show that the Aramaic of Daniel closely resembles that of Ezra and the Elephantine papyri, both of the latter part of the fifth century. Thus, Daniel's Aramaic section belongs to the sixth century, not the second century, B.C.

Though many alleged difficulties have been cleared up by archaeological and historical advancements, the book remains a battleground between faith and unbelief. The critics' reasons for dating the book of Daniel in the second century B.C. primarily fall into three assertions.

1. The predictions that have been fulfilled are too minutely correct to have been recorded before they occurred. Hence, it is considered a *vaticinium ex eventu*, a "prediction after the fact," in which the author creates a character of long ago and puts into his mouth predictions of important events that have already happened.

2. The language contains several Greek and Persian words that appear later in history. There are seventeen words from the Persian language, three Greek, and possibly one Egyptian.

3. The book is placed in the Hebrew canon among the Writings— after Esther and before Ezra-Nehemiah—instead of the Prophets. Therefore, it should be considered historical, not prophetic.

These three assertions, once thought to be supported by the strongest evidence, have in recent years given way to new discoveries of Aramaic documents and archaeology. Daniel's familiarity with the individuals as well as with the historical events and customs in the book necessitates a sixth-century date for the book (see bibliography for details).

There is no compelling reason not to date the completion of this book around 530 B.C. The clear testimony of the book itself is that Daniel was the author (Daniel 8:1; 9:20; 10:2). Without question, Jesus and His audience believed in Daniel's authorship of the book bearing his name.

So when you see standing in the holy place "the abomination that causes desolation," spoken of through the prophet Daniel—let the reader understand (Matthew 24:15).

Jewish and Christian traditions hold that Daniel is the author of the book.

Historical Background

The Time of Daniel

The sixth and fifth centuries B.C. was an active period in the ancient world. It was a time when some of the great religions of the world were being formed. Probably the first Persian king to recognize Zoroastrianism, the religion proposed by Zoroaster, was Darius I. Confucius in China and Buddha in India were establishing the religions to be known ultimately by their names. While all of this was taking place, Judaism was emerging among the Jews held captive in Babylon.

In the eighth century B.C., Yahweh had employed the Assyrian Empire to judge the northern kingdom of Israel. Near the close of the seventh century B.C., He raised up a new empire to judge the southern kingdom of Judah.

In 626 B.C. Nabopolassar, a Chaldean, rebelled against Assyria and established the Neo-Babylonian Empire.

In 612, along with Cyaxares the Mede and the king of the Scythians, Nabopolassar destroyed the city of Nineveh.

In 605, the Neo-Babylonian Empire was challenged by the Egyptians under the leadership of Pharaoh Necho, but the forces of Egypt were decisively defeated in the Battle of Carchemish by Nabopolassar's son and successor, Nebuchadnezzar (605-562).

Jehoiakim, King of Judah, whom Necho had placed upon the throne of Judah (2 Kings 23:34), became the vassal of Nebuchadnezzar (2 Kings 24:1), who now occupied Palestine. Nebuchadnezzar deported hostages of the royal family and nobility to Babylon; among those deported were Daniel and his three friends, Hananiah, Mishael and Azariah.

Nebuchadnezzar's great empire did not survive long after the death of its great king. The Neo-Babylonian Empire lasted for about seventy years after the first deportation from Judah in 605. On the 15th of Tishri of 539 B.C. (the Feast of Tabernacles on Israel's calendar), the great empire fell, without a battle, to the Medes and Persians. It had served its ordained purpose.

The Neo-Babylonian Empire

Ten Babylonian Dynasties stretch from Neo-Babylonia back to about 2230 B.C. Many kings of the first nine dynasties are unnamed. From time to time, the flow of these dynasties was interrupted by foreign powers. For instance, Assyrian kings often ruled over Babylon and the two powers were in conflict with one another for centuries.

Daniel lived during the last and greatest of the Babylonian dynasties, which ran from 625 to 539 B.C., a period of eighty-seven years.

The seven kings of this tenth and final dynasty of Babylon were:

Nabopolassar, founder of the Neo-Babylonian Empire.
> Reigned 21 years from 625-605 B.C.

Nebuchadnezzar, the greatest of earthly kings.
> Reigned 43 years from 605-561 B.C.

Evil-Merodach, who was kind to Jehoiachin.
> Reigned 2 years from 561-559 B.C.

Neriglissar, murderer of Evil-Merodach.
> Reigned 3-4 years from 559-556 B.C.

Labashi-Marduk, murdered by conspirators.
> Reigned 9 months in 555 B.C.

Nabonidus, who lived in his royal palace at Tema.
> Reigned 16 years from 555-539 B.C.

Belshazzar, governor of Babylon in Nabonidus' absence.
> Reigned 14 years from 553-539 B.C.

Nebuchadnezzar maintained his country's supreme position until he died. He was proficient in warfare, as well as being an active and successful builder. Architecture and literature flourished during his reign.

In absolute power and grandeur, Nebuchadnezzar ranks supreme until Christ reigns on His throne in Jerusalem. This preeminence was revealed by God in the king's dream of the enormous, dazzling statue, which depicted the king as the "head of gold." Daniel interpreted Nebuchadnezzar's place in history, saying, "You, O king, are the king of kings" (Daniel 2:37-38).

Nebuchadnezzar lived in a time of advancement. Observing the sky in the interest of astrology led to undreamed of advances. The astrologers were able to predict eclipses of the sun and moon. In the Babylonian school of Astronomy, about 750 B.C., observations of the heavenly bodies were recorded. Their studies continued without interruption for over 350 years, the longest series of astronomical observations ever made. The accuracy of their reckoning exceeded that of European astronomers until well into the 18th century.

In contrast to Nebuchadnezzar, Nabonidus, the last of the Babylonian rulers, neglected the empire for digging in ruins. He may well have been the first archaeologist in the world. He caused ruined shrines and temples to be excavated and old inscriptions to be deciphered and translated. However, his absence from the city and throne opened the way for the demise of the empire.

The Babylonian Empire had been raised up as the instrument of God's punishment of Judah. The empire would fall unexpectedly in one night. Babylon would be held accountable for the way it mistreated the apple of God's eye during its destruction of Jerusalem. Once Babylon served God's purpose, Isaiah 12:19-22 would be fulfilled:

> Babylon, the jewel of kingdoms, the glory of the Babylonians' pride, will be overthrown by God like Sodom and Gomorrah. She will never be inhabited or lived in through all generations; no Arab will pitch his tent there, no shepherd will rest his flocks there. But desert creatures will lie there, jackals will fill her houses; there the owls will dwell, and there the wild goats will leap about. Hyenas will howl in her strongholds, jackals in her luxurious palaces. Her time is at hand, and her days will not be prolonged.

The pomp and glory, the power and might of Babylon that "has sinned against the LORD" would be short-lived (Jeremiah 50:10-16). The lofty walls of the city, and its high towers, had been reflected in its waters for a short time. Today, the mighty Euphrates River turns its back on the site of the city; it has chosen a new bed. The little Arab settlement of "Babil" preserves in its name the memory of the proud city—but it lies some miles north of the ruins.

Ironically, by the time Daniel wrote his prophecy, Jerusalem lay in ruins. The Israelites were broken up and scattered everywhere throughout the "Fertile Crescent." Consequently, the book of Daniel was written to offer hope in the midst of despair.

The message of Daniel is that four empires will rise and fall. And yet God's people will not disappear, but will be preserved for a new millennium—"when the God of heaven will set up a kingdom that will never be destroyed, nor will it be left to another people" (Daniel 2:44).

The Babylonian Exile

There were two great watersheds in the history of Israel. The first was the Babylonian exile consisting of the four deportations of 605, 597, 586, and 581 B.C., marked by the destruction of Jerusalem and the Temple in 586 B.C. The second was the A.D. 70 destruction of Jerusalem and its Temple, and the *Diaspora* that accompanied the nation's rejection of Jesus Christ. Out of the first *Judaism* was born; *Zionism* rose from the second.

Apart from the prophetic books of the Bible, the Scriptures reveal little of the exile itself. The prophets Isaiah (distant) and Jeremiah (near) predicted the exile. Daniel and Ezekiel were written during the exile. The postexilic books of Nehemiah and Ezra focused on the return of the Jews and the rebuilding of Jerusalem. The Chronicler, writing after the exile, sketched the source, cause and consequence of the exile.

> The LORD, the God of their fathers, sent word to them through his messengers again and again, because he had pity on his people and on his dwelling-place. But they mocked God's messengers, despised his words and scoffed at his prophets until the wrath of the LORD was aroused against his people and there was no remedy. He brought up against them the king of the Babylonians, who killed their young men with the sword in the sanctuary, and spared neither young man nor young woman, old man or aged. God handed all of them over to Nebuchadnezzar. He carried to Babylon all the articles from the temple of God, both large and small, and the treasures of the LORD'S temple and the treasures of the king and his officials. They set fire to God's temple and broke down the wall of Jerusalem; they burned all the palaces and destroyed everything of value there.

> He carried into exile to Babylon the remnant, who escaped from the sword, and they became servants to him and his sons until the kingdom of Persia came to power. The land enjoyed its Sabbath rests; all the time of its desolation it rested, until the seventy years were completed in fulfillment of the word of the LORD spoken by Jeremiah (2 Chronicles 36:15-21).

Nebuchadnezzar besieged Jerusalem in 588 B.C., and destroyed the city in the summer of 586 B.C. The city of God, along with Solomon's magnificent Temple, was turned to burnt rubble. With the state destroyed, its cultic religion suspended, and the remnant exiled, history within Judah ceased for the next fifty years.

In 701 B.C., the Assyrian Sennacherib claimed to have deported 200,150 people from the northern kingdom of Israel. Only the choicest of Judah's political, ecclesiastical, and intellectual leadership were selected for deportation to Babylonia. A small country like Judah would not have had many educated and skilled citizens. For the three deportations, the number of 4,600 captives is recorded in Jeremiah 52:28-30. In 2 Kings 24:14-16, a higher number of 10,000 is given, which includes officials, fighting men, craftsmen and artists. It is conjectured that only adult males were included in Jeremiah's number.

Only a remnant of Judah was not killed and only the poorest people of the land were left behind. Unlike the Assyrians of the eighth century, Nebuchadnezzar did not import foreigners into the Promised Land. This was a significant benefit to Judah since it eliminated the danger of intermarriage with heathen Gentiles, a development which had become a reality in the North.

The exiles settled in villages and rural areas near the city of Babylon and lived normal lives. Many were content and became integrated into society as they found opportunities to get ahead.

Since the moving from place to place by individuals was dangerous, merchants traveled in caravans or by ship. Without government support and protection, the Jews were in Babylonia for the duration that God had ordained.

Back in Palestine, the prophet Jeremiah kept in touch with exiles by writing letters to them from 598 to 586. Ezekiel, both a priest and a prophet, ministered to the exiles in Babylonia, while Daniel, a statesman and a prophet, served the kings of two empires in the city of Babylon.

The City of Babylon

The name "Babylon" (בָּבֶל (*Babel*) is derived from בָּלַל (*balal*), which denotes "confusion (by mixing)" in Genesis 11:9. The city of Babylon was one of great wealth and magnificence. It was the center of a vast empire, which included all of Mesopotamia and the highlands beyond, as well as Syria and Palestine. The city was built on the monotonous plains, along the banks of the Euphrates River.

Ancient writers describe it as a city surrounded by four walls, each fifteen miles in length. Twenty-four streets ran north and south, and the same number east and west. Each street terminated at one of the one hundred gates in the inner walls. Hence, the city was made up of more than six hundred square blocks. It is said that in the center of each square there was a garden.

Two lines of walls protected the city. A twenty-four-foot wide roadway was between the walls. The inner walls were twelve feet thick, reinforced with towers at sixty-foot intervals. These walls ran three and one-half miles along the north, east and south sides of the city, with the Euphrates River guarding the west side. Similar walls enclosed the suburbs. The outer walls measured twenty-five feet high and eleven feet thick. They enclosed a triangular area occupied by suburbs and another royal palace. Their length was slightly over five miles. Outside the walls, a moat of 262 broad feet gave added protection. The walls were decorated with images of magical animals molded in relief in the brickwork. The animals were glazed yellow and brown against a blue background. For details, maps and pictures of Babylon; see *ISBE*, 1:349-355; *ZPEB*, 1:439-448.

According to the *Esagil Tablet*, the city walls enclosed a huge, seven-stage ziggurat, which rose to the height of 650 feet.

The city of Babylon under Nebuchadnezzar's reign reached the pinnacle of world power, displaying vulgar materialism in its political and religious systems, which were enlarged considerably through the king's conquests.

Babylonian merchants controlled all the trade that flowed across western Asia from the Persian Gulf to the Mediterranean Sea. Nebuchadnezzar spent the tolls of this trade, the tributes of these subjects, and the taxes of his people, in beautifying his capital and assuaging the hunger of the priests. "Is not this the great Babylon that I built?" He resisted the temptation to be merely a conqueror; he sallied forth occasionally to teach his subjects the virtues of submission, but for the most part he stayed at home, making Babylon the unrivaled capital of the Near East, the largest and most magnificent metropolis of the ancient world. Nabopolassar had laid plans for the reconstruction of the city. Nebuchadnezzar used his long reign of forty-three years to carry them to completion. Herodotus, who saw Babylon a century and a half later, described it as "standing in a spacious plain," and surrounded by a wall fifty-six miles in length, so broad that a four-horse chariot could be driven along the top, and enclosing an area of some two hundred square miles. Through the center of the town ran the palm-fringed Euphrates, busy with commerce and spanned by a handsome bridge. Practically all the better buildings were of brick, for stone was rare in Mesopotamia; but the bricks were often faced with enameled tiles of brilliant blue, yellow or white, adorned with animal and other figures in glazed relief, which remain to this day supreme in their kind. Nearly all the bricks so far recovered from the site of Babylon bear the proud inscription: "I am Nebuchadnezzar, King of Babylon" (*The Story of Civilization: Our Oriental Heritage*, 1:224).

This grandiose assertion is echoed by Nebuchadnezzar in Daniel 4:30:

He said, "Is not this the great Babylon I have built as the royal residence, by my mighty power and for the glory of my majesty?"

The ruins of Babylon reveal the grounds for the king's boast. The city contained many elaborate and expensive buildings. In addition, to relieve the homesickness of his wife for her native hills, Nebuchadnezzar constructed, at tremendous expense, the famous hanging gardens.

In 539 B.C., the city of Babylon was captured without a battle by Medo-Persia. Persia used the city as an administrative center. Desiring independence, the Babylonians revolted against Persia in 522, 521 and 482 B.C. The last revolt, during the reign of Xerxes, ended with the destruction and desolation of the magnificent city. Yahweh had executed His promise.

> Because of the LORD's anger she will not be inhabited but will be completely desolate. All who pass Babylon will be horrified and scoff because of all her wounds (Jeremiah 50:13).

The Religious Crisis

Daniel was taken as a captive to this magnificent city in the first deportation in 605 B.C. Some Israelites were deported elsewhere. The elderly Jeremiah, along with fellow citizens, were forced to go to Taphanhes (Daphnae), Egypt (Jeremiah 43:7). The exiles that went to Egypt fared well. They were hospitably received and apparently prospered, though they probably lived in segregation within its large cities. Interestingly, Yahweh advised the exiles to make the best of their situation.

> Build houses and settle down; plant gardens and eat what they produce. Marry and have sons and daughters; find wives for your sons and give your daughters in marriage, so that they too may have sons and daughters. Increase in number there; do not decrease. Also, seek the peace and prosperity of the city to which I have carried you into exile. Pray to the LORD for it, because if it prospers, you too will prosper (Jeremiah 29:5-7).

Compared to the Israelites' poor little country of Palestine, Babylonia was a big, rich and prosperous country. Here the exiles found an advanced culture, big business and materialistic splendor. For a long time, Babylon had been a center of trade. Ezekiel referred to it as "a land of merchants" and "a city of traders" (Ezekiel 17:4). The agricultural people of Palestine were introduced to a new way of life.

Life for the Hebrew exiles was comparatively pleasant—very different from their ancestors' life in Egypt. They maintained some of their own institutions, enjoyed freedom of movement as well as employment opportunities, and lived on fertile land. Still the captivity was intended as a punishment from God. The emotional trauma of being uprooted from their homes, and the humiliation of being forced to endure captivity, would have been felt most keenly at the beginning of the exile. At the end, relatively few Israelites desired to return to their homeland.

In spite of their comfortable life in Babylon, the Israelites questioned God's justice (Ezekiel 18:2, 25). Through tears, they cried out for mercy (Psalm 74), but could see no end to their fate because their ears and hearts were shut to God's prophets, especially to Jeremiah.

> This is what the LORD says: "When seventy years are completed for Babylon, I will come to you and fulfill my gracious promise to bring you back to this place (Jeremiah 29:10).

Wholesale loss of faith threatened the exiles. Compared to the undreamed of wealth and power around them and the magnificent temples of the pagan gods, what advantage did the worship of Yahweh have to offer? Besides, had not Yahweh failed to protect them from Nebuchadnezzar and his gods? Israel's faith was on trial for its life!

For many, life in Babylonia was not difficult; they grew wealthy and amalgamated with society as evidenced by archeological discoveries. Excavations at Nippur (a great mercantile center) which was situated on the great canal (Kebar River) unearthed a large number of tablets containing business transactions, which included the names of many Jews.

The exile was a time, not only of humiliation and sorrow, but also of radical changes in nearly every area of life for the Israelites. Many were from the southern kingdom of Judah and they adopted the nickname "Jews."

On the other hand, the hard core exiles remained sojourners in a strange land. They were filled with bitter hatred for those who had brought them to Babylon and longed for faraway Zion (Psalm 137). Clans and families lived together and the elders of Judah continued to be recognized. Hence, a national sense of pride was kept burning.

29

Daniel and his three friends illustrated what it meant to be in the world, but not of the world. They made the most of their situation, never compromising their faith in Yahweh while under the subtle and tenacious influences of Babylon. These four men were shining lights in a dark world; they were living examples that called for no compromise.

Another shining light was the prophet Ezekiel. He was God's messenger among the captives, rebuking them for sin and comforting them with promises of deliverance. His preaching made them realize their captivity was in no way the result of any limitation in God's power to protect them, but it was solely a punishment permitted by Him for their sin.

The seventy years of humiliation during their exile had some obviously beneficial results in the life of the Jews.

1. They were thoroughly cured of idolatry.
2. The synagogue came into existence.
3. They did a great deal of collecting of their literature during this time.
4. Religion became distinctly more spiritual and personal for them since they could not observe the elaborate ceremonies connected with the Temple.
5. The Law of Moses took on new significance in the fire of trials.
6. They became a people more genuinely united in ideals and purpose.
7. They came to a new understanding and appreciation of their destiny as a nation.

Ironically, Yahweh's people had been swallowed by a great fish and they found themselves in the very belly of idolatry. To cure the Israelites of idolatry, God gave them a bellyful of it! And it worked! The Israelites, who came to Babylon as idolaters, returned to their homeland as Jews, having been cleansed of idolatry. Undoubtedly, the prophet's great polemic (Isaiah 40-48) against apostatizing offered comfort to the sojourners.

The people would not be spit out upon the land until the Promised Land had enjoyed its Sabbath rests and the remnant had a change of heart concerning who actually rules history. That was the resounding message given by the two exilic prophets Ezekiel and Daniel, and was typified by the prophet Jonah.

Babylon was the cradle of false religion, with Satan working behind the scenes. False religion first appeared with the tower of Babel, on the plain of Shinar (Babylonia). It was man's first attempt to establish a central, one-world government without God as its king. *The Chaldean Mysteries* can be traced to the days of Semiramis, the wife of Nimrod, who lived a few centuries after the Flood. By the time of the exile, these mysteries permeated most areas of life. See Alexander Hislop's *The Two Babylons* for the extent that the Chaldean mysteries saturated the ancient world.

The Neo-Babylonian age may be properly designated as a religious age. In our culture, we cannot begin to fathom the intensity, depth, and importance that religion played in the lives of the people in the Ancient Near East. There were four-thousand gods in the Babylonian pantheon. These gods went through many changes in name, function and prominence through wars and mystical events.

The city of Babylon was a scene of idolatry. Inscriptions tell us there were 58 temples, 55 shrines dedicated to Marduk, 300 shrines for celestial divinities, 180 altars for the goddess Ishtar, 180 altars to the gods Negral and Adad, and 12 other altars to various deities (*Babylon and the Bible*, 53).

Entrance into the city of Babylon was through eight gates, each named for a deity. The Ishtar gate opened onto the Procession Way, which led to the great temple of Marduk. The gate's walls were decorated with enameled bricks portraying 120 lions, representing Ishtar, and 575 dragons, representing Marduk, and numerous bulls, representing Bel or Enlil (*Wycliffe Historical Geography of the Bible Lands*, 31). The cover photo of a winged-lion from the Ishtar Gate is an example of the enameled bricks.

A diagram, appearing in Alan Millard's *Treasures from Bible Times* (Lion Publishing Corp, 1985), shows nine gates passing through three sets of walls that open into the city. These gates are the Ishtar, Sin, Marduk, Zababa, Enlil, Urash, Shamash, Adad, and Lugalgirra. Each gate was named for a deity. Archeologists have excavated four of the gates. It should be noted that descriptions of the city sometimes disagree.

During the exile, the most important gods and goddesses in the Babylonian pantheon were:

> Marduk is the patron deity of the city of Babylon.
> Ishtar is the goddess of fertility and battle.
> Sin is the moon god.
> Nimurta is the god of hunting and warfare.
> Shamash is the sun god.
> Adad is a storm god.
> Enlil is the god of the wind and sky.
> Urash is the god of the city of Dilbat.

The thousands of gods in the pantheon were not worshiped in the same way, nor did they possess the same power. Marduk reigned as the supreme god in the pantheon, making Babylon's polytheism somewhat monotheistic as gods were identified as Marduk. This hypothesis is apparent from the following extract from the "Monotheist Tablet."

> Ninib is Marduk of the garden (or strength).
> Nergal is Marduk of war.
> Zagag is Marduk of battle.
> Enlil is Marduk of lordship and dominion.
> Nebo is Marduk of trading.
> Sin is Marduk the illuminator of the night.
> Shamash is Marduk of righteousness.
> Rimmon is Marduk of rain.
> (*In and Around the Book of Daniel*, 96).

Nebuchadnezzar rebuilt the temple, known as Esagila, for Marduk. It was the most important building in the city. In addition, the king's palace was a palace of heaven and earth, a palace of the lordship, a palace that was built to honor Marduk, where all deities came and paid homage.

The most important religious and political celebration in Babylon was Akitu, the New Year Festival. The chief figure in these rites was Marduk. Akitu provided an occasion for the annual re-investiture of the king as well as the symbolic reenactment of the creation of the world and the fixing of destinies for the coming year.

An excavated prayer of Nebuchadnezzar reveals the king's faith in Marduk prior to his encountering the Most High.

> To Merodach (Marduk) my lord I prayed, I lifted up my hands:
> 'O lord merodach (Marduk), wisest of the gods, mighty prince,
> thou it was that createst me,
> with sovereignty over multitudes of people that didst invest me.
>
> Like dear life I love thy exalted lodging place: in no place have I
> made a town more glorious than thy city of Babylon.
> According as I love the fear of thy divinity, and seek after thy
> lordship, favourably regard the lifting up of my hands, hear my
> supplication!
>
> I verily am the maintaining king, that maketh glad thine heart,
> the energetic servant, that maintaineth all thy town
> (*In and Around the Book of Daniel*, 97).

Other excavated inscriptions by Nebuchadnezzar, however, show that he saw himself as totally controlling his god Marduk. He believed that he could change the mind of his god by offering sacrifices of meat, fruit and vegetables to Marduk. Hence, his own fate was self-determined. Yet, the king said he organized his armies because "he trusted in the power of Nebo and Marduk." He neglected no opportunity to exalt Marduk above all other gods (*ANET*, 307). Consequently, Nebuchadnezzar should be viewed as having monotheistic tendencies when interpreting the events surrounding him in the book of Daniel.

From birth to death, the life of the Babylonian citizen was governed by religious conceptions and practices. Babylonians believed the future could be controlled and predicted. Everything that happened was a result of cause-and-effect relationships. Many things relating to life could be ascertained by observing the course of events, though the courses of events were in the hands of the gods. To the contrary, the very events and prophecies of the book of Daniel are a polemic against Babylon, the great prostitute of religion. Consequently, his book clarifies Yahweh's sovereignty in the affairs of humanity, not the pantheon of Babylon.

The Outline of Daniel

I. God's Sovereignty in the Rise of Four Hebrews, 1
(Written in Hebrew)

II. God's Sovereignty in the Rise of Five World Empires, 2-7
(Written in Aramaic)

   A. Nebuchadnezzar's Dream of the Great Image, 2
(God Sets the Times and Boundaries of Five World Empires)

      B. Nebuchadnezzar's Golden Image and Fiery Furnace, 3
(God Preserves Daniel's Friends in the Fiery Furnace)

         C. Nebuchadnezzar's Dream of the Tree, 4
(God Humbles Proud Nebuchadnezzar)

         C. Belshazzar's Blasphemous Feast, 5
(God Judges Blaspheming Belshazzar)

      B. Darius' Den of Lions and Decree, 6
(God Preserves Daniel in the Lion's Den)

   A. Daniel's Dream of the Four Beasts, 7
(God Judges Four World Empires)

III. God's Sovereignty in the Rise of Princes, 8-12
(Written in Hebrew)

   A. Daniel's Vision of the Ram, the Male Goat, and the Little Horn, 8
(Israel's Persecution)

   B. Daniel's Prayer and Vision of the Seventy Sevens, 9
(The Coming of Two Princes)

   C. Daniel's Vision of the Latter Days, 10-12
(Israel's Tribulation and Restoration)

      1. Invigorated for the Prophecy, 10
      2. Israel's Foreordained History, 11:1-12:3
         a. Two Empires:
            1. Medo-Persia, 11:1-4
            2. Egypt and Syria, 11:5-20
         b. Two Princes:
            1. Antiochus Epiphanes, 11:21-35
            2. The Wilful King—The Antichrist, 11:36-39
         c. Two Events:
            1. The Mid-Tribulation Crisis, 11:40-45
            2. The Final Deliverance of Israel, 12:1-3
      3. Instructions and Inquiries Concerning the Prophecy, 12:4-1

GOD'S SOVEREIGNTY

IN THE RISE OF FOUR HEBREWS

Daniel and His Friends' Captivity in Babylon (Daniel 1)

Time Line

YEAR B.C.	608	605	598	597	586
JUDAH	Jehoiakim		Jehoiachin	Zedekiah	Jerusalem's Fall
BABYLON		Nebuchadnezzar			
PROPHETS		Daniel & Ezekiel in Babylon			

Outline of Chapter One

Crisis Point: The Fulfillment of Prophecy, 1
Captive Situation: Humbled By God, 2
Crucial Test: Temptations to Conform, 3-7
Critical Choice: Yahweh or Marduk, 8-13
Commendable Decision: Way Out of Temptation, 14
Consequent Blessing: God's Response to Resolution, 15-20
Coincident Prophecy: Typical Fulfillment, 21

Background of Chapter One

In 722 B.C., the northern kingdom of Israel fell to the Assyrians. A century later, three powers beat the war drums to gain supremacy in the Middle East. In 616, Napolassar, king of Babylon, invaded Assyria. With the help of the Medes, he besieged Nineveh in 612. In 610, the fall of Haran to Babylon prompted Egypt and Assyria to join forces. In 609, Pharaoh Necho marched north and Josiah, king of Judah, was killed attempting to block his way at Megiddo, resulting in Necho's domination of Palestine and Syria. In Jerusalem, the prophet Jeremiah delivered God's decree.

> Therefore the LORD Almighty says this: "Because you have not listened to my words, I will summon all the peoples of the north and my servant Nebuchadnezzar king of Babylon," declares the LORD, "and I will bring them against this land and its inhabitants and against all the surrounding nations. I will completely destroy them and make them an object of horror and scorn, and an everlasting ruin. I will banish from them the sounds of joy and gladness, the voices of bride and bridegroom, the sound of millstones and the light of the lamp. This whole country will become a desolate wasteland, and these nations will serve the king of Babylon for seventy years. But when the seventy years are fulfilled, I will punish the king of Babylon and his nation, the land of the Babylonians, for their guilt," declares the LORD, "and will make it desolate forever" (Jeremiah 25:8-12).

In December 604 B.C., Jehoiakim had cut to pieces Jeremiah's prophetic scroll (Jeremiah 36:9-32), including this prophecy of the seventy-year captivity under Babylon. One can rip and tear prophecy from the pages of Scripture, but it changes nothing. Judah's days were numbered.

By 607 B.C., the young and energetic Babylonian crown prince, Nebuchadnezzar, had begun his attempt to dislodge the Egyptians and Syria. Napolassar lay sick in Babylon when his son Nebuchadnezzar led a surprise attack against Pharaoh Necho and the Egyptian Army at Carchemish. Routing the Egyptians, the Babylonian crowned prince pursued them through Syria, Phoenicia, and Palestine and stopped to besiege Jerusalem in 605 B.C. Yahweh gave Jehoiakim, king of Judah, into his hands.

God Rewards Those Who Fear Him

CRISIS POINT: THE FULFILMENT OF PROPHECY (1:1). Jehoiakim became the vassal of Nebuchadnezzar in the summer of 605 B.C. The king of Judah might have been deported if the conqueror had not received bad news; his father had died on August 15 or 16.

37

Nebuchadnezzar hastily returned to Babylon by way of the Arabian Desert to secure the throne for himself. He arrived either on September 6 or 7, 605 B.C., and on the same day ascended to the throne. Now the conquering hero was king of Babylon, which would become the greatest empire of history under his shrewd leadership.

Nebuchadnezzar took the fastest way to Babylon. The members of the royal family of Judah, along with the articles from the temple of God, were taken on the longer trek around the Fertile Crescent. This exportation began the fulfillment of the prediction Isaiah made to King Hezekiah, more than a century earlier.

> Hear the word of the LORD: The time will surely come when everything in your palace, and all that your fathers have stored up until this day, will be carried off to Babylon. Nothing will be left, says the LORD (2 Kings 20:16-17). The prophetic future had arrived for Judah—God rules!

CAPTIVE SITUATION: HUMBLED BY GOD (1:2). It is through the trials and tribulations of life that God molds men for times of crisis. Among the royal family taken captive was a young man of about fourteen to seventeen years of age named Daniel. Like Joseph, Daniel would be tempted, tested and approved for service to God's glory in two pagan empires.

Daniel was born during the reign of the godly king Josiah about 620 B.C. Nothing is known of his parents, except that they were of royal ancestry. He had had opportunity to observe apostasy and was now experiencing firsthand what happens to a people when their leaders are ungodly and compromise God's Word. In 609, death came to Josiah and his religious reforms. The three kings that succeeded Josiah all did evil in the eyes of the LORD. Jehoahaz reigned in Jerusalem three months (2 Kings 23:31-32). He was followed by Jehoiakim, who reigned eleven years (2 Kings 23:36-37). Jehoiachin sat on the throne when Jerusalem was besieged.

> Nebuchadnezzar took Jehoiachin captive to Babylon. He also took from Jerusalem to Babylon the king's mother, his wives, his officials and the leading men of the land (2 Kings 24:15).

Since Daniel revealed and interpreted Nebuchadnezzar's Dream of the Image in the second year of the king's reign (602 B.C., Daniel 2:1), he must have been deported in 605 B.C.

In all likelihood, Daniel knew the predictions of Isaiah and Jeremiah. Now he was witnessing as well as experiencing the fulfillment of prophecy. What impact would this fulfillment have on his life? It was time to find out—and one of God's methods of revealing the impact of His Word on one's life is through testing.

> Remember how the LORD your God led you all the way in the desert these forty years, to humble you and to test you in order to know what was in your heart, whether or not you would keep his commands (Deuteronomy 8:2).

Certainly, captivity would have been a humbling experience. All the grand illusions that might have filled Daniel's heart would have been knocked out of him during the long trek to Babylon. A few descendants of Hezekiah arrived with the kind of heart that God seeks. Four of the royal youths proved to be men of conviction, courage and commitment, displaying an uncompromising character. The rest of the royal family faded from Scripture because they lacked these three essential qualities of faith.

CRUCIAL TEST: TEMPTATIONS TO CONFORM (1:3-7). Ashpenaz, the chief of Nebuchadnezzar's officials selected several handsome, brilliant, teenage boys from the royal family to train for service to the king. The teenagers came from Judah; they still were Israelites, but not for much longer, if Nebuchadnezzar had his way. Temptations for the youths to convert to the ways of Babylon were often subtle.

The king's goal was clear—change their way of thinking! Babylon stamped its mark of ownership on these young men. The chief official gave them new names. From the time that Adam had named the animals in Eden, the right to name had been the mark of dominion. The change of names was the first step in the process of making these men

Babylonians. The four young men mentioned had either the shortened form for God (*el*) or Yahweh (*iah*) in their given Hebrew names.

DANIEL (God is Judge or God is my Judge) changed to
BELTESHAZZAR (The god Bel favors).

HANANIAH (Beloved of Yahweh) changed to
SHADRACH (Illuminated by the Sun God).

MISHAEL (Who is as God) changed to
MESHACH (Who is what the Moon God is).

AZARIAH (Yahweh is my help) changed to
ABEDNEGO (Servant of Nebo/Marduk).

Their names were changed but their allegiance remained faithful to Yahweh

Their changed names reflected that the youths now belonged to the Babylonian gods. The king intended to obliterate any reference to the true God of Israel and to place before the four youths a continuous reminder of the gods of the Chaldeans. Their names were changed, but not their character or allegiance; they would remain faithful to Yahweh.

Placed in a different environment, they were vulnerable to all kinds of influences and temptations. The allurements of the world's luxury, prestige and power were a crucial test of their faith in Yahweh.

Nebuchadnezzar's brainwashing program was to fill the stomach with the sensual, the mind with knowledge and understanding, and the ego with eminence. Here are echoes of the serpent's temptations, first to Eve in the Garden of Eden, and later to Christ in the Judean desert.

Often the adversary's temptations are the same; his methods and packaging of temptation may vary. Jesus was led by the Spirit into the desert to be tempted by the Devil (Matthew 4:1). God had placed Eve in a beautiful garden and allowed the Devil to beguile her. Now Yahweh had brought Daniel and his three friends to the magnificent palaces of Babylon to be tempted by the deceiver.

Temptations Common to Humanity, Eve, Christ and the Exiles

1 John 2:16 Humanity	Genesis 3 Eve	Luke 4 Christ	Daniel 1 Exiles
Lust of the Flesh (*Gratification*)	Good for Food	Turn Stones to Bread	Partake of choice food and drink
Lust of the Eyes (*Greed*)	Pleasant to eyes	Shown the kingdoms of the world for the taking by compromise	Power and prestige for the taking by compromise
Pride of Life (*Gratification*)	Make one wise	Cast yourself down and prove you are the Son of God	Seek the king's approval and be highly esteemed

Consider the difficulty of this test.

1. The king ordered a menu that violated God's Law; the inexperienced youths would have to stand firm against the most powerful adult who ever lived.
2. Disobedience meant severe punishment; obedience to the king's orders would please everyone but God.
3. Disobedience, even if not punished, could work to their disadvantage in respect to future positions.
4. The king's menu appealed strongly to the natural appetites of the four young men.
5. There would be the temptation to reason:

   a. God has not been good to us. Why should we be faithful to His laws?
   b. We were taught to obey those in authority so let's obey King Nebuchadnezzar.
   c. Under normal circumstances, God's Law is to be obeyed, but we are in abnormal circumstances.
   d. Mom and Dad will never know. We're far away from home—who would ever know?
   e. Hey! We're only kids!

These teenagers knew what was right and good under God's Law and its consequences. "Anyone, then, who knows the good he ought to do and doesn't do it, sins" (James 2:4). Their decision not to sin was wise in God's eyes and He would add to their wisdom.

Temptations are tests. This is apparent from the dual meanings of the Hebrew (נסה *nacah*) and Greek (πειρασμος *peirasmos*), which are translated either "tempt" or "test" depending on their context. When Satan tempts one to sin, God tests that person for faith. James 1:2-12 offers insights into the dual temptation and testing of these youths.

Nebuchadnezzar was as much an instrument of the Devil as of God. His motives were worldly and his methods were shrewd attempts: (1) to solicit the good will of the youths; (2) to maintain and develop healthy bodies for his service; (3) to convert them to his religion; and (4) to make them into magnificent statesmen. The youths were to be indispensable assets in building his new empire; and God planned to help him!

CRITICAL CHOICE: YAHWEH OR MARDUK (1:8-13). Nebuchadnezzar was looking to these young men for service in his palace and so was Yahweh. The king was looking on the outward appearance and God was looking at the heart. Both sovereigns wanted the finest to grace the royal court. The chosen royal youths would be without defect, handsome, intelligent, knowledgeable, quick to learn and qualified to serve. How many measured up to the king's qualifications we are not told; only four met God's standard of holiness. The others succumbed to logic, psychology and the temptation to conform.

Human logic would say, "Marduk, Nebuchadnezzar's god, had won. Since Marduk is superior to Yahweh, why obey God's commands?" Psychology would have the youths conform to the present world system: "When in Babylon, do as the Babylonians do!" However, God's people are not to be conformed to the world; they are the salt of the earth and light of the world (Matthew 5:13-16).

When tested to conform, or to not conform, the exiles had an outstanding example from their past to follow. Moses might have been brainwashed in Egypt. He was educated in all the wisdom of the Egyptians and was powerful in speech and action (Acts 7:22), but he would not be corrupted (Hebrews 11:24-26). Likewise, Daniel and his three friends chose not to be brainwashed and corrupted in Babylon.

Many secular universities and colleges are like the Babylonian school— they attempt to have their students conform to a humanistic and atheistic system of values. These values are designed to whitewash God out of the picture, and render young minds brainwashed to serve the adversary of God. The NT urges the believer to "abstain from all appearance of evil" (1 Thessalonians 5:22, KJV).

To eat the king's fare would have the appearance of giving allegiance to the Babylonian gods, especially if the meats came from sacrificial offerings. At the same time, the youths would have been disobeying God's Law regarding the eating of only "clean" foods (Leviticus 11) and meat without blood (Leviticus 19:26; Deuteronomy 12:23).

Why did the youths reject wine since only high priests and kings were not to drink wine nor strong drink (Leviticus 10:8-11; Proverbs 31:4-6)? It is noteworthy that the angel Gabriel said that John the Baptist was not to drink wine nor strong drink (Luke 1:15). There was no prohibition against such drinking for these lads. They chose the uncompromising life, which is characterized by opting for the highest, noblest, and best.

Great men have fallen to the power of strong drink. Belshazzar lost the Babylonian Empire while involved in a drunken feast. History records that Alexander the Great, in a similar vein, lost his world empire at the age of thirty-three. Daniel stands as a polemic against these two rulers in his book.

Daniel and his three friends knew that Yahweh's prophets predicted their coming to Babylon. The youths were still under God's rule. They would pass the crucial test of faith because they feared the LORD.

They chose to eat vegetables, probably edible seeds of leguminous plants, such as peas, beans, and lentils, instead of royal food. Wine and food affect disposition and muscle tone; however, the rapid and favorable results of abstaining were of God, not the diet!

Daniel resolved (literally, "set in his heart") not to defile himself with the royal food and wine and his three friends agreed. The heart is the center of life according to Proverbs 4:23: "Above all else, guard your heart, for it is the wellspring of life." Disobedience defiles the whole person, which is why Daniel says "himself" in 1:8.

Apparently, the four youths had hidden God's Word in their heart. Faithful Jews repeated daily "the Shema" of Deuteronomy 6:4-6:

> Hear, O Israel: The LORD our God, the LORD is one. Love the LORD your God with all your heart and with all your soul and with all your strength. These commandments that I give you today are to be upon your hearts.

Hence, one's heart, soul, mind and strength are defiled by rebellious disobedience. To keep God's commands is to love Him. This crucial test required a crucial decision. Fear man or fear the LORD. It called for strength and courage as well as wisdom. This chapter illustrates the key verse of the Bible.

> The fear of the LORD is the beginning of wisdom, and knowledge of the Holy One is understanding (Proverbs 9:10).

Daniel feared the LORD and in return, he received the wisdom to make his way out of this temptation. The text says, "God had caused the official to show favor and sympathy to Daniel." God led Daniel into trial but provided a way out of temptation.

> No temptation has seized you except what is common to man. And God is faithful; he will not let you be tempted beyond what you can bear. But when you are tempted, he will also provide a way out so that you can stand up under it (1 Corinthians 10:13).

Daniel's request to Ashpenaz, the chief official, was courageous, polite and persistent. It displayed faith and fairness. Nevertheless, Ashpenaz feared the king. If his charges lost weight because of a change of diet or appeared pale and undernourished, he could be beheaded. He was answerable to his superior, who was in this case the hot-tempered monarch of the empire. The official feared the king, but the lads feared

Yahweh. In Acts 5:29, Peter and the other apostles stated what these four knew and understood at a young age: "We must obey God rather than men!"

Daniel was young and daring, but were the odds against him? No! "If God is for us, who can be against us?" (Romans 8:31).

> Dare to be a Daniel,
> Dare to stand alone;
> Dare to have a purpose firm!
> Dare to make it known!

Daniel's courage sets the stage for the upcoming events in his book. The Word of God is plain; one must take a positive stand; dare to stand with the few, or perhaps alone, and trust the grace and power of our faithful God—dare to be a Daniel!

COMMENDABLE DECISION: WAY OUT OF TEMPTATION (1:14). Having his request turned down, Daniel made another sincere effort to keep from sinning against his knowledge of God's Law and therefore against his conscience. Instead of going up the ladder of authority, Daniel appealed to a subordinate of Ashpenaz.

Daniel expected the impossible in ten days—he knew all things are possible with God—his request was made with much more faith than a mustard seed (cf. Matthew 17:20; Luke 17:6). The guard, who was appointed by the chief official, respected Daniel's convictions. Daniel's request was polite and fair; the guard agreed and tested the four youths for ten days. Of course, the foursome never ate the king's fare.

CONSEQUENT BLESSING: GOD'S RESPONSE TO RESOLUTION (1:15-20). Daniel resolved not to defile himself, and God provided a way out of the temptation. The official's heart was supernaturally touched by Yahweh, who had metaphysically touched the bodies and minds of the teenagers. He had given the youths a healthier appearance as well as minds with wisdom and understanding. Why? They feared the LORD!

Daniel attributed his learning as well as his understanding of visions and dreams of all kinds to be gifts from God: "To these four young men God gave knowledge and skill in every aspect of literature and wisdom" (NRSV).

Science began in Egypt and Babylon with the birth of mathematics, metallurgy, anatomy, and astronomy. To the Babylonians we owe the exact measurements of the lunar and solar cycles, the tracing of the paths of the planets, the division of the circle into 360 degrees, and the designation of constellations, notably those of the zodiac. Daniel was no doubt trained in all these sciences.

Daniel learned many language skills. The students would have learned the letters of the Chaldeans, a form of cuneiform or wedge-shaped script used throughout Mesopotamia. Mastering this form of writing was a long and difficult process, which only professional scribes and scholars learned. The language of the Chaldeans was Sumerian, an ancient language of Mesopotamia, which was used as the language of religion and learning, just as Latin was preserved as the language of liturgy in the Roman Catholic tradition. Daniel knew Hebrew, but most likely was taught the Aramaic used in this prophecy.

The extant inscriptions show that there was a palace school with elaborate arrangements for special education. There is no indication in the Babylonian records at what age this education began. The Persians commenced similar education at the age of fourteen and it lasted until the youth was sixteen or seventeen.

Nebuchadnezzar was looking for court advisors with humanistic qualifications; God was seeking a prophet with distinct qualifications, which are inferred by the text. Daniel met the first qualification to become a prophet with his resolute purpose to be holy, undefiled, and separate from sin. The second qualification was met by giving himself diligently to his studies. The third qualification was met when God gave him the gift of knowledge and understanding.

Graduation day for Daniel's class of 602 B.C. came at last. They were ushered into the presence of Nebuchadnezzar with all the royal pomp and circumstance that the occasion demanded. After an intense oral examination, the king found no one was equal to Daniel, Hananiah, Mishael and Azariah among all the magicians and enchanters in his whole kingdom. Final exam completed with flying colors! The students had excelled beyond their teachers. It was time for promotion—the four entered the king's service.

King Nebuchadnezzar was pleased with the results of his training program and so was God. Ten days of trusting God for a better appearance and now ten times better in every matter of wisdom and understanding. Imagine their joy—wiser and firmer in their faith.

> Consider it pure joy, my brothers, whenever you face trials of many kinds, because you know that the testing of your faith develops perseverance (James 1:2).

If Daniel had failed or compromised in his first test, how great would have been his loss! However, he did not fail; he persevered and lived to see the downfall of the empire.

COINCIDENT PROPHECY: TYPICAL FULFILLMENT (1:21). "And Daniel remained there until the first year of King Cyrus." This statement is prophetic in its typical interpretation. Daniel typified the Jewish exiles, remaining in captivity until Cyrus became king.

There is a basic rule of interpreting Scripture, which is often stated:

> All Scripture has but one primary interpretation.
> All Scripture may have several practical applications.
> Many Scriptures have also a prophetic revelation.

Recognizing this basic rule of interpreting Scripture, a few applications and prophetic revelations are interpreted at the end of each chapter. The people and events of the first six chapters are a foreshadowing of future people and events. Hence, the entire book of Daniel is prophetic.

Applications and Typical Prophecies of Chapter One

Daniel and his godly friends foreshadow the nation of Israel to which they belonged. The events in their lives become Israel's history and

47

hope during the "times of the Gentiles." God's people would survive the captivity; they will continue through the times of the Gentiles until the Messiah's reign, which is foreshadowed by Cyrus. At the beginning of Cyrus' reign in 538 B.C., he issued a decree that the Israelites could return to the Promised Land and rebuild the Temple (Ezra 6:3-5). This coincident prophecy is extremely important in light of God's revelation of the "times of the Gentiles" in chapter two. The dream in that chapter provides hope to Israel until the time of the end.

Throughout the Scriptures, God tests His people. Every Christian should anticipate trials, temptations and testing at various times in life. There will be difficult times of distress and suffering. These hardships are like the wind that blows against the young tree and the drought that sends its roots deep to seek moisture. The hardships cause the tree to grow sturdy and strong. Likewise, hardships produce the Christian's personality, faith and hope.

> And we rejoice in the hope of the glory of God. Not only so, but we also rejoice in our sufferings, because we know that suffering produces perseverance; perseverance, character; and character, hope. And hope does not disappoint us, because God has poured out his love into our hearts by the Holy Spirit, whom he has given us (Romans 5:2-5).

The foursome had no hope of returning home, at least not for seventy years. They had every reason for embracing the customs of Babylon. Yet, they believed in Yahweh and acted accordingly, not knowing that the end would be prosperity. Hebrews 11:6 would be illustrated in the life of Daniel beginning with this crucial test.

> And without faith it is impossible to please God, because anyone who comes to him must believe that he exists and that he rewards those who earnestly seek him.

Three men in the OT foreshadow Christ in His anointed offices. Yahweh placed in the palaces of kings at crucial points in the life of His people Israel: Joseph (savior), Moses (king), and Daniel (prophet). Each was endowed with wisdom from above because they rejected the pleasures of this world. Moses rejected Egypt's riches; Joseph rejected Potiphar's wife; and Daniel rejected the king's food and wine. Solomon stands in sharp contrast to these three men. At a young age, God endowed Solomon with wisdom, but the king failed to apply it to his life. As he grew older, he sought the pleasures of this world instead of God and His righteousness. Let us be numbered with Joseph, Moses and Daniel since Christ Jesus has become for us wisdom from God and we have the mind of Christ (1 Corinthians 1:30; 2:16).

Daniel and his friends were some of the best Jerusalem had to offer; they were "the good figs," that would be the hope of the future for Israel according to the LORD in Jeremiah 24.

Daniel stands tall among the heroes of faith in the Bible. His whole life was pure, obedient, and blessed. Daniel shows us what it means to live courageously. His example challenges us to stand true to our Lord and His teachings regardless of the cost. It is easy to fit in with the culture, but the road to blessing is rarely easy. There is a definite connection between the eighth and twenty-first verses of the first chapter: "Daniel resolved" and "Daniel remained."

Psychology would have us conform to the present world system, but the Bible admonishes the Christian not to be conformed to this world.

> Therefore, I urge you, brothers, in view of God's mercy, to offer your bodies as living sacrifices, holy and pleasing to God—this is your spiritual act of worship. Do not conform any longer to the pattern of this world, but be transformed by the renewing of your mind. Then you will be able to test and approve what God's will is—his good, pleasing and perfect will (Romans 12:1-2).

The great lesson of this chapter is "the fear of the LORD is the beginning of wisdom, and knowledge of the Holy One is understanding" (Proverbs 9:10). If we fear the LORD, it is possible to succeed in high school, college, or business and remain a truly separated Christian according to the standard taught in God's Word—Dare to be a Daniel!

GOD'S SOVEREIGNTY IN THE RISE

OF FIVE WORLD EMPIRES

Nebuchadnezzar's Dream of the Great Image
(Daniel 2)

Time Line

YEAR B.C.	609	603	598	597	586
JUDAH	Jehoiakim	Jehoiachin		Zedekiah	Jerusalem's Fall
EVENT		Dream of Dreams			

Outline of Chapter Two

The Aftermaths of Nebuchadnezzar's Dream, 2:1-23
    Nebuchadnezzar's Dream and Distress, 1-3
        Nebuchadnezzar's Unreasonable Request, 4-11
            Nebuchadnezzar's Folly, 12-13
            Daniel's Wisdom, 14-16
        Daniel's Reasonable Request, 17-18
    Daniel's Vision and Praise, 19-23
The Interpretation of Nebuchadnezzar's Dream, 2:24-45
The Declaration of Nebuchadnezzar, 2:46-47
The Advancement of Daniel and His Three Friends, 2:48-49

Background of Chapter Two

THE CHRONOLOGICAL PUZZLE. This chapter opens with a chronological puzzle. Daniel was carried to Babylon in 605 B.C., received three years of training, interpreted Nebuchadnezzar's dream in the second year of the king's reign (602 B.C.), and is promoted to a high position. An inspired writer of Daniel's ability would not make such an obvious contradiction. What happened to the third year?

In their second year of exile (603 B.C.), Daniel and his three friends were examined by Nebuchadnezzar and they entered the king's service. It is reasonable they completed their academic training ahead of schedule since they were ten times better than were their teachers in every matter of wisdom and understanding.

Another solution to this chronological puzzle is that the youths were taken captive in August 605 B.C., but Nebuchadnezzar did not begin his first official year as king of Babylon until the first of Nisan in the following spring (April 4, 604).

Consequently, the youths completed their third year just before Nisan 602, which would still have been the second official year of Nebuchadnezzar (ending April 9, 602).

THE SWITCH OF LANGUAGES. Among the most spectacular discoveries in the Dead Sea Scrolls is the transition in the book of Daniel from Hebrew to Aramaic and then back again to Hebrew. This section (Daniel 2:4b-7:28) was written in Aramaic, whereas the rest of the book was written in Hebrew. Since the Aramaic section covers the "times of the Gentiles," Daniel wrote in the international language so his message could not be missed by the Gentiles of that time.

There are three periods of Aramaic: Old Aramaic (10th-7th centuries B.C.), Official or Imperial Aramaic (6th-4th centuries B.C.), and Western and Eastern Aramaic (3rd century B.C. forward). Aramaic was the language spoken by the Jews coming out of captivity. The Levities had to translate and interpret the Hebrew Scriptures in order for the people to understand what was being read (Nehemiah 8:8). In Jesus' day, the Jews spoke both Aramaic and Greek.

In the Aramaic section, an amazing revelation of world history is set forth from the time of Daniel until the second coming of Christ. In particular, the imagery in Nebuchadnezzar's dream reveals the empires that arise during this period of history. In the Hebrew section, Daniel 9:24-27 provides the outline of Israel's future during the "times of the Gentiles."

God Sets the Times and Boundaries

The Aftermaths of Nebuchadnezzar's Dream

In our day, dreams are usually attributed to physical, emotional and psychological causes. Yet, dreams given by God in order to reveal the future were nothing new in history as can be seen with Abimelech (Genesis 20:3), Jacob (Genesis 28:13), Joseph (Genesis 37:5), Pharaoh (Genesis 44:1, 25), and Gideon (Judges 7:13-15).

The time was ripe for God to reveal the future. His people were captives in a foreign land. The captives and Nebuchadnezzar were faced with an inescapable question, "Who really controls the present and the future— Marduk or Yahweh?" The king was about to find out what Paul declared six centuries later.

> From one man he made every nation of men, that they should inhabit the whole earth; and he determined the times set for them and the exact places where they should live. God did this so that men would seek him and perhaps reach out for him and find him, though he is not far from each one of us (Acts 17:26-27).

Nebuchadnezzar's dream is like a skeleton to which one attaches the tendons and flesh of Biblical prophecy. Many prophecies of Isaiah and Jeremiah are brought together in the book of Daniel. The subsequent visions and dreams in Daniel add many details. In addition, the book of Revelation completes the image and God's forecast of history. Therefore, God gave to Nebuchadnezzar the dream of dreams! God's plan for the times of the Gentiles are encoded in Nebuchadnezzar's dream and decoded in Daniel's interpretation of it.

NEBUCHADNEZZAR'S DREAM AND DISTRESS (2:1-3). Not all or any sum of the world's wealth and power can cure a troubled mind. In a brief moment, God can take away one's peace of mind. He terrified Nebuchadnezzar with dreams as He did Job (Job 7:14).

The king dreamed a recurring dream; its various aspects were so troubling that he could not sleep. Nebuchadnezzar knew his dreams did not come from a bedtime snack. God impressed the dream so deeply on his mind that Nebuchadnezzar awoke in a highly agitated state. Troubled and perplexed, the king called the כַּשְׂדִּי (*kasday*, Aramaic for "Chaldeans," translated as astrologers), to make known the dream and its meaning. Originally an ethnic term, Chaldeans is a generic term for all Babylonians as well as a special term for the cult of temple priests and scholars.

The magicians, enchanters, sorcerers and Chaldeans employed herbs, charms, potions, and stars in league with evil forces to interpret dreams. Such practices are strongly condemned in the OT (Exodus 22:18; Deuteronomy 18:10; Isaiah 47:9, 12; Jeremiah 27:9).

NEBUCHADNEZZAR'S UNREASONABLE REQUEST (2:4-11).

King Nebuchadnezzar was one of history's shrewdest monarchs. The king most likely attributed the dream to his god Marduk, but he did not trust the ability of his religious advisors; yet they were his only recourse. To be certain of the validity of the interpretation, he would test them.

> This is what I have firmly decided: If you do not tell me what my dream was and interpret it, I will have you cut into pieces and your houses turned into piles of rubble. But if you tell me the dream and explain it, you will receive from me gifts and rewards and great honor. So tell me the dream and interpret it for me (Daniel 2:5-6).

Nebuchadnezzar's negative consequences are fearful, and his positive rewards are desirable. God also motivates His people with His blessings and curses. The king's threat "to cut into pieces" should be taken literally. He was equally as cruel as other Ancient Near Eastern rulers were as we easily can detect from 2 Kings 25:6-7:

> He was taken to the king of Babylon at Riblah, where sentence was pronounced on him. They killed the sons of Zedekiah before his eyes. Then they put out his eyes, bound him with bronze shackles and took him to Babylon.

A good day turned bad in Babylon. The advisors could expect no sympathy from Nebuchadnezzar—the head of gold—they had met their match. One can imagine the advisors had welcomed this opportunity until they heard the king's request and terms. They could see the king was firmly set on carrying out his threat and asked him again to tell them the dream so they could interpret it.

Nebuchadnezzar had not forgotten the dream; he could only know that the interpretation was correct if he remembered it. God does not give forgettable dreams. The whole dream was still troubling the king and the agitation spilled out in his demand.

The caliber of advisors in Nebuchadnezzar's court was the very best the world had to offer. Yet, their worldly wisdom was insufficient to solve even the most basic spiritual problems of the human mind. It is clear from this episode that Satan has no power to read minds, or else these advisors would have honored the king's demand.

The brilliant and shrewd young king suspected his advisors had conspired to tell him misleading and wicked things. His mistrust was confirmed. In NT terminology, "they are wild waves of the sea, foaming up their shame; wandering stars, for whom blackest darkness has been reserved forever" (Jude 1:13).

Unwittingly, the Chaldeans told the king point blank that his request was unreasonable and their explanation was accurate. The interpretation of the dream did go beyond man's ability. Unfortunately, these men revealed that they could not do the job they were supposed to do—their business was to contact the divine realm and find out such information. With unsuspecting boldness, they had just confessed. Their evaluation was correct and so was the king's—they were frauds!

With their declaration, "No one can reveal it to the king except the gods, and they do not live among men," the astrologers have set the stage for Daniel and his God. Only super intelligence belonging to deity could reveal this kind of information. The advisors gave the right answer, but it was the wrong thing to say to a man not known for self-control.

NEBUCHADNEZZAR'S FOLLY (2:12-13). The answer of the advisors made the king so angry and furious that he ordered the execution of all the wise men of Babylon, including Daniel and his three friends. "This" at the beginning of verse 12 might refer to:

1. The king's disappointment in not having the dream interpreted.
2. The king's confirmation of his suspicions about the advisors.
3. The king's faith in his god Marduk being shaken.
4. The king's reaction to the audacity of these frauds to criticize him.

No law, no judge, no jury—the will or whim of this king governed all things. One can imagine the unsettling effect of this hasty execution on the subjects of the kingdom. It is of no consequence to Satan that many should be killed in accomplishing his ends. Usually the decisions made when infuriated are folly. In the heat of the moment, Nebuchadnezzar would foolishly wipe out his future. He could do without the Chaldeans, but not without Daniel!

It is noteworthy that Daniel, Hananiah, Mishael and Azariah were not among the advisors. Apparently, they had separated themselves from the pagan religious leaders of Babylon.

In a cooler state of mind, Nebuchadnezzar would have realized that his wisest advisors were not present. Fury blurs one's ability to think clearly.

DANIEL'S WISDOM (2:14-16). In contrast to the king, Daniel acted with wisdom and tact when he learned of the King's decree. Innocent of any crime and confronted with death, there is no panic, no despair, no frustration, but instead, the wisest words in response to Arioch, the commander of the king's guard. Held in high esteem by Nebuchadnezzar, Daniel was granted an audience and he asked for time to do exactly what the king had requested. His calmness rubbed off on Nebuchadnezzar.

Daniel admitted that he did not presently have the answer, but it would be forthcoming. He had no information about the dream and he had never experienced this kind of miraculous contact with God—all Daniel had was faith and hope. In the midst of crisis, one should recognize the following basic promises of Scripture:

Commit to the LORD whatever you do, and your plans will succeed.

✗ The LORD works out everything for his own ends—even the wicked for a day of disaster (Proverbs 16:3-4).

✗ And we know that in all things God works for the good of those who love him, who have been called according to his purpose (Romans 8:28).

God had perfectly prepared the stage of history as well as Daniel for this moment. Daniel knew that all things are possible with God. Yahweh had tested Daniel, but he, in turn, had tested God. It was apparent that God was with him; he already had experienced what David urged: "Taste and see that the LORD is good; blessed is the man who takes refuge in him" (Psalm 34:8).

Deep down Daniel must have realized that God had a plan and a purpose for his life as He does for every believer.

For it is by grace you have been saved, through faith—and this not from yourselves, it is the gift of God—not by works, so that no one can boast. For we are God's workmanship, created in Christ Jesus to do good works, which God prepared in advance for us to do (Ephesians 2:8-10).

The dream would be revealed to him; he would reveal and interpret God's most significant revelations about the future.

DANIEL'S REASONABLE REQUEST (2:17-18). The advisors claimed powers to reveal secrets and make known divine revelations, but in a crisis, they could not produce. Daniel's secret to success is revealed in this crisis—prayer! His concern was not for the wise men of Babylon, but for three friends and himself. At Daniel's urging, the four friends pleaded for God's mercy concerning this mystery. Prayer meetings are especially effective when urgent and earnest pleas come from the righteous.

Therefore confess your sins to each other and pray for each other so that you may be healed. The prayer of a righteous man is powerful and effective (James 5:16).

Daniel knew the supreme importance of praying with other believers as did the early church (Acts 4:23-31). It is obvious from Daniel's episode that prayer is indispensable in knowing and understanding spiritual truth. The secrets of God are not revealed to those who do not know Him or pray to Him. It behooves every believer to cultivate a prayer life based on God's many promises.

> Call to me and I will answer you and tell you great and unsearchable things you do not know (Jeremiah 33:3).

> If any of you lacks wisdom, he should ask God, who gives generously to all without finding fault, and it will be given to him (James 1:5).

Truly, "He reveals deep and hidden things; He knows what lies in darkness, and light dwells with him." Wisdom is a reflection of everlasting light. God is light and in Him is no darkness at all. There is nothing so hidden or mysterious that it is inaccessible to God (cf. Psalm 139). God is willing and able to reveal wisdom to the wise. Nebuchadnezzar and his advisors lacked wisdom; one must have spiritual insight to understand God's revelations according to 1 Corinthians 2:14:

> The man without the Spirit does not accept the things that come from the Spirit of God, for they are foolishness to him, and he cannot understand them, because they are spiritually discerned.

As you continue to read, observe several amazing things that occur between 2:18-2:30:

In 2:18   Daniel and his friends prayed for themselves.

In 2:24   God expanded Daniel's heart to include concern for others—enemies.

In 2:30   Nebuchadnezzar was the target of God's mercy and compassion—His love. Since God reveals His plans to His friends, the presupposition is that Yahweh wanted Nebuchadnezzar as a friend (cf. Genesis 18:18-19; John 15:15).

DANIEL'S VISION AND PRAISE (2:19-23). Nebuchadnezzar took his worries to bed with him; Daniel took his worries to God in prayer. During the night, the mystery was revealed to Daniel in a vision. He was awake, not asleep. Dreams occur during the transition stage between waking consciousness and sound sleep. Visions occur during moments of being awake.

Here Daniel's response to answered prayer is praise. He includes his three friends in his prayer of thanks (2:23), though the answer was given to him alone. The combined, corporate prayer of the four brought the answer. Daniel's praise is eightfold, as he acknowledges that:

1. God's name is hallowed.
2. God's kingdom resides over the earth.
3. God exercises His will on earth.
4. God gives wisdom to the wise.
5. God reveals deep and hidden things.
6. God gave him wisdom and power.
7. God makes known what we ask for.
8. God made known the king's dream.

Now Daniel understands. Though the kingdom of Israel is broken up and dispersed, God's plans for His people remain intact. He is the first to know what God is planning for the world and His people from the captivity forward. The curtain has been drawn on history. The script is written; the stage and characters are set. Everything is ready for the actors; however, they will perform their parts of their own free will. The first member of the cast, with the leading role, is Nebuchadnezzar.

THE INTERPRETATION OF NEBUCHADNEZZAR'S DREAM (2:24-45). Arioch and Daniel are contrasts. The commander of the guard lied, taking credit for finding the interpreter; Daniel gave all the glory to God for what he was about to reveal to Nebuchadnezzar. It is not stated whether the monarch saw right through Arioch's deception. Clearly, Daniel's humility is contrasted with Arioch's boast.

Nebuchadnezzar's heart must have sunk as Daniel spoke until the prophet uttered one of those great "buts" of Scripture.

> But there is a God in heaven who reveals mysteries. He has shown King Nebuchadnezzar what will happen in days to come. Your dream and the visions that passed through your mind as you lay on your bed are these (Daniel 2:28).

With absolute confidence and skill, Daniel unfolded the dream while informing the king that God in heaven has the whole world in His hands and that it is He who rules the future. Nebuchadnezzar might have been surprised at having his dream revealed, but Daniel knew that God was able to reveal mysteries. After all, Yahweh had declared through the prophet Isaiah a century earlier:

> I make known the end from the beginning, from ancient times, what is still to come. I say: My purpose will stand, and I will do all that I please (Isaiah 46:10).

"To come" is the Aramaic אחרית (*'achariyth*), which denotes "end." Hence, Daniel revealed "the days to the end." The Hebrew expression for this period is "the Day of the Lord" or "that day." The interpretation of the dream covers the period from Nebuchadnezzar to Christ's second coming.

> You looked, O king, and there before you stood a large statue—an enormous, dazzling statue, awesome in appearance. The head of the statue was made of pure gold, its chest and arms of silver, its belly and thighs of bronze, its legs of iron, its feet partly of iron and partly of baked clay. While you were watching, a rock was cut out, but not by human hands. It struck the statue on its feet of iron and clay and smashed them. Then the iron, the clay, the bronze, the silver and the gold were broken to pieces at the same time and became like chaff on a threshing-floor in the summer. The wind swept them away without leaving a trace. But the rock that struck the statue became a huge mountain and filled the whole earth (Daniel 2:31-35).

The enormous, dazzling statue (צלם *tselem*, image, form or idol) signifies the dawn, duration, deterioration and doom of "the times of the Gentiles" —a specification by Christ for the period covered by the statue.

> They will fall by the sword and will be taken as prisoners to all the

nations. Jerusalem will be trampled on by the Gentiles until the times of the Gentiles are fulfilled (Luke 21:24).

The image portrays history from man's perspective. In chapter seven, the same period of history is portrayed from God's perspective with beasts. From head to toes, the image reveals four trends that will occur with each succeeding empire until Christ's kingdom comes:

1. Deteriorating power of the king
2. Increasing power of the military
3. Increasing size of territory
4. Increasing duration of rule

The image depicts that the longer man attempts to rule the world apart from God, the more that rule will be characterized by military power. Therefore, we are not surprised to hear Jesus predict that there will be wars and rumors of war until the end (Matthew 24:6).

The dazzling appearance of the image speaks of the outward glory of the nations in their worldly pomp and splendor (cf. Luke 4:4-6). The enormous size of it equates to the length of the "times of the Gentiles."

Whether this period is characterized as "awesome," "excellent," or "terrible" (יַתִּיר *yattiyr*) depends on one's own circumstances and perspective; each of the meanings fit. Indeed, there is an underlying ruthless power and beastly ferocity that is exposed in chapter seven, indicating that "terrible" is the best choice.

The image or statue that Nebuchadnezzar saw in his dream conveys significant information about the future from his day to Christ's kingdom. The following chart, *The Times of the Gentiles*, reflects some of this information about this period.

The Times of the Gentiles

(Dawn, Duration, Deterioration, Doom)
The God in Heaven is Sovereign
Romans 13:1: Acts 17:26

The Future from Man's Perspective
(Daniel 2)

FROM HEAD TO TOES

Deteriorating Power of the King
Increasing Strength of the Army
Increasing Size of the Territory
Increasing Duration of the Rule

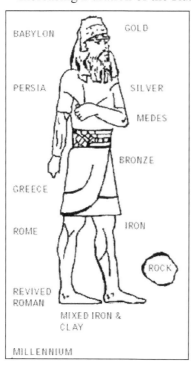

Babylon (605-539 B.C.)

Unlimited Power of the King
Gold (19) – Economic Standard

Medo-Persia (539-330 B.C.)

Limited Power by Decree
Silver (11) – Economic Standard

Greece (330–63 B.C.)

Military Power
Bronze (8.5) – Military Shields

Rome (63 B.C.–A.D. 1453)

Imperialistic Power
Iron (7.8) – Military's Iron Rule

Revived Roman Empire (?)

Unable to Hold Together
Mixed Iron & Clay (Brittle)
Ten Toes – Confederation

There was a partial assimilation of the political, religious, and culture of each succeeding empire from Babylon; however, there will be no assimilation in Christ's millennial kingdom.

The boundaries of the Babylonian, Medo-Persian, Grecian and Roman empires increased in land mass in proportion to their representation on the image as shown on the following four maps.

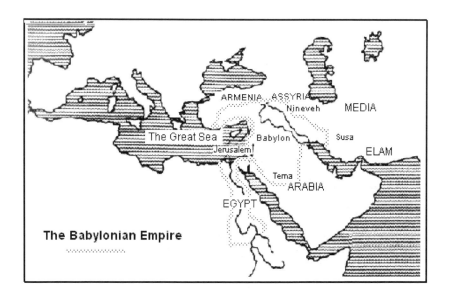

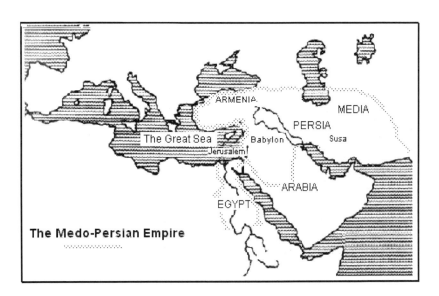

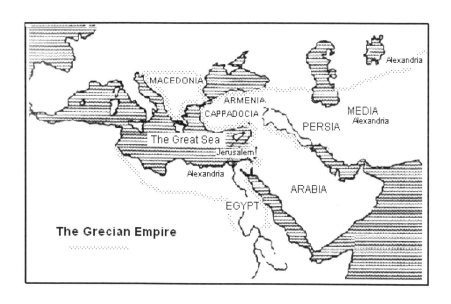

The Grecian Empire

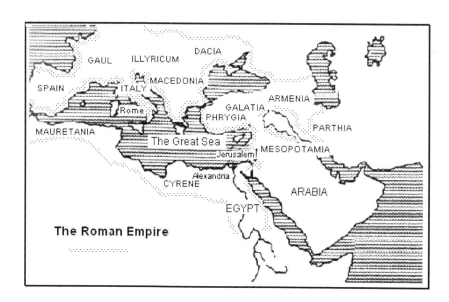

The Roman Empire

The Dawn, Duration, Deterioration, Doom of Four Empires

Having revealed the dream, Daniel turned to its interpretation. The young prophet moved progressively from the top of the image to the bottom, since the head represented current history and the successive parts portrayed later history, all in sequential order.

> You, O king, are the king of kings. The God of heaven has given you dominion and power and might and glory; in your hands he has placed mankind and the beasts of the field and the birds of the air. Wherever they live, he has made you ruler over them all. You are that head of gold (Daniel 2:36-38).

Marduk, the chief god of Babylon, was called "the god of gold." Gold was used exclusively in the city's buildings, images and shrines. Herodotus, the Greek historian who was at Babylon ninety years after the era of Nebuchadnezzar, was astonished at the amount of gold there. Even the walls and buildings were overlaid with gold (see "Babel, Babylon," *ISBE*). Being identified as the head of gold should have registered with Nebuchadnezzar.

It took courage for Daniel to speak this way to the king. He declared that it was the God of heaven, not the Babylonian gods nor the king himself, who had made Nebuchadnezzar the ruler of the world. Daniel made it clear that the God of heaven is sovereign.

One element in the interpretation of the dream is that God is the Bestower of dominion, power, might and glory. Gold, being the most precious of the image's metals, represents King Nebuchadnezzar, who possessed those four things to a greater degree than any other monarch did.

> Everyone must submit himself to the governing authorities, for there is no authority except that which God has established. The authorities that exist have been established by God (Romans 13:1).

Nebuchadnezzar is "the king of kings," because like no other monarch after him, he had absolute authority and unlimited power. He was subject to neither men, nor their laws, and so he prefigures Christ.

Then Jesus came to them and said, "All authority in heaven and on earth has been given to me" (Matthew 28:18).

And you have been given fullness in Christ, who is the Head over every power and authority (Colossians 2:10).

To the only God our Savior be glory, majesty, power and authority, through Jesus Christ our Lord, before all ages, now and for evermore! Amen (Jude 25).

Then I heard a loud voice in heaven say: "Now have come the salvation and the power and the kingdom of our God, and the authority of his Christ" (Revelation 12:10).

The Ancient Near East regarded kings and their kingdoms as being synonymous with each other. Hence, the head of gold represents Babylon as well as Nebuchadnezzar. This dual concept is important to remember when interpreting apocalyptic imagery in the Bible.

John McArthur, Jr. has observed that there is a decreasing specific gravity of the image's metals (gold, 19; silver, 11; bronze, 8.5; iron 7.8) as well as preciousness (*The Rise and Fall of the World,* 24). The descending metals picture the deteriorating authority and power of each successive empire's ruler.

The *gold head* signifies the absolute authority and power of Nebuchadnezzar, the king of kings. The *silver chest* signifies the kings of Medo-Persia who were limited by the power of decree. Their rule sprang from the power of nobles. The *bronze belly and thighs* signify the military heads of the Greek empire, and its rulers were elected by the popular vote of the military. The *iron legs* signify the imperialistic power of Rome that occurred with colonization—a commonwealth of nations.

The *feet of mixed iron and clay* signify democratic rule—the rule of the people is an inferior quality of government. Today all races, religions, and rationalizations are clamoring for a hearing, insisting upon their rights. The United States of America has become a melting pot for the peoples of all nations. There is no mistaking the present trend and the end depicted by the image.

A democracy will produce the Antichrist, consummating in the lawlessness and wickedness of the satanic world system. Then the smashing Rock will strike, becoming a mountain that fills the whole earth with God's kingdom. This event answers the second petition of the Lord's Prayer—"Your kingdom come!"

The dream, therefore, reveals the course of world rule from *autocratic* (Babylon) to *oligarchic* (Medo-Persia) to *militaristic* (Greece) to *imperialistic* (Ancient Rome) to *democratic* (Revived Rome) to *theocratic* (God's Kingdom).

The strength of Rome was not a moral or religious strength, nor the strength of inner unity, but a destructive strength that ruthlessly "smashes everything" (2:40). With the notable exception of the clay and iron feet, the metals become progressively harder.

The feet of iron mixed with clay may be seen in the rider of the four horses of Revelation 6:1-8 along with other biblical prophecies. The Antichrist will rise to power by peaceful means (economics and the power of the people) before he unleashes his military on an unsuspecting world.

The world powers rise, only to fall. The decreasing weight of the image supported by feet of mixed clay and iron indicates the image is top-heavy and destined to topple. The iron, the bronze, the clay, the sliver and the gold are smashed to pieces when the Rock strikes the image.

The four metals are characteristic of each empire. *Gold* was the standard of Babylon; *silver* the standard of Medo-Persian; the Greek military was known for its *bronze* implements of war; and iron was used by Rome's military, which was known for its *iron*-rule. Additionally, iron is able to crush gold, silver and bronze because it is stronger. Ancient Rome did just that through its military strength.

When Nebuchadnezzar dreamed his dream, Media and Persia were not a threat to Nebuchadnezzar; Greece was barely anything, and Rome was merely a little village on the banks of the Tiber. Yet, the details of

Daniel's interpretation fit these empires like fingers in a glove. So much so, liberal scholars deny the authenticity of Daniel.

Each section of the image represents proportionally the duration of four empires from the shortest to the longest. *First*, the head is the shortest duration: Babylon (605-539 B.C.); *second*, the chest: Medo-Persia (539-330 B.C.); *third*, the belly and thighs: Greece (330-63 B.C.); and *fourth*, the legs, which are the longest: Rome (63 B.C. to A.D. 1453). In A.D. 455, the Western Roman Empire fell to the Vandals, and in A.D. 1453, the Eastern Roman Empire fell to the Ottomans.

Likewise, the image from head to toes represents proportionally the land area each empire ruled. Each successive empire conquered and ruled more land mass and more people than the empire preceding it (see maps on pages 46 and 47).

The two arms of the image represent the twofold division of the Medes and the Persians. The belly represents the Greek Empire united under Alexander the Great. After his death, the kingdom was divided among his four generals, but only two of the divisions, Egypt and Syria (typified by two thighs), played an important part in history. The two legs typify the division of the Roman Empire in A.D. 364: *The Western Roman Empire* (Mediterranean and Western Europe) with Rome as its capital and the *Eastern Roman Empire* (Western Asia) with Constantinople as its capital.

This last part of the image is the eschatological portion. The legs are separated from the feet and toes in Daniel's interpretation. No hint is given as to the duration of the intervening period, which also occurs between the sixty-ninth and seventieth sevens of Daniel 9:26-27. The fourth empire would have two distinct stages of existence: *Ancient Roman Empire* (iron legs) and *Revived Roman Empire* (feet and toes of mixed iron and clay).

The toes are only mentioned by Daniel in his interpretation (2:41-43). The toes represent the tenfold division of the final form of the Roman Empire. Such a division has never occurred in history. These toes are the same as the ten horns (kings) of Revelation 17:12. Out of this predicted ten-nation confederacy, the Antichrist will arise and he will seek to rule the world prior to the second coming of Christ.

The feet and toes of iron and clay imply that the Revived Roman Empire will be weak and vulnerable. This weakness will be due to its composition of the firm and brittle. The original Roman Empire was strong in that its government was solidly organized, its armies well disciplined, and it policies well defined as evidenced by the *Pax Romana*. The weakness was not located in the iron legs (Ancient Rome), but in the feet and toes (Revived Rome) according to verse 43:

> And just as you saw the iron mixed with baked clay, so the people will be a mixture and will not remain united, any more than iron mixes with clay.

Solidarity will be brittle in the final stage of the Roman Empire. The ten toes of mixed iron and clay represent the ultimate in deterioration of the character of sovereignty. A democracy of mixed nationalities and races, each with their own agenda is naturally weak. At the top of the image is the gold head, the only part that is identified as a ruler and not as an empire. The more government becomes decentralized; the more it becomes susceptible to internal problems. The Revived Roman Empire will be fragile because of the mixture of people.

There has been no world empire since Rome. Napoleon tried to rule the world, Hitler tried it, and neither of them could do it. The Roman Empire simply faded away to await its comeback. During the end times, religious and state powers will join forces for the sake of world dominion.

> He exercised all the authority of the first beast on his behalf, and made the earth and its inhabitants worship the first beast, whose fatal wound had been healed (Revelation 13:12).

In our time, "the beast coming out of the sea" (Revelation 13:1), might be starting to breathe in the European Union. "Sea" most likely stands for the rise of ten nations around the Mediterranean, which sets the stage for man's last effort to rule the world apart from God. Hereafter, this confederation of nations is referred to as "the Revived Roman Empire."

Out of the Revived Roman Empire will arise "the ruler who will come" of Daniel 9:26, who is "the Wilful King" of 11:36-39, and who is better known as "the Antichrist." He will come on the scene in Europe in order to pull together the ten-nation coalition. Once the ten kings submit to the Antichrist, it will not be very long until the final kingdom comes.

In the time of those kings, the God of heaven will establish His kingdom on earth. It will never be destroyed, nor will it be left to another people. It will crush the remnants of the previous kingdoms and put an end to them, but it will itself endure forever. That is the meaning of the vision of the rock cut out of a mountain, but not by human hands—a rock that broke the iron, the bronze, the clay, the silver and the gold to pieces (Daniel 2:44-45).

The Everlasting Empire

The fifth kingdom will not be another attempt by man to rule the world apart from God. It will not come into existence by human hands. The אֶבֶן (*'eben*; "rock" or "stone") is none other than the Lord Jesus Christ, "the stone the builders rejected has become the capstone" (Psalm 118:22; Matthew 21:42; 1 Peter 2:8). "Rock" is a symbolic name applied to the Messiah.

> For they drank from the spiritual rock that accompanied them, and that rock was Christ (1 Corinthians 10:4).

Zechariah, the prophet of the sixth century B.C., describes the arrival of the Rock that will crush the Revived Roman Empire and scatter it to the wind.

> On that day his feet will stand on the Mount of Olives, east of Jerusalem, and the Mount of Olives will be split in two from east to west, forming a great valley, with half of the mountain moving north and half moving south (Zechariah 14:4).

Christ's kingdom, a mountain, not cut by human hands, will fill the earth. All commentators agree that this verse describes the founding of the Kingdom of God. Those who do not believe that Jesus Christ is going to come and reign over His earthly Kingdom for a thousand years are called

"Amillennialists" and "Covenant Theologians." They claim this verse is referring to the spiritual Kingdom of Christ, which is being set up in the hearts of men. They see the Church as the mountain that fills the whole earth and crushes the Ancient Roman Empire, not the revived one of the last days. However, there is no coexistence of Rome and the Kingdom of God depicted in the dream. The exact opposite is the case.

Moreover, the striking of the image is not gradual, it is sudden, violent, catastrophic and complete, totally deviating from the Church and its great commission (Matthew 28:18-20).

"Postmillennialists" believe that the world will be converted by the Church prior to Christ's return. However, the Church has not been promised any victory over the world (cf. Matthew 13:24-30, 36-43; 2 Timothy 2:1-12). The opposite is predicted. The present age will end in apostasy and rebellion, winding down with the rise of the man of lawlessness, rather than with the Church overcoming the world (2 Thessalonians 2:1-12).

To apply this prophecy to the Church is to invite confusion. The Church has been here for almost two thousand years and pagan Gentile sovereignty has not been destroyed. The Church will never overcome the world; it will be raptured prior to the Lamb's wrath. This wrath begins with Christ's opening of the seven-sealed scroll and ends with His return to strike down the nations (Revelation 5-19). Paul asserts that those in God the Father and the Lord Jesus Christ are excluded from wrath.

> For God did not appoint us to suffer wrath but to receive salvation through our Lord Jesus Christ (1 Thessalonians 5:9; cf. 5:1-8).

The Rock that smites the image does not begin to grow until the image has entirely disappeared; then it fills the whole earth. Thus are portrayed the events prior to the Millennial Kingdom of the Lord Jesus Christ when He returns as "KING OF KINGS AND LORD OF LORDS" (Revelation 19:16).

Each of the four empires are literal, political, physical, and earthly kingdoms, and therefore, the fifth and final kingdom should be interpreted the same. It does not make sense to have a spiritual kingdom introduced into a prophecy that is dealing with physical kingdoms in history. Unlike all other kingdoms, the earthly Kingdom that God establishes will neither be destroyed, nor fade away, nor be taken over by another people.

It is important to recognize that Nebuchadnezzar saw in his dream the iron, the clay, the bronze, the silver and the gold broken to pieces at the same time and becoming like chaff on a threshing-floor in the summer. The wind swept them away without leaving a trace. History shows that the political, religious and cultural characteristics of each kingdom were assimilated by succeeding empires, not so with Christ's kingdom. The characteristics of the preceding empires will be swept away like chaff in the wind without leaving a trace.

"Summer" is a code word for the Tribulation Period, the Time of Jacob's Trouble (cf. Jeremiah 30:4-11). During the Mount Olivet Discourse, Jesus referred to this period as summer in His *Parable of the Fig Tree*.

> Now learn this lesson from the fig tree: As soon as its twigs get tender and its leaves come out, you know that summer is near. Even so, when you see all these things, you know that it is near, right at the door. I tell you the truth, this generation will certainly not pass away until all these things have happened (Matthew 24:32-34).

After pronouncing seven woes on the teachers of the law and the Pharisees (Matthew 23:1-36) and lamenting over faithless Jerusalem (23:37-39), Christ once again announced the forthcoming judgment on Jerusalem.

> Jesus left the temple and was walking away when his disciples came up to him to call his attention to its buildings. "Do you see all these things?" he asked. "I tell you the truth, not one stone here will be left on another; everyone will be thrown down." As Jesus was sitting on the Mount of Olives, the disciples came to him privately. "Tell us," they said, "when will this happen, and what will be the sign of your coming and of the end of the age?" (Matthew 24:1-3).

The first question, "when will this happened?" had a near future fulfillment. On July 28, A.D. 70, Titus' army destroyed the Temple.

With distant future predictions, Jesus answered their second question, "What will be the sign of your coming and of the end of the age?" Moving chronologically through the Mount Olivet Discourse, He revealed God's eschatological plan for both the nation of Israel and the world in Matthew 24:4-25:46.

The following chart, *Eschatology of the Mount Olivet Discourse,* decodes chronologically Christ's discourse from a futurist and premillennial perspective.

Eschatology of the Mount Olivet Discourse

24:4-28   The seven years of Tribulation, also known as the Time of Jacob's Trouble (Jeremiah 30:4-10)
The First Half of the Tribulation, 4-14
The Second Half of the Tribulation, 15-28
24:29-31 The signs accompanying His second coming to the earth
24:32-35 The Parable of the Fig Tree—the rebirth of the nation of Israel
24:36-44 The unexpectedness of His return
24:45-51 The reward for faithfulness and the judgment for unfaithfulness
25:1-13   The Parable of the Ten Virgins, which illustrates 24:36-44
25:14-30 The Parable of the Talents, which illustrates 24:45-51
25:31-46 The separation of the sheep and goats, ending this present age and beginning the millennial kingdom

In His discourse, Christ forecasts the end of man's rule over the earth and the beginning of His rule. Even the second law of dynamics calls for His rule. This law is apparent in the image's portrayal of mankind; man left to himself over time will deteriorate. Thus, the image that Nebuchadnezzar saw in his dream is a polemic against evolution—man and his ability to rule is declining, not rising! Such deterioration demands the coming of a radical new rule. Revelation 19:15-16 describes the end of man's rule with the coming of Christ:

Out of his mouth comes a sharp sword with which to strike down the nations. "He will rule them with an iron scepter." He treads the winepress of the fury of the wrath of God Almighty. On his robe and on his thigh he has this name written: KING OF KINGS AND LORD OF LORDS.

The exposition of the final three chapters of Revelation is arguably the chief controversy in eschatological studies. The four interpretive approaches (made by the *Historicists, Preterists, Idealists, and Futurists*) to the first nineteen chapters of the book of Revelation fade into an *amillennial, postmillennial or premillennial* interpretation at chapter 20.

Amillennialists believe there will be no thousand-year reign of Christ on earth. They hold that the thousand years is a symbolic term for the preaching of the Gospel and the control of Satan's power between the first and second coming of Christ. Satan was bound at the Cross, but not entirely. He cannot stop the advancement of the Gospel (Luke 11:17-23; Colossians 2:15; Hebrews 2:14). Amillennialists hold that Satan will be loosed briefly to wreak havoc and to persecute the Church at the end of this present age. The new heavens and new earth will be created immediately after this present age without the reign of Christ on earth. The reign of the departed saints will take place in heaven prior to their resurrection. The older view of the Amillennialists is that of the spiritual reign of believers on earth in the present age (Romans 8:37).

Postmillennialists believe that the thousand years (literal or symbolic) immediately precede the return of Christ. Hence, the Gospel will be triumphant in the last thousand years of Church history. Satan will be bound at some future time when the Gospel reduces the Evil One's influence to nothing. His final attempt to win the world will fail and a general resurrection and judgment will occur at the coming of Christ.

Premillennialists believe Christ will come immediately before His thousand-year reign on the earth. He will sit on the throne of David in Jerusalem. There will be a restoration of the earth. Satan will be bound during this period and his loosing will close the Millennium.

A final battle ("Gog and Magog") is followed by the resurrection of the dead and the judgment of the unrighteous before the Great White Throne. The new heavens and new earth will be created after the Millennium (Revelation 20-22).

Revelation 20 asserts six times that Christ's rule will last one thousand years. During these thousand years, Satan will be bound in the Abyss and kept from deceiving the nations. How long is a thousand years? The phrase "a thousand years" appears three times outside of the book of Revelation.

> For a thousand years in your sight are like a day that has just gone by, or like a watch in the night (Psalm 90:4).

> Even if he lives a thousand years twice over but fails to enjoy his prosperity. Do not all go to the same place? (Ecclesiastes 6:6).

> But do not forget this one thing, dear friends: With the Lord a day is like a thousand years, and a thousand years are like a day (2 Peter 3:8).

Amillennialists and Postmillennialists say a "thousand years" is never used elsewhere in Scripture for an actual number of years, but only to suggest the idea of a very long time; hence, the entire Church Age. Premillennialists say a "thousand years" is to be taken as literally as "three and one half years," "forty-two months," and "1,260 days." No number in the book of Revelation is supported by evidence that would cause it to be taken other than literally.

The unmistakable teachings of the NT reveal that the adversary, the Devil, opposes the kingdom of God and His people during this present age (cf. Matthew 13; Ephesians 6:10-18; 1 Peter 5:8). Furthermore, two resurrections separate the thousand years.

> They came to life and reigned with Christ for a thousand years. (The rest of the dead did not come to life until the thousand years were ended.) This is the first resurrection. Blessed and holy are those who have part in the first resurrection. The second death has no power over them, but they will be priests of God and of Christ and

will reign with him for a thousand years (Revelation 20:4-6).

Thus, this writer concludes that the literal thousand-year reign of Christ has not yet begun.

When the thousand years are over, Satan will be released from his prison and will go out to deceive the nations in the four corners of the earth—Gog and Magog—to gather them for battle" (Revelation 20:7).

Then the end will come, when he [Christ] hands over the kingdom to God the Father after he has destroyed all dominion, authority and power" (1 Corinthians 15:24).

At that time, the new heaven and the new earth will be created (Isaiah 66:17-19; 2 Peter 3:10-13; Revelation 21:1-2) and the earthly kingdom of Christ will merge into the eternal kingdom of God.

The Scriptures describe in some detail what the millennial kingdom will be like. During the thousand-year reign of Christ, the earth returns to conditions prior to the Fall. Animals and nature will have been redeemed as well as man. It will be a time of great joy, rejoicing and deliverance for the people of God, but death and sin will still be present. Christ will "rule all the nations with an iron scepter" (Revelation 12:5), suggesting that all rebellion will be squashed immediately.

The greatness of Christ's Kingdom will be characterized by universal change in the structure and operation of society in seven areas.

SPIRITUAL IN NATURE. God's laws will be written on the hearts and minds of the saints by the Holy Spirit as the New Covenant is realized in the areas of forgiveness, righteousness, spiritual cleansing, regeneration, and direct knowledge of God (Isaiah 59:20-21; Jeremiah 31:31-34; Ezekiel 26:24-27).

ETHICAL CONDUCT. Spiritual orientation will bear fruit of ethical conduct. There will be a proper recognition of moral values. The vile person will be recognized for what he is (Isaiah 32:5), and good men and things will be approved. Life's inequalities will be reversed (Isaiah 40:3-11; Psalm 73) and retribution for sin will become wholly an individual matter (Jeremiah 31:28-30).

SOCIAL RELATIONS. Christ's Kingdom will restore perfect social relations. In this society war will be eliminated (Zechariah 9:10) and an era of peace will be ushered in that will last forever (Isaiah 9:7). The resources used for the arts and industries of war will be employed for the blessing of humankind (Isaiah 2:4). The Lord's antipoverty program will work (Isaiah 65:21-23).

PHYSICAL WHOLENESS. Not only will spiritual healing occur, but tangible effects will be experienced physically. There will be the healing of physical ills (Isaiah 33:24; 35:5-6), the restoration of long life (Isaiah 65:20, 22), the elimination of physical hazards (Isaiah 65:23; Ezekiel 34:23-31), great geological changes from the Tribulation along with changes in climate (Isaiah 32:15-16; 35:7), increased fertility (Isaiah 35:1-2; Amos 9:13), and changes in the animal world (Isaiah 11:6-9; 65:25). All of creation came under God's curse when Adam fell and all will be restored to Garden of Eden-like conditions at the return of Christ (Romans 8:19-22).

POLITICAL CHANGE. The form of government will be a theocracy. God Himself will rule over the earth in the person of Jesus Christ, the Son of David, thereby fulfilling the Davidic Covenant (2 Samuel 7:8-17). A central authority will exist for the settling of international disputes (Isaiah 2:4; Micah 4:3). National security will be assured (Isaiah 32:18). Israelites will be restored permanently to the Promised Land (Amos 9:14-15), resulting in the reestablishment and unification of the nation of Israel (Ezekiel 37), and guaranteeing its place of priority among the nations (Isaiah 60:10-14). The government will be one of peace, tranquility and blessedness. On the other hand, there will be instantaneous destruction of those who are insubordinate or rebellious (Isaiah 11:1-4).

RELIGIOUS PURIFICATION. The Ruler of this realm will be both King and Priest (Psalm 110). A central sanctuary will be established in Jerusalem (Ezekiel 37:27-28). The Shekinah glory will return to the Temple (Ezekiel 43:1-7). Israelites will become the priests and ministers of Yahweh in religious matters (Isaiah 61:6). There will be universal worship of Yahweh (Isaiah 66:23), and this worship of the true God will be compulsory (Zechariah 14:16-19).

EXTENT OF RULE. "The LORD will be king over the whole earth. On that day there will be one LORD and His name the only name" (Zechariah 14:9; cf. Psalms 96-100). Christ's Kingdom will include all nations (Psalm 72:8-11). After the thousand years, Christ's kingdom will merge into the eternal state (Micah 4:7; Psalm 45:6; Daniel 7:13-14; Revelation 22:1-5). Therefore, Christ's kingdom will never be destroyed and will endure forever (Daniel 2:44).

The ultimate purpose of Nebuchadnezzar's dream was to assert God's sovereign rule over the affairs of men. In doing so, the dream revealed God's superiority over the pagan gods. It also revealed the characteristics of the four empires, which end with Christ's kingdom that endures forever.

THE DECLARATION OF NEBUCHADNEZZAR (2:46-47). There are two great presuppositions in the Bible: (1) God exists and (2) God reveals Himself to man. The title "God of heaven" is used four times in this chapter (2:18, 19, 37, 44). That Yahweh is God in heaven was revealed to Israel seven centuries earlier.

> Acknowledge and take to heart this day that the LORD is God in heaven above and on the earth below. There is no other (Deuteronomy 4:39).

Nebuchadnezzar understood from Daniel's interpretation that "there is a God in heaven who reveals mysteries." However, the Word of God was sown on a hard heart and the evil one snatched it away (Matthew 19:4, 13). More cultivation of the king's heart would be necessary before the king would acknowledge the reign of Yahweh in his heart. The seed will not have good soil in which to take root (cf. Matthew 13:23) until chapter four, yet Daniel may have been thrilled with the king's response.

> Surely your God is the God of gods and the Lord of kings and a

revealer of mysteries, for you were able to reveal this mystery (Daniel 2:47).

Is this an inspired utterance pertaining to the Trinity?

> First Person of the Trinity is the God of gods.
> Second Person of the Trinity is the Lord of kings.
> Third Person of the Trinity is a revealer of mysteries.

An outward confession or profession does not always reveal the heart, even if inspired by the Holy Spirit (cf. Caiaphas' prophecy in John 11:49-52). The events of chapters three and four show that, instead of this experience and revelation turning him to Yahweh, Nebuchadnezzar grew more proud and defiant.

THE ADVANCEMENT OF DANIEL AND HIS THREE FRIENDS (2:48-49). True to his promise, the king showered gifts, rewards, and great honor upon the teller and interpreter of the dream. He made Daniel ruler over the entire province of Babylon and placed him in charge of all its wise men. The captive from Judah was living in luxury. Daniel never sought nor asked anything for himself. Nevertheless, because he exalted God and humbled himself, he was in God's timing, exalted and honored. Such will be the fate of every Christian who glorifies God in this life (cf. Matthew 25:14-30; Luke 19:12-17; Revelation 2:7, 13, 17, 26; 3:5, 12, 21).

At Daniel's request, Nebuchadnezzar appointed Shadrach, Meshach and Abednego administrators over the province of Babylon, while Daniel remained at the royal court.

Applications and Typical Prophecies of Chapter Two

This chapter illustrates the fact that symbolic imagery carries a significant amount of information in apocalyptic prophecy. Daniel understood the basic meaning of Nebuchadnezzar's dream, which God revealed to him. However, Yahweh did not explain the prophetic details of the image seen in the dream.

Today, most of the precise details of this image are understood since they have been literally fulfilled. On the one hand, we cannot expect to understand beforehand all details of unfulfilled apocalyptic imagery. In the upcoming portions of Daniel as well as the book of Revelation, there are many details yet to be fulfilled. On the other hand, God has revealed, since the time of Daniel, significant information about what the future holds.

Sound exegesis and hermeneutics, which rightly divide the Word of God, along with prayer and the Spirit's illumination, will yield an abundance of understanding.

Daniel and his friends prayed together in the midst of crisis. The power of praying with other Christians in order to gain knowledge, understanding and wisdom from above cannot be overstated. The world offers many solutions to life's problems, but God has the answers!

God placed Daniel in the court of Nebuchadnezzar, the most powerful monarch of history, to be a testimony and witness of His existence and power. The LORD uses those of His people who are faithful and prepared to give an answer. How might God use you?

On the surface, it seems strange that God would reveal the future to an ungodly, Gentile king, until one realizes that Gentiles are the main players and recipients of God's favor and graciousness during this present age. In chapter three, the portraiture of Nebuchadnezzar foreshadows Gentiles who turn to God while Jews reject Him.

Daniel's attitude and actions in the first two chapters sublimely illustrate the sage's advice.

> Trust in the LORD with all your heart and lean not on your own understanding; in all your ways acknowledge him, and he will make your paths straight. Do not be wise in your own eyes; fear the LORD and shun evil. This will bring health to your body and nourishment to your bones (Proverbs 3:5-8).

Nebuchadnezzar's Golden Image and Fiery Furnace
(Daniel 3)

Time Line

YEAR B.C.	598	597	586
JUDAH	Jehoiachin	Zedekiah	Jerusalem's Fall
EVENTS	Dream of Dreams		Golden Image & Fiery Furnace

Outline of Chapter Three

The Creation, 1
The Ceremony, 2-3
The Command, 4-7
The Conspiracy, 8-12
The Coercion, 13-15
The Courage, 16-18
The Coolness, 19-27
The Confession, 28
The Canon, 29
The Commission, 30

Background of Chapter Three

The Greek Septuagint of the Old Testament (LXX), translated around the third century B.C., places chapter three in the eighteenth year of Nebuchadnezzar's reign, which corresponds with his final siege of Jerusalem during the years of 587-586 B.C.

The key word of chapter three is "worship," (סְגִד *segid*) occurring ten times (5, 6, 7, 10, 11, 12, 14, 15, 18, 28). Worship is not incidental; it is fundamental in the events of this chapter. Here state and religion merge, with terrifying results.

At verse 23, the Septuagint (LXX) inserts sixty-eight extra verses, which are understood to be apocryphal. This appendix includes: (1) a prayer of Azariah; (2) an added heating of the furnace followed by the Angel of the LORD putting out the fire; (3) and a song of praise by the three Jews for their deliverance.

At the time of this chapter, Nebuchadnezzar had hardened his own heart towards Yahweh, but God responded differently to the Babylonian king than He did to the Egyptian Pharaoh, whose heart He hardened (Exodus 8:32; 9:12; 10:1, 20, 27; 11:10; 14:8). Yahweh was determined to reveal to this pagan monarch that He is the God of heaven.

- Chapter 1 teaches the king: there is a God in heaven, who makes four teenagers physically and mentally superior.

- Chapter 2 teaches the king: there is a God in heaven, who gives dreams and reveals their interpretations, and controls history.

- Chapter 3 teaches the king: there is a God in heaven, who works miracles on behalf of His people who obey God rather than men.

Moreover, God's dealings with Nebuchadnezzar affected Daniel and his three friends.

- Chapter 1 involves the test of the unclean foods.
- Chapter 2 involves the test of the unfair decree.
- Chapter 3 involves the test of bow or burn.

In the first three chapters, it becomes obvious that God works for good in diverse ways in the very same events. While God used these events to test the youths, He also used these events to forecast the future.

In these chapters, Yahweh interacts in the affairs of men for His glory without violating man's free will. Of their own free will, Daniel and His friends made God-centered choices, which resulted in Yahweh acting on their behalf, and their being elevated to high positions in accordance with God's purposes. This is the best way to understand the sovereignty of God.

81

God Preserves Daniel's Friends in the Fiery Furnace

THE CREATION (3:1). Many ancient rulers made statues of themselves to symbolize their dominion. The golden image fashioned by King Nebuchadnezzar, however, was not just a statue or image. It was an enormous golden idol—sixty cubits (ninety feet) high and six cubits (nine feet) wide. The Colossus of Rhodes by comparison was seventy feet high. The image would have looked grotesque, since in normal human proportions, the height is four to five times the width, whereas in this image, the height was ten times the width.

The king's idea for this idol appears to have come from his dream of dreams. On the other hand, it does have links to Babylonian worship since Marduk was the god of gold. In any case, the idol is definitely meant to represent a god, since people are commanded to worship it.

Overwhelmed by pride, Nebuchadnezzar's thinking became futile and defiant. He made the image of gold to express what he considered his own power and glory. In doing so, the king rejected the God of heaven, who had bestowed greatness on him (cf. 2:36; Romans 1:21-23).

Nebuchadnezzar realized that the dream forecasted his kingdom would end in a short period. Filled with pride, he rejected the image from his dream, with only a head of gold, and made this one entirely of gold. Perhaps he rationalized, "Why should my great empire end with the head? I will make it gold from head to toes! Babylon will be the everlasting kingdom!"

If the Septuagint's date ("in *his* eighteenth year" (586 B.C.)) is correct, the Babylonian army burned both the city and Temple of Daniel's God to the ground the same year Nebuchadnezzar erected the golden image. From the king's viewpoint, it turns out that Marduk is stronger and greater than Daniel's deity is—if his God exists at all! One can understand the king's rationale, but he is unequivocally wrong!

Behind the scene of every event in Daniel, there is Yahweh! And of course, on the opposite side, there are demons, working in the events to promote the Babylonian religion. Even though man is the maker of the idol, and the religion associated with it, all idolatry is demonic (Isaiah 44:6-20; Revelation 9:20). Ultimately, the worship of any image is the worship of man and demons.

Additionally, the golden image portrays humanism, materialism and religion wrapped up in one package. The image was extremely costly for it was very large. It would not have been solid gold, but overlaid with gold plates (cf. Isaiah 30:22). Set on the plain of Dura in the province of Babylon, the golden image would have been a dazzling sight in the sunlight and seen for miles.

Much like Adam, who typifies both fallen man and Christ (cf. Romans 5:12-19), Nebuchadnezzar typifies Jesus Christ—the King of kings—in the previous chapter, and in this chapter, the Antichrist—the man who will attempt to unite the world by force under one religion (Revelation 13). Like Nebuchadnezzar, the Antichrist will set up his image and those who do not worship it will be killed (Revelation 13:15). Jesus calls this image "the 'abomination that causes desolation,' spoken of through the prophet Daniel" (Matthew 24:15; Daniel 12:11).

THE CEREMONY (3:2-3). Such dedicatory rites were frequently observed in the Ancient Near East. Solomon's dedication of the Jerusalem Temple is an example (2 Chronicles 7:1-10).

Those summoned to the ceremony were official personnel, not common people. Several hundred, dressed in their finest uniforms, were probably present on the plain of Dura. There is no indication that the participants knew the king's purpose for summoning them. They might have been under the impression that it was a patriotic or political service.

Daniel may have been absent from the ceremony, perhaps carrying out business elsewhere for the king, or possibly, too ill to attend. The statesman did not have a perfect attendance record on the job.

> I, Daniel, was exhausted and lay ill for several days. Then I got up and went about the king's business (Daniel 8:27).

Significantly, Daniel's office is not listed among the satraps, prefects, governors, advisers, treasurers, judges, magistrates and all the other provincial officials. If Daniel were present at the ceremony, the king's Prime Minister might not have been required to bow down to the image; the king himself remained seated. The Chaldeans would not have been courageous enough to attack the king's chief advisor if he was present at the ceremony.

THE COMMAND (3:4-7). Nebuchadnezzar expected obedience at this ceremony. With the finest fanfare of pomp and all kinds of music, the crucial test for the Hebrews was announced: bow or burn!

> As soon as you hear the sound of the horn, flute, zither, lyre, harp, pipes and all kinds of music, you must fall down and worship the image of gold that King Nebuchadnezzar has set up. Whoever does not fall down and worship will immediately be thrown into a blazing furnace (Daniel 3:5-6)

Satan, the great counterfeiter, employs music to set the mood. He uses music to stir the congregation to an emotional fervor in order to plunge them into false religion. All men are religious by nature, and are easily carried away by anything that excites and stirs the emotions.

The command to fall down and worship the golden image violated God's first and second commandments (Exodus 20:2-6). Bowing down to the image signified an allegiance to whichever false god it represented.

The Babylonian kings were noted for burning people alive (Jeremiah 29:22). Little wonder there was an overwhelming response to Nebuchadnezzar's command: "Bow or burn!" Once again, Hananiah, Mishael and Azariah are tested. There are three components to this test:

1. Fear man or fear God.
2. Sacrifice truth on the altar of expediency or take a stand for it.
3. God is able, but will He save?

Any number of excuses to conform could have been employed, such as:

1. Why not join the system, you can't fight city hall.
2. We'll cooperate with Nebuchadnezzar and win him to the Lord.
3. A live dog is better off than a dead lion (Ecclesiastes 9:4).

4. Daniel our leader is not here to make the right decision for us.
5. Our key positions in the government should not be sacrificed.
6. Nebuchadnezzar has treated us well; he deserves our obedience.
7. We can always ask God to forgive us afterwards.

THE CONSPIRACY (3:8-12). Satan loomed behind the scenes; he is always ready to point his finger and accuse God's people. Offstage lurked those ready to make their grand entrance in order to perform the Devil's evil plans and purposes. Jealousy and envy are often his tools. Green with envy, the Chaldeans waited for this opportunity and they pounced on it. Years before, the prayers of Daniel and his friends had saved the Chaldeans. Now they came forward, denouncing the Jews. Such was the ingratitude of the Chaldeans!

The Chaldeans brought three charges against the three Jews who did not bow:

1. They have not regarded you.
2. They serve not your gods.
3. They do not worship the golden image you have set up.

All others bowed; the fact that three did not was very conspicuous. (It can be assumed that any other Hebrews present bowed). Three stood alone! What a testimony by Shadrach, Meshach and Abednego! Their courageous act is one of the great examples in Scripture: they trusted and obeyed God rather than man. They did not cave in to peer-pressure. Talk about boldness. Moses' instruction to Israel might have been echoing in their minds.

> Be strong and courageous. Do not be afraid or terrified because of them, for the LORD your God goes with you; he will never leave you nor forsake you (Deuteronomy 31:6).

What a contrast these Jews are to the apostle Peter, when he denied Christ Jesus three times in the dark. Moreover, Peter was not required to be there (John 18:15-18, 25-27)!

The Chaldeans were swift to point out that the king had set Shadrach, Meshach and Abednego over the affairs of Babylon. This charge was added to infuriate the king. They were successful; they "pushed his button."

THE COERCION (3:13-15). Furious with rage—the king was intensely angry at being defied and embarrassed in this way. He may have put forth a great effort to keep such rebellion from occurring. The king, older and wiser than when he ordered the execution of all the wise men of Babylon, summoned the three men, questioned them and offered them another opportunity to bow or burn.

Unwittingly, Nebuchadnezzar put God to the test. There is little difference between this test on the plain of Dura, and the test of Elijah and his God versus the false prophets of Baal on Mount Carmel (1 Kings 18:16-40). Defiant words spilled out of the king's mouth, "Then what god will be able to rescue you from my hand?"

THE COURAGE (3:16-18). It appears the command to bow down and worship the idol came as a surprise to those summoned, otherwise the three men might have avoided the dedication ceremony. If a surprise, they had no time to prepare their response to the king. The Spirit of God might have prompted their words for Jesus told His disciples:

> When you are brought before synagogues, rulers and authorities, do not worry about how you will defend yourselves or what you will say, for the Holy Spirit will teach you at that time what you should say (Luke 12:11-12).

Actions usually speak louder than words, but one can hear the Holy Spirit in their reply to the furious king.

> O Nebuchadnezzar, we do not need to defend ourselves before you in this matter. If we are thrown into the blazing furnace, the God we serve is able to save us from it, and he will rescue us from your hand, O king. But even if he does not, we want you to know, O king, that we will not serve your gods or worship the image of gold you have set up.

Two matters stand out in their reply: (1) The will of God might be different from what they desire; and (2) their obedience was not conditioned upon God doing what they desired. Undoubtedly, when they were back in Jerusalem, they had heard what Yahweh said through the prophet Jeremiah.

> Do not pray for this people nor offer any plea or petition for them, because I will not listen when they call to me in the time of their distress (Jeremiah 11:14).

Certainly, this was a time of distress; would God listen if they called on Him?

THE COOLNESS (3:19-27). The three Hebrews possessed the faith and hope of Job: "Though he slay me, yet will I hope in him" (Job 13:15). Their confidence in God made Nebuchadnezzar furious and his attitude toward them changed; they had challenged him and his gods. He ordered the furnace to be heated seven times hotter than usual. Literally, the text reads, "one times seven beyond," which is heat raised to a factor of seven. Symbolically, this phrase indicates extremely hot. This extraordinary heating of the furnace opens the door for the performing of a miracle by God, who specializes in the impossible (Luke 1:37).

Babylonian stone and brick furnaces were made like recent-day limekilns, with one opening at the top and a large opening at the bottom, for the withdrawing of burned substances. Charcoal normally served as the fuel. This furnace had a ramp leading to its top since the soldiers "took up" the condemned men. This furnace may have been constructed to smelt the gold used in making the image. God used it for another purpose—to overrule evil for good.

Nebuchadnezzar is intensely hot, the furnace is intensely hot, and the three victims are amazingly cool! Firmly tied, they dropped down the shaft to the bottom of the furnace.

The strong soldiers, who threw the three Jews into the furnace, were incinerated by the flames. Nebuchadnezzar looked into the furnace and sprang to his feet.

Five things amazed the king:

1. Four persons were seen instead of three.
2. No one was bound.
3. Four persons were walking in the fire; no one was lying down.
4. All four persons were unhurt.
5. The fourth person looked supernatural—"a son of the gods."

When God performs a miracle, He overrules natural order so that His power is unmistakable, and there is no other explanation for what occurred.

Unwittingly, Nebuchadnezzar almost made the correct identification: "the fourth looks like a son of the gods." Whom did the king see? An angel sent by God or one who looks like "a son of the gods." Of course, that is what the king said he saw. Most likely, the king saw a theophany. In the OT, Yahweh sometimes appeared in human form as He appeared before Samson's parents (Judges 13:10-22). It is probable that such appearances are the Second Person of the Trinity.

Moses had encountered the angel of Yahweh, who appeared in the burning bush that was not consumed (Exodus 3:2). Keeping the flames of the fiery furnace from consuming the three Jews was nothing new. Figuratively, we might say that God had permitted the Jews to be cast into the horrifying furnace of Babylon, but in so doing, He had literally gone with them!

Interestingly, the meanings of the Hebrew names of the three men are fulfilled by God's presence, protection and power in the fiery furnace.

Hananiah	Beloved of Yahweh.
Mishael	Who is as God.
Azariah	Yahweh is my help.

Yahweh is God, He loves His people, and He helps them. Where were the king's gods? Not in the fiery furnace! Nebuchadnezzar must have recognized their absence when he confessed "the Most High God" along with his cry of defeat: "Come out! Come here!"

Humiliation! How would the king handle it? His strongest soldiers dead; unbound Hebrews alive; the only thing associated with the three men that suffered harm in the furnace had been the king's rope; the hair of the three men was not singed; and their clothing did not even smell of smoke. Ironically, on the day that had been set aside for the dedication and worship of the golden image, the Most High God received the glory!

THE CONFESSION (3:28). Instead of the Jews bowing down to Nebuchadnezzar's gods, the king confessed the God of the three men.

> Praise be to the God of Shadrach, Meshach and Abednego, who has sent his angel and rescued his servants! They trusted in him and defied the king's command and were willing to give up their lives rather than serve or worship any god except their own God.

The king testified, directly or indirectly, to five things in verses 29-30.

1. God has sent His angel.
2. God delivers those who trust in Him.
3. God made him change his boast, "Then what god will be able to rescue you from my hand?"
4. The three were willing to die in order to remain true to their God.
5. There is no other God able to deliver this way.

What is lacking in the king's testimony? God is the God of Shadrach, Meshach and Abednego, but not the God of Nebuchadnezzar! There is a song that says, "I am a great big bundle of potentiality" and another song that says, "He's still working on me." God is working on Nebuchadnezzar as evidenced by the next chapter. He is a great big bundle of potentiality and God is not about to let go of him.

What a revolting development for Nebuchadnezzar. The king assembled his officials to bring glory to his god and ends up glorifying the God of Israel. One can almost hear the laughter in heaven (cf. Psalm 2:4).

THE CANON (3:29). The Bible clearly states that the nations will be judged for their treatment of Yahweh's people (Genesis 12:3; Matthew 25:31-46). Such a great fear of the LORD must have been sown into the king's heart to account for his adding to Babylon's canon of laws, the official decree of toleration towards the God of Shadrach, Meshach and Abednego. With this decree, he saved his people from the wrath of God. God brought about two miracles that day: the deliverance and the decree.

Decrees like this one are found in nonbiblical sources of Babylon and Persia. The *Council of Wisdom*, which comes from this period reads:

> Every day worship your god.
> Sacrifice and benediction are the proper accompaniment of incense.
> Present your freewill offering to your god,
> For this is proper towards the gods.
> Prayer, supplication, prostration
> Offer him daily, and you will get your reward.
> Then you will have full communion with your god.
> In your wisdom study the tablet.
> (*Documents from Old Testament Times,* 106).

As surmised from the *Council of Wisdom*, one could choose his or her god or gods. Since the king acknowledged the Most High God, it was not difficult for Nebuchadnezzar to add the God of Israel to the Babylonian pantheon. The king has not yet recognized Yahweh as sovereign. Keep in mind that God is still working on him. The king is about to discover that there are not many gods, but one!

THE COMMISSION (3:30). One can imagine how the already envious Chaldeans felt when the king promoted Shadrach, Meshach and Abednego in the province of Babylon. Faith is rewarded!

Application and Typical Prophecies of Chapter Three

In this chapter, faithfulness and fearlessness, in the face of extreme adversity, are modeled by Shadrach, Meshach and Abednego. Following their example, believers during times of turmoil and tribulation should be encouraged to hold to the faith.

This chapter is prophetic, foreshadowing the ultimate preservation and restoration of Israel in spite of the wrath of the Antichrist during the Tribulation Period.

The near future is typified by the three men from Judah (Jews) and the fourth person in the fiery furnace. Herein is portrayed God's presence and His protection of the faithful remnant during the Babylonian exile. The Jews will not perish as a people but will come out of the furnace when the king commands. What is typified here was fulfilled in King Cyrus' decree in 538 B.C.

Subsequent history of the Jews shows that the courage of Daniel's friends encouraged the Jewish patriots during the time of the Maccabean revolt against Antiochus Epiphanes, who foreshadows the Antichrist. He commanded the Jews to violate the regulations of their sacred law and apostatize from their ancestral faith on pain of death.

> And the king sent letters by messengers to Jerusalem and the towns of Judah; he directed them to follow customs strange to the land, to forbid burnt offerings and sacrifices and drink offerings in the sanctuary, to profane sabbaths and festivals, to defile the sanctuary and the priests, to build altars and sacred precincts and shrines for idols, to sacrifice swine and unclean animals, and to leave their sons uncircumcised. They were to make themselves abominable by everything unclean and profane, so that they should forget the law and change all the ordinances. He added, "And whoever does not obey the command of the king shall die" (1 Maccabees 1:44-50, NRSV).

In his last words, Mattathias said:

> Elijah, because of great zeal for the law, was taken up to heaven. Hananiah, Azariah and Mishael believed and were saved from the flame" (1 Maccabees 2:59, NRSV).

The courage and faith of such men encouraged the Jews to fear God, not man. This will be the ultimate test in the end times for "faith is the victory that overcomes the world!"

The nation of Israel is a miracle—a far greater miracle than three

Hebrews saved from the flames and heat of the fiery furnace. The very fact of Israel's existence, after three thousand years of passing through the fires of satanic opposition, is proof there is a God of heaven who rules. Israel is God's polemic against false gods (Isaiah 41). The fiery furnace is symbolic of the saving of Israel.

> They will know that I am the LORD, when I disperse them among the nations and scatter them through the countries. But I will spare a few of them from the sword, famine and plague, so that in the nations where they go they may acknowledge all their detestable practices. Then they will know that I am the LORD (Ezekiel 12:15-16).

God's protection and preservation of the Jews, while they are in the fires, is proof that He continues to be the God of Israel during periods of chastisement according to Isaiah 43:1-7:

> But now, this is what the LORD says—he who created you, O Jacob, he who formed you, O Israel: "Fear not, for I have redeemed you; I have summoned you by name; you are mine. When you pass through the waters, I will be with you; and when you pass through the rivers, they will not sweep over you. When you walk through the fire, you will not be burned; the flames will not set you ablaze. For I am the LORD, your God, the Holy One of Israel, your Savior; I give Egypt for your ransom, Cush and Seba in your stead. Since you are precious and honored in my sight, and because I love you, I will give men in exchange for you, and people in exchange for your life. Do not be afraid, for I am with you; I will bring your children from the east and gather you from the west. I will say to the north, 'Give them up!' and to the south, 'Do not hold them back.' Bring my sons from afar and my daughters from the ends of the earth—everyone who is called by my name, whom I created for my glory, whom I formed and made."

Just as chapter two's panorama of history is followed by the persecution of the faithful remnant in chapter three, so will the times of the Gentiles end with the persecution and salvation of Israel.

The sixth century prophet Zechariah announced God's purpose behind the yet future fiery furnace for Israel.

"In the whole land," declares the LORD, "two-thirds will be struck down and perish; yet one-third will be left in it." This third I will bring into the fire; I will refine them like silver and test them like gold. They will call on my name and I will answer them; I will say, 'They are my people,' and they will say, 'The LORD is our God'" (Zechariah 13:8-9).

Thus, the fiery furnace is a type of the Great Tribulation, which constitutes the second half of the seventieth "seven" revealed and recorded in Daniel 9:24-27. This period will be seven times hotter for the Jews than any previous times of distress. It is "*A Time for Jacob's Trouble*" according to the prophet Jeremiah. This period serves multiple purposes of God as manifested by the following outline of Jeremiah 30:4-11.

A TIME FOR JACOB'S TROUBLE

A Time of Travail, Jeremiah 30:4-6
A Time of Terror, 7a
A Time of Triumph, 7b-11b
    End of the times of the Gentiles, 8
    Beginning of Christ's Kingdom, 9
        Restoration of Israel to the Land, 10a
        Rest for Israel, 10b
        Salvation for Israel, 11a
        End of All Nations, 11b
A Time of Training, 11c

Shadrach, Meshach and Abednego are by inference in *The Faith Hall of Fame*: "Who through faith . . . quenched the fury of the flames" (Hebrews 11:33). When we consider that Yahweh gave light and protection to His people in the desert by means of a pillar of fire (Exodus 13:21; 14:19-20), it is not surprising to find His presence also in the burning bush (Exodus 3:1-4), or the fiery furnace.

The application for the Christian is that God saves us in the fire but not from the fire. He takes us through the fire to test and refine our faith as well as to manifest His glory before an unbelieving world. To all who will stand firm in faith, there is the promise of persecution. No saint in any age has been popular with the world. Therefore, "consider it pure joy, my brothers, whenever you face trials of many kinds, because you know that the testing of your faith develops perseverance" (James 1:2-3).

Nowhere in the whole Bible is there a verse that supports the contention that this present age is going to get better and better, until at last, through mutual understanding between men and nations the Gospel will banish war and bring about an age of peace and contentment. Instead, David describes this present age as a time of rebellion against God.

> Why do the nations conspire and the peoples plot in vain? The kings of the earth take their stand and the rulers gather together against the LORD and against his Anointed One. "Let us break their chains," they say, "and throw off their fetters (Psalm 2:1-3).

Nebuchadnezzar foreshadows the Antichrist who will conspire against God in the end times. He will set up his image on the wing of the Temple in Jerusalem; then he will demand that everyone worship it or die. The images erected by Nebuchadnezzar and the Antichrist represent the state and its monarch. One religion for all people, nations, and languages during the end times is foreshadowed in Daniel 3:4. All must conform to state worship or die.

Paradoxically, God's government disallows separation of state and religion. Yahweh instituted state religion when he created the nation of Israel. The millennial reign of Christ will be a state religion. Many of man's efforts to combine state and religion have been devastating. Constantine corrupted the Church with state religion. In the Dark Ages, the popes, through abuse of their religious power, usurped the authority of kings, all in the name of religion.

America's forefathers, in the Bill of Rights, legislated against the tyranny of the state religions of England and Europe. State religion will reach its darkest moment under the Antichrist in the end times and its brightest day during Christ's millennial reign.

The dimensions of the image are not without significance. Its height was sixty cubits and its width was six cubits. The number of man is six. Six stops short of perfection. Six then is the number of human incompleteness. Man was made on the sixth day; the seventh day is a Sabbath to the LORD. Revelation 13:18, speaking of the number of the beast, says:

> This calls for wisdom. If anyone has insight, let him calculate the number of the beast, for it is man's number. His number is 666.

One of the sixes is missing in Nebuchadnezzar's image, possibly because the religious system is incomplete. On the other hand, six musical instruments are mentioned with the worship of the image (Daniel 3:15). Little did Nebuchadnezzar know that the golden image he erected on the plain of Dura would foreshadow the image and number of the beast.

Babylon embodies the religious system of man. It began with the erection of a tower on the Plain of Shinar; it continued with Nebuchadnezzar's golden image on the plain of Dura; and it will end with the beast's image on the wing of the Temple.

The image is of gold (materialism) and of a man (humanism), possibly the main elements of the religion forced on the inhabitants of the world by the false prophet, during the end times (cf. Revelation 13:11-17). The golden image also foreshadows Satan's attempt to sidetrack God's plan for the future. The Antichrist, like Nebuchadnezzar, will attempt to make the whole image gold (the end time empire), not just its head. He will almost achieve his goal as indicated by the title given to his empire.

> This title was written on her forehead: MYSTERY BABYLON THE GREAT THE MOTHER OF PROSTITUTES AND OF THE ABOMINATIONS OF THE EARTH (Revelation 17:5).

The three faithful men in the fiery furnace prefigure the Jews saved in the midst of the fire. The Jews' bonds will be burned off in the end times. Just as God preserved the 7,000 Israelites who did not bow to Baal in Elijah's day, so He is going to preserve 144,000 Jews during the

Tribulation Period (1 Kings 19:18; Revelation 7:1-8). They will be victorious over the beast and his image (Revelation 14:1-6). When God delivers, He does it miraculously.

Not one Israelite perished in the Red Sea. Not one Jew perished in the fiery furnace. Not one of the 144,000 will perish in the Tribulation. Those who stand with the Lamb will be sealed and safely delivered. The soldiers, who died while throwing the three Jews into the fire, foreshadow the fate of those who will persecute the Jews in the end times.

Nebuchadnezzar's royal decree provides the basis for Christ's separation of the people one from another as a shepherd separates sheep from goats. Those separated as sheep will enter the millennial kingdom and eternal life. Those separated as goats will go away into eternal punishment (cf. Matthew 25:31-46). Opposition to God's people ends in terrifying consequences, as we will see in chapter six.

Nebuchadnezzar is a dual type of the Antichrist and Christ. Verse 26 is exhilarating from the Christian's perspective.

> Nebuchadnezzar then approached the opening of the blazing furnace and shouted, "Shadrach, Meshach and Abednego, servants of the Most High God, come out! Come here!" So Shadrach, Meshach and Abednego came out of the fire (Daniel 3:26).

The unquenchable and non-consuming flames of Hell are the destiny of everyone until Christ issues the invitation to "Come out! Come here! Enter My kingdom." According to the NT, every believer is to follow suit, extending Christ's invitation to the perishing.

> Be merciful to those who doubt; snatch others from the fire and save them; to others show mercy, mixed with fear—hating even the clothing stained by corrupted flesh (Jude 22-23).

Shadrach, Meshach and Abednego were tested by fire; survived the fire; and received their reward. That sounds very much like the Christian at the Judgment Seat of Christ.

His work will be shown for what it is, because the Day will bring it to light. It will be revealed with fire, and the fire will test the quality of each man's work. If what he has built survives, he will receive his reward. If it is burned up, he will suffer loss; he himself will be saved, but only as one escaping through the flames (1 Corinthians 3:13-15).

This chapter emphasizes the truth that the wise fear the LORD, not people. Ultimately, those who trust and obey God will be rewarded. In the intervening time, every "fiery furnace" trial can produce within a believer a stronger faith, resulting in spiritual maturity.

{Let us} also rejoice in our sufferings, because we know that suffering produces perseverance; perseverance, character; and character, hope (Romans 5:3-4).

Consider it pure joy, my brothers, whenever you face trials of many kinds, because you know that the testing of your faith develops perseverance. Perseverance must finish its work so that you may be mature and complete, not lacking anything (James 1:2-4).

Every believer, who perseveres in testing, has the potential to be a bold witness of the power of God in his or her life.

Nebuchadnezzar's Dream of the Tree
(Daniel 4)

Time Line

YEAR B.C.	586	(?)	562
JUDAH	Jerusalem's Fall		
EVENTS	Golden Image & Fiery Furnace	The Tree Dream-Vision	Nebuchadnezzar's Death

Outline of Chapter Four

The King's Praise, 1-3
The King's Perplexity, 4-7
The King's Positiveness, 8-9
The King's Problem, 10-18
The King's Punishment, 19-26
The King's Procrastination, 27-29
The King's Pride, 30
The King's Perversion, 31-33
The King's Preservation, 34-37

Background of Chapter Four

There is a common thread running through the first four chapters of Daniel. Throughout the events of these chapters, God is revealing to King Nebuchadnezzar His existence and sovereignty.

In Chapter 1, the king learns of a God in heaven who makes four teenagers physically and mentally superior.

In Chapter 2, the king learns of a God in heaven who gives dreams and reveals their interpretation and overrules history.

In Chapter 3, the king learns of a God in heaven who works miracles on behalf of His people, who trust and obey Him rather than men.

In Chapter 4, the king learns of a God in heaven who humbles the proud and saves the humble person who calls on Him.

People have favorite Bible chapters and characters. For this writer, Nebuchadnezzar and his testimony ranks among the top. It is the climax of one of the greatest love stories ever penned—telling how God demonstrated His love toward a sinner until he became a saint.

One can write four little words over this chapter: "The Love of God." For God saves the King! Nebuchadnezzar might have been on the mind of Jesus in Matthew 5:43-45:

> You have heard that it was said, "Love your neighbor and hate your enemy." But I tell you: Love your enemies and pray for those who persecute you, that you may be sons of your Father in heaven.

Few Jews would have prayed "God Save the King!" or even said those words on behalf of King Nebuchadnezzar, especially, in light of the events of the summer of 586 B.C. Nebuchadnezzar's army had destroyed Jerusalem and the Temple, leaving the Holy City as burnt rubble.

Undoubtedly, the faithful remnant had had a bellyful of Nebuchadnezzar's Babylon by now. Their noses had been rubbed in idolatry. Their hatred of the Gentiles grew so great; they would not even eat with them after the exile.

To the Jew, this king was a vile pagan—one's worst nightmare! They would have liked to cast him into the fiery furnace. To God, this proud shepherd was a lost sheep that was perishing. Unquestionably, Daniel, Ezekiel and Jeremiah would have been praying for the king so things would go well for their people (Jeremiah 29:7). God answered someone's prayers!

Nebuchadnezzar's last recorded words in Scripture summarize chapter four: "And those who walk in pride he is able to humble."

God Humbles Proud Nebuchadnezzar

THE KING'S PRAISE (4:1-3). Chapter four is very unique for it was written by Nebuchadnezzar himself—a Gentile! It is the king's own testimony of how God saved him. No doubt, Daniel had copied it from the state papers of Babylon and preserved it in the original language. The king began where every testimony should—by giving God the glory. These are the words of a saved man.

> King Nebuchadnezzar, To the peoples, nations and men of every language, who live in all the world: May you prosper greatly! It is my pleasure to tell you about the miraculous signs and wonders that the Most High God has performed for me. How great are his signs, how mighty his wonders! His kingdom is an eternal kingdom; his dominion endures from generation to generation (Daniel 4:1-3).

The introduction of his testimony is actually a conclusion! These words grow out of the king's personal experience. He acknowledged that the Most High God had performed miraculous signs and wonders for him, such as the dream of dreams; the amazing deliverance of Shadrach, Meshach and Abednego from the fiery furnace accompanied by the appearance of the preincarnate Christ; and the events described in this chapter. They surpass all human power.

We are not surprised by the apostle Paul's greeting of peace, but Nebuchadnezzar's? "May you prosper greatly!" literally reads in the Aramaic "Peace multiplied to you." These are strange words from the mouth of this mighty king, who had spent his life in warfare, suppression, and enslavement of people in order to build his world empire to satisfy his ego and pride. This greeting of peace comes from a man with a changed heart.

The Aramaic שְׁלָם (*shelam*, "peace") is equivalent to the Hebrew word for peace (שָׁלוֹם *shalom*). The OT and NT writers view peace as a gift from God and the meaning of salvation is closely related to it in passages like Psalm 85:9-11 and Romans 5:1. Nebuchadnezzar wanted his subjects to experience the peace of the Most High God.

He acknowledged that God is the eternal King, His dominion is everlasting, and every generation is a proof of His all-governing influence. How did the king arrive at such knowledge? Proverbs 9:10!

Nebuchadnezzar could never be accused of being private with his faith. He broadcasted it to everyone.

THE KING'S PERPLEXITY (4:4-7). In the thirty-fifth year of his reign, Nebuchadnezzar was at home in his palace, contented and prosperous. He had conquered and subjugated Syria, Phoenicia, Judah, Egypt, and Arabia. His song could have been "*It Is Well With My Soul!*" He possessed power, prestige, wealth and health.

After all is said and done, "the heart is deceitful above all things and beyond cure. Who can understand it?" asks the prophet (Jeremiah 17:9). "No one" is the answer. However, the LORD searches the heart and all is not well with the king; he is puffed up with pride and at enmity with God. Therefore, Yahweh gives the monarch something to worry about—a perplexing dream of images and visions that terrify him. Based on his first dream, he must have known that it concerned him.

The unsaved king, still trusting in his gods, called for all the wise men of Babylon. Again, Daniel is a no show. This time he told the wise men the dream, but they admitted that they could not interpret it. No attempt is made to pull the wool over the eyes of this shrewd king. For all they knew, he might have talked to Daniel and learned the correct interpretation, and now was testing them.

The king may have called these wise men instead of Daniel, desiring a positive and comforting interpretation. King Jehoshaphat knew that the prophet Micaiah would give him a negative prediction about going to war so he called four hundred prophets who told him what he wanted to hear (1 Kings 22). Nebuchadnezzar would have expected no less than a straightforward prediction from the prophet Daniel.

THE KING'S POSITIVENESS (4:8-9). Finally, Daniel came into his presence. Keep in mind that Nebuchadnezzar is giving his testimony. At this point in the testimony, he is still trusting in Marduk. Bel in Belteshazzar is an alias for Marduk. The name "Daniel" (God is Judge) must have unsettled the king.

The Aramaic אלהה (*'elahh*) corresponds to the Hebrew אלוהה (*'elowahh*). Both terms are first person singular nouns and should be translated "God" instead of "gods" in Daniel 4:8, 9, 18; 5:11, 14. Nebuchadnezzar observed the Spirit of the Holy God in Daniel. Some translators assumed that Nebuchadnezzar meant "the spirit of the holy gods." This is unlikely, since no pagan worshipers claimed purity or holiness of their deities. In fact, just the opposite was believed. Since the king was rehearsing his conversion, he was able to identify the Holy Spirit in Daniel as he wrote.

Based on more than thirty-five years of observations and interactions, Nebuchadnezzar was positive that Daniel could interpret his dream. This time images (mental pictures) and visions accompanied the dream, adding to his dismay.

THE KING'S PROBLEM (4:10-18). The dream and visions have four sections.

1. The exceedingly great tree, 10-12
2. The cutting down of this tree, 13-15a
3. The seven-year drenching and animalistic behavior, 15b-16
4. The messenger's decree, 17

The king saw a עיר (*`uwr*, "watcher," "messenger," or "angel") and a קדיש (*qaddiysh*, Aramaic for "holy one"). Did the king see two beings or one? The Aramaic construction can be translated either "behold, a watcher and a holy one came down from heaven" or "there before me was a messenger, a holy one, coming down from heaven." *Watchers* and *holy ones* are of different orders in the Chaldean oracles. Verses 17 and 23 infer that *watchers* judge human actions, with the power to determine the lot of men, and *holy ones* executed their judgment. Hence, the king's case was tried in the Judicial Court of Watchers and the sentence was executed by the holy ones. The decree of the messengers (watchers) terrified the king.

Let him be drenched with the dew of heaven, and let him live with the animals among the plants of the earth. Let his mind be changed from that of a man and let him be given the mind of an animal, till seven times pass by for him (Daniel 4:15-16).

The change of pronouns from "it" and "its" (10-15a) to "his" and "him" (15b-16) is significant—the tree signifies "a man." A person of Nebuchadnezzar's intelligence might have suspected that he was the tree. Great men and princes are often represented, in the language of the prophets, under the similitude of trees; see Psalm 1:3; 37:35; Ezekiel 17:5-6; 31:3; Jeremiah 22:15. The tree symbolizes his pride and imperial self-exaltation as well as God's sovereignty in raising him up and bringing him down (cf. Ezekiel 17:22-24; 31:3-9).

Interestingly, Jesus employs a tree in one of His kingdom parables to represent the Kingdom of Heaven in its present mystery form.

> He told them another parable: "The kingdom of heaven is like a mustard seed, which a man took and planted in his field. Though it is the smallest of all your seeds, yet when it grows, it is the largest of garden plants and becomes a tree, so that the birds of the air come and perch in its branches" (Matthew 13:31-32).

In Jesus' parable, the great mixture of good and evil commonly called "Christendom" is symbolized by the perversion of an herb becoming a tree. Earlier in Matthew 13, the birds of the air are seen typifying the evil one, who snatches away the seed from men's hearts before it takes root. Now that the birds have fled in Nebuchadnezzar's dream, God's Word will take root!

This man is to live with animals and to eat like them. He will have the mind of חֵיוָא (*cheyva'* Aramaic for "animal" or "beast") till seven times pass by him. In other words, "Let him conceive of himself as a beast, and act as such, herding among the beasts of the field till seven years pass by for him." The Aramaic phrase עִדָּנִין (*`iddan*, "times") שִׁבְעָה (*shib`ah*, "seven") appears in this chapter only and denotes seven literal years.

> The decision is announced by messengers, the holy ones declare the verdict, so that the living may know that the Most High is sovereign

103

over the kingdoms of men and gives them to anyone he wishes and sets over them the lowliest of men (Daniel 4:17).

Here we gain insight into the invisible realm. Messengers (watchers, angels) oversee the affairs of men, enabling them to bring about the will of God on earth (Daniel 4:17; 10:10-21; 11:1; 12:1; Matthew 18:10; Hebrews 1:14). Angels will be the harvesters at the end of this present age (Matthew 13:39).

In Nebuchadnezzar's dream, God's decision to cut down the king is announced by heavenly messengers. Angels are the bearers of both good and bad news in the book of Revelation. The angel Gabriel announced the births of John the Baptist and Jesus; angels announced Christ's birth to shepherds; an angel told Joseph, in a dream, to take Mary as his wife; an angel warned the Magi, in a dream, to return home another way; two angels announced the resurrection and ascension of Jesus; etc.

This dream revealed to Nebuchadnezzar that the Most High is sovereign in the affairs of man and that He does as He wishes, even setting the lowliest of men over them. The throne enhances the status of man, but to be properly filled, the man must be noble. Some of the greatest men and some of the meanest men have sat on a throne or headed nations. Kings and leaders seldom differ in wisdom from their subjects. Ultimately, each ruler derives his power and authority from God.

THE KING'S PUNISHMENT (4:19-26). Like Nebuchadnezzar, Daniel is perplexed, but only for a little while. The prophet is terrified by thoughts of what will happen to the king, and his compassionate alarm is apparent to the king. Daniel would have applied the dream to the king's enemies if possible!

Did Daniel love Nebuchadnezzar? Obviously he did, as seen from his own reaction to the interpretation. Yet, as with the prophet Nathan, he had to tell the king, "You are the man!" (2 Samuel 12:7). That is tough love!

Because Daniel's interpretation of this dream and visions is so self-explanatory, only a brief summary follows.

1. Nebuchadnezzar, you are the tree.

2. The watcher, a holy one sent down from heaven, is an angel announcing the decree of the Most High.

3. It is decreed that you will become mentally deranged and men will drive you from your kingdom. You will imagine yourself one of the beasts of the field, eating and sleeping with them for seven years, until you learn that the Most High rules in the kingdom of men, giving it to whomsoever He wills.

4. The stump and its roots, bound with iron and bronze, remain in the ground. This indicates that Nebuchadnezzar's kingdom shall be secured for him until the lesson is learned. The fact that the stump is not uprooted indicates the preserving of his own life, as well as his kingdom.

5. The seven times (years) of malady will end with Nebuchadnezzar knowing that the Most High God rules in the kingdom of men.

Nebuchadnezzar does not record whether Daniel interpreted the meaning of "let the animals flee from under it and the birds from its branches." The probable interpretation is that those around the king would abandon him as soon as his insanity appeared. They would give up on him, never anticipating his return to the throne. How many people view Christ this way? Amazingly, Jesus' own family thought He was out of His mind (Mark 3:21), while others thought He was raving mad (John 10:19). C. S. Lewis has correctly pointed out that "either Jesus is a lunatic, a liar or He is Lord." There are no other choices!

THE KING'S PROCRASTINATION (4:27-29). The prophet understood God's ways. Through the reading of his OT Scriptures, Daniel would have been familiar with the prophet Jonah's testimony concerning God's character, in particular His willingness to save even the Ninevites, a most despicable people.

I knew that you are a gracious and compassionate God, slow to anger and abounding in love, a God who relents from sending calamity

(Jonah 4:2).

Therefore, the decree of the Most High God, in Nebuchadnezzar's dream, is not fixed in stone. God's character does not change; but His holiness and love necessitate a change in plans when man changes his heart. Therefore, Daniel warns the king that it is better to repent today rather than waiting until tomorrow.

> Therefore, O king, be pleased to accept my advice: Renounce your sins by doing what is right, and your wickedness by being kind to the oppressed. It may be that then your prosperity will continue.

"Renounce your sins by doing what is right," literally reads, "break off your sins by righteousness." Significantly, the word "break off" (פְּרַק *peraq*) is the same word used later in the Targums and in the Syriac language to denote "redeem."

In OT terms, Daniel advises the king to repent and receive God's salvation. The king is to practice righteousness, the chief virtue of a good ruler. Faith and righteousness are manifested by good works. God's fundamentals never change: "Faith without deeds is dead" (James 2:20-26).

Over the centuries, God's prophets, apostles and preachers have urged people to repent and believe, not tomorrow—but today. For instance, Paul writes in 2 Corinthians 6:1-2:

> As God's fellow-workers we urge you not to receive God's grace in vain. For he says, "In the time of my favor I heard you, and in the day of salvation I helped you." I tell you, now is the time of God's favor, now is the day of salvation.

The king took the hard road to humility. Like so many others, the stubborn-hearted king chose procrastination. Bad choice! When "the Hound of Heaven" picks up the scent and seeks, He is tenacious. God's patience with Nebuchadnezzar ran out one year after the king dreamed the dream of a tree, heard its interpretation and Daniel's call for repentance.

THE KING'S PRIDE (4:30). Humanly speaking, and from a worldly perspective, the king had every reason to be proud. He had conquered his whole world and had built the great Babylonian Empire. In addition, he had built the spectacular city of Babylon, whose massive walls, hanging gardens, temple of Marduk and royal palace made it the greatest city in the world. All had been done to glorify his majesty. *Power* plus *possessions* plus *prestige* plus *pride* equal *poverty of soul* for Nebuchadnezzar and a multitude of others.

THE KING'S PERVERSION (4:31-33). At the highest point of self-glorification, Nebuchadnezzar's mind snapped; for seven years, he remained insane. Nebuchadnezzar's understanding and memory were gone, and all the powers of the rational mind were broken. How careful we should be to not do, or say, anything that might provoke God into putting us out of our senses!

The mental disease Nebuchadnezzar suffered from is rare. It is called "lycanthropy" (from the Greek word λυκοσ (*lukos*, wolf) and αντηροποσ (*anthropos*, man), or wolfman, because the person imagines himself to be a wolf, a bear, or some other animal. This disease is known to have afflicted, among others George III of England and Otto of Bavaria. Lycanthropy is the basis of the "werewolf" legends. Nebuchadnezzar thought and acted like cattle (תור *towr*; Aramaic for "oxen" or "bulls") for seven years.

In obvious reference to the king's unusual malady, Berossus, a Babylonian priest of the third century B.C., records that Nebuchadnezzar, having reigned forty-three years, was suddenly invaded by sickness (*Contra Apionem* 1:20).

According to Megasthenes, who lived form 313-280 B.C., the Chaldeans had told him that Nebuchadnezzar, while on the roof of his palace, having completed his military conquests, "was possessed by some god or other."

Eusebius, in his *Praeparatio Evanelica* (9:41), quotes Abydenus concerning Nebuchadnezzar in his last days "being possessed by some god or other" and who, having uttered a prophecy concerning the coming

Persian conqueror, "immediately disappeared."

Sir Henry Rawlinson recovered a damaged, Babylonian inscription by Nebuchadnezzar, which is translated as follows:

> For four years the seat of my kingdom in my city . . . did not rejoice my heart. In all my dominions I did not build a high place of power, the precious treasures of my kingdom I did not lay out. In the worship of Merodach my lord, the joy of my heart in Babylon, the city of my sovereignty, I did not sing his praises and I did not furnish his altars, nor did I clear out the canals (*Historical Evidences of the Truth of the Scriptural Records,* 185, 440 n. 29).

Nebuchadnezzar's malady is a historical fact, documented from various quarters. His case seems much like that of the man with an evil spirit in Mark 5, whose dwelling was among the tombs, and who was shunned by society. God's rule extends over the demonic forces and He is able to overrule their evil for His good purposes, which are always righteous and just. In Saul's case, God used an evil spirit to punish the king for his apostasy.

> Now the Spirit of the LORD had departed from Saul, and an evil spirit from the LORD tormented him (1 Samuel 16:14).

Nebuchadnezzar munched on grass for the predicted amount of time. Whether demon-possessed or mentally ill, his appearance was as grotesque as his pride was in the eyes of God. His body, no longer clothed in purple and fine linen, grew hairs like feathers of an eagle. He was wet with the dew of heaven; his fingernails and toenails like the claws of birds.

The iron and bronze surrounding the stump may indicate that Nebuchadnezzar munched on grass in one of the palace's parks where animals were kept, much like a modern zoo.

God probably used this dream to prepare Daniel for his vision of the four beasts, described in chapter seven. Daniel must have watched in horror as the most powerful monarch humankind would ever offer went mad—

acting like a beast. It seems likely that Daniel remained prime minister, and protected Nebuchadnezzar during his seven-year malady.

THE KING'S PRESERVATION (4:34-37). Nebuchadnezzar learned the hard way that God does as He wills. The Most High rules as He pleases and no one can stop Him or question His right to do what He does.

> At the end of that time, I, Nebuchadnezzar, raised my eyes towards heaven, and my sanity was restored. Then I praised the Most High; I honored and glorified him who lives forever. His dominion is an eternal dominion; his kingdom endures from generation to generation. All the peoples of the earth are regarded as nothing. He does as he pleases with the powers of heaven and the peoples of the earth. No one can hold back his hand or say to him: "What have you done?" (Daniel 4:34-35).

Here Nebuchadnezzar admitted that God's actions in dealing with him had been proper and that he, Nebuchadnezzar, was not about to question them. Job was taught the very same lesson by the LORD (Job 38:1-42:6).

As one studies and decodes the prophecies of the book of Daniel, it is paramount to seek literal fulfillment. Every prophetic detail of the king's dream and visions, as interpreted by Daniel, was literally fulfilled.

> At the end of that time, I, Nebuchadnezzar, raised my eyes towards heaven, and my sanity was restored. Then I praised the Most High; I honored and glorified him who lives forever. His dominion is an eternal dominion; his kingdom endures from generation to generation.

The prodigal son, having come to his senses, has come home; God having waited and waited, has welcomed him with open arms (cf. Luke 15:17-20). Nebuchadnezzar finally had a beatitude attitude heart: "Blessed are the poor in spirit, for theirs is the kingdom of heaven (Matthew 5:3-5). One cannot enter God's kingdom with a proud and self-sufficient heart. Jesus said, "I tell you the truth, anyone who will not receive the kingdom of God like a little child will never enter it" (Mark

10:15).

Meet Nebuchadnezzar, the king of kings, the greatest king in history—poor in spirit and humble like a little child—a citizen of the kingdom of God. He has a changed heart and a new song to sing—the praises of the Most High instead of himself.

Seven blessings were restored to Nebuchadnezzar:

1. His understanding returned.
2. His reason returned.
3. The glory of his kingdom was restored.
4. His honor and brilliance returned.
5. His advisers and nobles sought him out again.
6. He was reestablished in his kingdom.
7. Splendor was added to him.

Miraculously, no new king ascended to the throne during the seven-year malady; however, his son, Evil-Merodach, might have been regent during his father's insanity. As with Job (Job 42:10-15), God's blessings bestowed on Nebuchadnezzar increased after his walk through the fires of suffering.

There is a progression in Nebuchadnezzar's understanding of the Most High God (4:2). The king recognizes Him as:

1. Revealer, 2:47
2. Deliverer, 3:28
3. Eternal God, 4:34
4. Sovereign, 4:35
5. King, 4:37

By the end of chapter four, Nebuchadnezzar should have learned at least twenty-one things about the Most High God.

1. Praise, honor and glory belong to God alone.
2. God is the King of heaven who rules the earth.
3. All God's works are truth.
4. God's ways are just.

5. God blesses those who fear Him rather than man.
6. God is Lord of kings.
7. God is the revealer of mysteries.
8. God's presence is with those who put their trust in Him.
9. God can silence man's boasts and reduce him to a beast.
10. True servants of God will not worship any other god.
11. There is no other god who can deliver people like the true God.
12. There is no other god who can do miracles like the true God.
13. God's kingdom is everlasting.
14. Generations of men will continue on the earth for a long time.
15. The Spirit of the Holy God can dwell in man.
16. God gives rule to whomsoever He wills.
17. The wise men of earth are incapable of knowing and understanding spiritual truth unless God reveals it to them.
18. Sin does not pay.
19. Pride is the cause of downfalls.
20. Anyone that walks in pride, God is able to humble.
21. God demonstrates His love to us while we were still sinners, even to the most arrogant, wicked, and cruelest of tyrants.

It is not known how long Nebuchadnezzar reigned after he was restored, but long enough to become greater than before. In 562 B.C., King Nebuchadnezzar died a man of faith—an OT saint! One day we will meet in heaven. To talk and sing with Nebuchadnezzar about the amazing grace that flows from the love of God—that will be glory!

Applications and Typical Prophecies of Chapter Four

Yahweh's dealings with Nebuchadnezzar offer practical insight on how much God hates pride and insight on its destructive results. When pride results in jealousy and disdainful behavior or treatment of others, it becomes a serious sin, which is condemned repeatedly in the Bible.

Pride was the downfall of the guardian cherub Lucifer, who is Satan (Isaiah 14:12-15; Ezekiel 28:13-17). Pride moved Cain to slay his brother Abel. Pride was Nebuchadnezzar's downfall. Pride will be the downfall of the Antichrist (Proverbs 16:18).

The book of Proverbs offers seven warnings against pride (6:17; 8:13; 11:2; 13:10; 16:5, 18; 29:23). Pride is an abomination to the LORD because it desecrates His name and His rightful place. It leads to shame, brings about destruction, and ends with judgment.

God works in many ways to break pride. Like Nebuchadnezzar, we tend to ignore His signs. God dropped Daniel and his friends into the king's lap to confront the monarch and to give him opportunities to turn away from himself to the true and living God.

Finally, the LORD used one of His most effective means—a malady that comes in the forms of infirmity, sickness, disease, debilitation, etc. Some people have to lose their "grip on life" in order for reality and eternity to come into clearer focus. Such was the case with Nebuchadnezzar.

We might say that God went "the second mile" with Nebuchadnezzar, not wanting him to perish but to come to repentance. Yahweh's dealings with the king are the quintessence of His patience spoken of by the apostle Peter.

> He is patient with you, not wanting anyone to perish, but everyone to come to repentance (2 Peter 3:9).

Nebuchadnezzar typifies a strong-willed person, along with what is often necessary to bring about the conversion of such a heart. Note the sequence in Nebuchadnezzar's conversion.

A false sense of significance
A false sense of security
A target of God's mercy and compassion
A warning of coming judgment
An invitation to repent
A drastic event prior to conversion
An attitude and behavior like a beast
A humbling by God
A turning from self to God

If God could bring about a change in Nebuchadnezzar's heart, no one is

112

beyond repentance and belief. Therefore, as opportunities arise to tell the unsaved world what God has planned for the lost, Christians are to be as bold and courageous as Daniel. Because, for the perishing, their fate will be far worse than Nebuchadnezzar's seven years of madness if they do not repent and believe in Christ.

If you find it too hard to tell a friend about Christ, write a letter to him or her. In that letter tell your friend how the Lord saved you, and give all the glory to God. That is what Nebuchadnezzar did. The king wanted to teach to all the people of the earth the lesson that God had taught him. Should we not want to do the same?

It is incorrect to view the prophetic writings of Daniel as merely heroic accounts of a man, named Daniel, which have been compiled into a book of twelve disconnected and unrelated chapters. Instead, they are related accounts of God's progressive revelation concerning those things He wants His people to know.

During the end of his reign, Nebuchadnezzar typifies Christ, the Ruler of the millennial reign. When Daniel told the king to break off sin and practice righteousness, a ruler's chief virtue, the king acted accordingly. He proceeded to proclaim peace, one of the blessings of righteousness, to all his subjects. The One who brings righteousness and peace came and will come again to fulfill what the prophet Isaiah predicted.

> For to us a child is born, to us a son is given, and the government will be on his shoulders. And he will be called Wonderful Counselor, Mighty God, Everlasting Father, Prince of Peace (Isaiah 9:6).

Nebuchadnezzar typifies Christians also. Like the king, unsaved unbelievers walk in pride and are at enmity with God, who sees them in a state of insanity—unless, and until—they humble themselves, call on the LORD, and have their sanity restored. Both Nebuchadnezzar and Christians have been rescued from the dominion of darkness ruled by Satan.

> For he has rescued us from the dominion of darkness and brought us into the kingdom of the Son he loves, in whom we have redemption,

the forgiveness of sins (Colossians 1:13-14).

Once you were alienated from God and were enemies in your minds because of your evil behavior. But now he has reconciled you by Christ's physical body through death to present you holy in his sight, without blemish and free from accusation (Colossians 1:21-22).

Our alienation from God, and the enmity we had in our minds for Him, have both been vanquished, and replaced with the righteousness that is of, and from, God. Our evil deeds are superseded by good works.

In addition, Nebuchadnezzar foreshadows the Antichrist, who, in his madness and pride, will attempt to build a kingdom by his mighty power, for the glory of his own majesty. At that time, God will deal with the nations as He dealt with Nebuchadnezzar. Either the people of nations will humble themselves and come under the subjection of His Son, or they will be gone with the wind. As predicted in the dream of dreams, the whole earth will be filled with the everlasting kingdom.

Nebuchadnezzar addressed his edict "to the peoples, nations and men of every language, who live in all the world." The edict points to the time of the Tribulation, when a great multitude that no one can count, coming from every nation, tribe, people and language, are saved (Revelation 7:9).

As with Nebuchadnezzar, God's judgment on the nations during the Tribulation concludes with the subjugating of the earth to the One who has been given all authority and the right to rule.

As with Nebuchadnezzar, the earth will not be restored until the seven years of the Tribulation (Malady) have passed. Then the saved will be restored to the kingdom of God on earth, which was forfeited by Adam's self-centeredness.

During this present age, the conversion of Nebuchadnezzar foreshadows the fact that while salvation is being experienced by Gentiles, the Jews are being despised among the nations.

Just as the Gentile king proclaimed the glory of the Most High God to his empire, so it will be primarily the responsibility of Gentiles to proclaim the Gospel of God during the "times of the Gentiles." In this period, God will preserve a remnant of Jews as foreshadowed by His miraculous deliverance of Shadrach, Meshach and Abednego from the fiery furnace. However, since the Jews have forfeited their position as the light of the world—a kingdom of priests, and a holy nation, it is not their place to ask, "What have You done?

Belshazzar's Blasphemous Feast
(Daniel 5)

Time Line

YEAR B.C.	562	559	555	555-539	553-539
BABYLONIAN KINGS	Evil-Merodach	Neriglassar	Labash-Marduk	Nabonidus	Beleshazzar
EVENTS	Kind to Jehoiachin	Murders Evil-Merodach	Murdered	At Tema	Vice-Regent

Outline of Chapter Five

Sacrilege of Belshazzar, 1-4

Shock of Belshazzar, 5-6

Summons of the Wise Men, 7-9

Solution of the Queen, 10-17

Sermon from Daniel, 18-25

Significance of the Handwriting, 26-28

Sequel of Events, 29-31

Background of Chapter Five

Most likely affected by his father's conversion, Nebuchadnezzar's son, Amel-Marduk (known in the Bible as Evil-Merodach) showed kindness to the Judean king Jehoiachin, who had been imprisoned by Nebuchadnezzar (2 Kings 25:27-30). This kindness could be an indication that Evil-Merodach had been converted. This action may have led to his being killed by Neriglissar, his brother-in law, in 559 B.C. Neriglissar's biblical name is Nergal-sharezer, the official under Nebuchadnezzar, who apparently was involved in helping release Jeremiah from prison (Jeremiah 39:3, 13). Time had not been good to Neriglissar; instead of ascending in virtue, he descended.

After the death of Evil-Merodach, war broke out between Babylon and the Medes and Persians. Neriglissar ascended to the throne of Babylon, reigned for about four years, and died in battle in 556 B.C. Then his son, Labashi-Marduk, having reigned for less than a year, was beaten to death by conspirators and the throne was seized by Nabonidus, who reigned from 555 B.C. to the fall of Babylon in 539 B.C.

In a libel known as *The Verse Account of Nabonidus*, the king is accused of being a madman, a liar boasting of victories he had never won, and a heretic who blasphemed Marduk and worshiped the deity Sin. Because of his lengthy excavations in search of written documents, Nabonidus has been called "the Royal Archaeologist." While he devoted himself to excavating ruins, his own realm was falling into ruins.

In contrast to Nabonidus stands Cyrus II, who ascended the Persian throne in 559 B.C. He lacked neither ambition nor intelligence.

The Persians were an Indo-European speaking people, who had entered Iran from the north at the end of the second millennium—at the same time as the Medes, who were closely related to the Persians. By the time of Cyrus II, the Persians had reversed the role of being a vassal of the Medes. In 550 B.C., Cyrus II became ruler of both the Persian and Media kingdoms (*Ancient Iraq,* 352-354).

When Nabonidus captured Tema, the oasis city which lies south of Edom in Arabia, he set up his palace there. While Nabonidus was establishing a new military and commercial fortress at Tema, Belshazzar was left in full control of the army of Babylon from at least 553 to 539 B.C. Because of this, the famous *Nabonidus Chronicle* inferred correctly that the "crown prince" (obviously Belshazzar) was regarded as "king." In A.D. 1919 and 1924, oaths were found between Nabonidus and Belshazzar entrusting the kingship in Babylon to Belshazzar while Nabonidus reigned from Arabia.

The liberal scholarship that denied the historicity of major portions of Daniel had been wrong. Daniel is solidly grounded upon historical realities. Only a person writing from this period could have known correctly this detail about these two rulers. All should take to heart Jesus' rebuke of Cleopas and the other traveler on the road to Emmaus,

"How foolish you are, and how slow of heart to believe all that the prophets have spoken!" (Luke 24:25).

The main character of this chapter is Belshazzar, the son of Nabonidus and grandson of Nebuchadnezzar. There is no word in Aramaic for grandfather. So the word "father" is often used of ancestors.

This chapter covers the last night of the Babylonian Empire. The date is the fifteenth of Tishri (October 12/13) 539 B.C. On Israel's calendar, it is the first day of the Feast of Tabernacles, which typifies the Millennial Kingdom. The prophet Jeremiah had predicted this time would come.

> All nations will serve him and his son and his grandson until the time
> for his land comes; then many nations and great kings will subjugate
> him (Jeremiah 27:7).

This chapter is similar to the book of Esther. It begins with a great banquet; the queen plays an important role in the outcome; then it ends with the villain killed and its hero rewarded.

The most dramatic moments in this chapter are the supernatural appearance of the fingers of a human hand, writing on the wall, and Daniel's interpretation of the cryptic writing.

Chapter one and chapter five are contrasts. In chapter one, there is restraint in eating and the drinking of wine; Daniel is on the rise in the Babylonian empire. In chapter five, there is no restraint in feasting and the drinking of wine; Belshazzar falls with the Babylonian empire.

God Judges Blaspheming Belshazzar

SACRILEGE OF BELSHAZZAR (5:1-4). As the events of this chapter unfold, we see the irony of Belshazzar's name, which means "Bel protect the king." Belshazzar was the son of Nabonidus ("the god Nabu is to be revered"), who was last of the Babylonian kings. The designation "Belshazzar, the king" has been criticized as historically inaccurate since he did not reign as sole king and was never directly called "king" in the inscriptions from Babylon. However, the Aramaic word for "king," מֶלֶךְ (*melek*), does not necessitate the coronation of a sole monarch. Furthermore, a cuneiform source expressly states that Nabonidus entrusted the kingship to his son, Belshazzar. Hence, he was king of Babylon.

The Prayer of Nabonidus, found with the *Dead Sea Scrolls,* indicates the king had been "smitten with a serious inflammation, by the command of the Most High God, in the city Tema," and was quarantined until "seven times" had passed. This disease may be the reason Nabonidus was absent from Babylon when the kingdom fell. On the other hand, this prayer might be apocryphal genre drawn from Nebuchadnezzar's malady.

Great feasts were characteristic of antiquity. Persian kings frequently dined with as many as 15,000 guests. The Assyrian king Ashurnaspiral II entertained 69,574 guests at the dedication of his new capital city of Calah in 879 B.C. Alexander the Great had 10,000 guests at his wedding feast and the story line in the book of Esther encompasses ten banquets.

It was the custom at Ancient Near Eastern feasts for the king to sit on a raised platform, apart from the guests. Excessive drinking after the dinner was common in this period. Many feasts became drunken orgies, since people who are overly excited by alcohol are apt to lose control of their thoughts and actions. History is replete with costly mistakes made by people while under the influence of alcohol.

While Belshazzar was drinking his wine and becoming inebriated, he did a most foolish and blasphemous thing. He gave orders to bring into the licentious, idolatrous festivities the sacred articles from the Temple of God that Nebuchadnezzar had brought back from Jerusalem in 605 B.C.

Nebuchadnezzar had been drunk with pride; his grandson was drunk with wine and corruption. However, their eternal destinies are opposites. The patience of God has run out; there is no time to repent! The justice of God is righteous and it is beyond question, as seen in His declaration to Moses, which is quoted by Paul.

> I will have mercy on whom I will have mercy, and I will have compassion on whom I will have compassion (Exodus 33:19; Romans 9:15).

Nebuchadnezzar received God's mercy and compassion, but Belshazzar had blasphemed God, thereby crossing over the line of God's grace to judgment. Jesus taught that "whoever blasphemes against the Holy Spirit will never be forgiven; he is guilty of an eternal sin" (Mark 3:29). Belshazzar may have blasphemed against the Holy Spirit by rejecting His revelation of God's sovereignty. Daniel points out in this chapter that Belshazzar had rejected the truth about the Most High God, which he had received from his grandfather Nebuchadnezzar.

The drunken feast was symbolic of the moral condition of the empire and its king. The feast was an outrageous, sacrilegious affair and its participants were reprobate. Such debauchery called for swift and irrevocable judgment. Babylon's moral degradation had filled the cup of iniquity, just as the Amorites had centuries before (Genesis 15:16). As the king and his nobles, wives and concubines drank from the sacred goblets, they were symbolically drinking of Yahweh's cup of wrath.

> Therefore hear this, you afflicted one, made drunk, but not with wine. This is what your Sovereign LORD says, your God, who defends his people: "See, I have taken out of your hand the cup that made you stagger; from that cup, the goblet of my wrath, you will never drink again. I will put it into the hands of your tormentors, who said to you, "Fall prostrate that we may walk over you." And you made your back like the ground, like a street to be walked over" (Isaiah 51:21-23).

> In the hand of the LORD is a cup full of foaming wine mixed with spices; he pours it out, and all the wicked of the earth drink it down to its very dregs (Psalm 75:8).

Intemperance, impropriety, impiety, idolatry, immorality and finally *indifference* to the things of God marked this feast—the whole affair pictured Babylon ripe for God's judgment.

Man is intuitively religious; if the true God is not worshiped, man will be dominated by Satan and turn to idolatrous worship. The moment the guests "praised the gods of gold and silver, of bronze, iron, wood and stone" with the golden and silver goblets in hand, they crossed over the line of God's patience with their blasphemy. These goblets had been dedicated and sanctified to Yahweh, and they had desecrated them.

SHOCK OF BELSHAZZAR (5:5-6). The Bible teaches that God's judgment may come with the unexpected suddenness of a thief in the night.

> Suddenly the fingers of a human hand appeared and wrote on the plaster of the wall, near the lampstand in the royal palace. The king watched the hand as it wrote (Daniel 5:5).

If not the actual fingers of the hand of God, they certainly represent His fingers. Earlier, in the miracles of Moses, the finger of God was recognized by the Egyptians (Exodus 8:19); the Ten Commandments were written by the finger of God (Exodus 31:8); and Jesus said, "But if I drive out demons by the finger of God, then the kingdom of God has come to you" (Luke 11:20).

Excavations of this palace corroborated that its large hall (173 by 56 feet) was covered with white plaster. The walls were beautifully decorated with painted stucco designs, to which God adds His own sketch of the immediate future.

It is likely that "the lampstand" came from the Holy Place of God's Temple. Among other things, this article typifies judgment, which is symbolic of God's light exposing good and evil. In the NT, there are "the seven golden lampstands" that appear in the midst of the seven churches of Asia Minor. The lampstands symbolize the scrutiny of Christ as He reveals His commendations and condemnations of the seven churches (Revelation 2-3).

Here the light from the lampstand illuminated the king's face, the writing hand, and the writing on the wall. "His face turned pale and he was so frightened that his knees knocked together and his legs gave way."

God's dreams and visions had terrified Nebuchadnezzar, but nothing like what the writing hand did to Belshazzar. Definitely, "it is a fearful thing to fall into the hands of the living God" (Hebrews 10:31). Belshazzar's reactions are a vivid description of terror.

1. His face turned pale.
2. He was so frightened.
3. His knees knocked together.
4. His legs gave way.
5. He called out in distress.

SUMMONS OF THE WISE MEN (5:7-9). The king called for the wise men (the enchanters, Chaldeans and diviners). For the third time their fakery is exposed. The tongues of the godless are powerless to tell the meaning of God's message even when marvelous rewards are to be gained.

> Whoever reads this writing and tells me what it means will be clothed in purple and have a gold chain placed around his neck, and he will be made the third highest ruler in the kingdom (Daniel 5:7).

Belshazzar does not offer the second highest office in the kingdom since he holds that position. Sometime following Nebuchadnezzar's death, Daniel ceased being the prime minister of the empire. This is not surprising since darkness hates the light.

Amazingly, these well-educated wise men cannot even read the writing. It might have been written in a script unknown to them.

SOLUTION OF THE QUEEN (5:10-17). Who is the queen? Not Nabonidus' wife, she is at Tema. And Belshazzar's wives are in the banquet hall. It is Nebuchadnezzar's widow, Amytis, the grandmother of Belshazzar. His ancestral line was from Nitocris and Nabonidus, who in turn came from Nebuchadnezzar and Amytis.

Neither the queen nor Daniel attended the feast. Both are the salt of the earth and the light to the world. The queen had the spiritual discernment of her husband, recognizing the Spirit of the Holy God in Daniel. She presented a sevenfold favorable testimony concerning Daniel.

1. He has the Holy Spirit in him.
2. He has a keen mind.
3. He is full of knowledge.
4. He has great understanding.

5. He has the gift of interpreting dreams.
6. He can explain riddles.
7. He can solve difficult problems.

Why does Daniel have such great knowledge, understanding and wisdom? Proverbs 9:10.

Amytis' testimony to her grandson indicates she was converted also. With the same confidence her husband had displayed, she said, "Call for Daniel and he will tell you what the writing means." Ironically, her evaluation of the outcome of the circumstances is unequivocally wrong. She said, "O king live forever! Don't be alarmed! Don't look so pale." Daniel would decisively reverse the queen's comfort with condemnation.

SERMON FROM DANIEL (5:18-25). It is difficult to know exactly what Belshazzar meant by "I have heard the spirit of the gods is in you and that you have intelligence and outstanding wisdom." He may have learned this fact from his grandparents long before this night. If so, he is doubly culpable.

Daniel was offered the same reward for reading and interpreting the writing, as the king offered to the wise men. The prophet wanted no part of his gifts. Before the night is over, they would be worthless. In addition, he may have been saying, "Keep your gifts, I cannot be bribed."

Before Daniel interpreted the handwriting on the wall, the bold and courageous prophet preached a sermon to Belshazzar that recounted the conversion of Nebuchadnezzar and condemned Belshazzar.

Here, the boldness and courage of Daniel is apparent. The OT prophets often made predictions concerning the future. But primarily, the prophets were covenant enforcers. The Israelites were assured of God's blessing if they repented, and warned of His curses if they did not. The prophet's sermon demonstrates that even Gentiles, such as Belshazzar, are responsible for what has been made known to them. Belshazzar had sinned against knowledge, blasphemed God, committed idolatry, and that he is cursed. The day of reckoning had arrived.

Daniel's Sermon to Belshazzar

The Progress of Nebuchadnezzar was God given, 18.

The Power of Nebuchadnezzar was God given, 19.

The Pride of Nebuchadnezzar was his downfall, 20.

The Punishment of Nebuchadnezzar was God taking his throne away, 20.

The Poor in Spirit Nebuchadnezzar had acknowledged God's rule over him, 21.

The Points of the Sermon are aimed at Belshazzar, 22-23:

    He did not humble himself.

    He did not profit by the dealings of God with his grandfather.

    He set himself against God.

    He desecrated the sanctified vessels of the house of God.

    He praised idol gods.

The Pronouncements of God are in the handwriting, 24-28.

SIGNIFICANCE OF THE HANDWRITING (26-28). In four little words, divine judgment was pronounced against Belshazzar, who had set himself up against the Most High God. The pronouncement consists, however, of three Aramaic words, since one is repeated: תקל ופרסין מנא מנא. In our script, the writing looks like *MN'MN'TKLUPRSUN*, and with the words separated and vowels added, it reads *MENE MENE TEKEL UPARSIN*. In his interpretation, Daniel dropped the conjunction "*U*" and the plural ending of "*IN*" from the last word and made it *PERES*.

Some commentators have attempted to make these words stand for "a mina, a shekel and two half-minas." Literally, the writing means "to number," "to weigh," and "to divide." Therein resides a cryptic message, which Daniel decoded and revealed.

    MENE: *God has numbered the days of your reign and brought it to an end.* MENE indicates that Belshazzar's and Babylon's numbers are up! God's calculations are not carelessly arrived at—duration of the king's life and empire's existence is perfectly timed and not left to chance (Daniel 2:21; 4:17).

    TEKEL: *You have been weighed on the scales and found wanting.* It indicates God's scales are accurate, exact and just. The king is lacking righteousness.

PERES: *Your kingdom is divided and given to the Medes and Persians.*   PARSIN (PERES) has a double sense. Daniel discerns the kingdom will be given to the Medes and Persians and afterwards be broken up.

Belshazzar had been found too light in moral and spiritual worth to balance God's scales—the standard being righteousness.   Numbered, counted out and measured—weighed and divided, the king is found deficient by God.   The scales of God are accurate, exact, just and fair. Abraham recognized these things about God, when He said to the LORD:

> Far be it from you to do such a thing—to kill the righteous with the wicked, treating the righteous and the wicked alike. Far be it from you! Will not the Judge of all the earth do right? (Genesis 18:25).

Why did Babylon fall? Its time was up! The period that God allotted to Babylon had been revealed by the head of gold in the Dream of Dreams. The predicted seventy years of captivity for the Jews was ending (Jeremiah 29:10). Having challenged God's patience and having passed His deadline for repentance, Belshazzar would be plunged into eternal destruction.

There is a last night for every nation and there is a last night for every individual. God rules; He determines the times and boundaries of the nations, and every person is utterly dependent upon God for his or her next breath. With the unexpectedness of a thief, the Babylonian Empire and Belshazzar's life ended that night. Everyone should take to heart Yahweh's warning to Israel.

> Therefore this is what I will do to you, Israel, and because I will do this to you, prepare to meet your God, O Israel (Amos 4:12).

SEQUEL OF EVENTS (5:29-31). Like Mordecai (Esther 8:15), Daniel wears the purple robe of royalty, and like Joseph in Egypt (Genesis 41:42), he wears a golden chain of honor around his neck, both articles being symbolic of rule. A similar reward is promised to overcomers by

Christ.

> To him who overcomes, I will give the right to sit with me on my throne, just as I overcame and sat down with my Father on his throne (Revelation 3:21).

How insignificant is the end of the greatest world empire in God's eye; He inspires Daniel to record it in a single sentence.

> That very night Belshazzar, king of the Babylonians, was slain, and Darius the Mede took over the kingdom, at the age of sixty-two (Daniel 5:30).

Daniel was about eighty-one years old when Darius the Mede at age sixty-two began to reign at Babylon. However, it is not the time for Daniel to retire. There is much to do and more for God to reveal to him.

Scholars disagree on the identification of Darius. Most recent research, however, favors the view that he was Gubaru (Gobryas), the man whom King Cyrus appointed governor of Babylon (see *A Survey of Old Testament Introduction*, 372-374). Gubaru was born in 601 B.C., thus he would have been sixty-two as Daniel indicated.

Archaeological discoveries from this period, and historians near to it, provide a vivid picture of what happened that night. A brief summary of the fall of Babylon follows.

> In the last year of Nabonidus, the Babylon Chronicle records that the gods of the cities around Babylon, except Borsippa, Kutha and Sippar, were brought up in, and action taken only at the sign of impending war. The Persian army clashed with the Babylonians at Opis. While in the city Nabonidus seems to have quelled a popular uprising with much bloodshed. Sippar fell to the Persian army led by Ugbaru, the district governor of Gutium, who entered Babylon the next day without a battle. This ease of entry may have been due to action by fifth columnists or, as Herodotus, asserts, to the diversion of the River Euphrates which rendered the flood defenses useless and enabled the invaders to march through the dried up river bed to enter by night. Belshazzar was killed and Gutean soldiers guarded the

temple area of Esagila where services continued without a break. Sixteen days later on 29 October 539 Cyrus himself entered amid public rejoicing. A peace settlement was reached quickly and Gubaru appointed sub-governor. The fall of Babylon and coming of Cyrus is mentioned frequently in the OT (Isaiah 13:14; 21:1-10; 44:28; 47:1-5; Jeremiah 50-51). Cyrus decreed religious freedom and the restoration of national shrines. Since Judah had no statues to be restored, compensation was granted (Ezra 1) (*ZPEB*, 1:446).

An inscription made by Cyrus reads, "Without any battle, he (that is Marduk) made him enter his town Babylon, sparing Babylon any calamity. He delivered into his hands Nabonidus, the king, who did not worship him." This inscription also tells how Cyrus was welcomed by the entire population (*ANET*, 315-316).

The Nabonidus Chronicle tells of Cyrus' approach to Babylon, of his defeating one city after another as he came, and of Nabonidus' flight from before him at Sippar on the fourteenth of Tishri (October 10, 539 B.C.). Cyrus' commander Ugbaru (often called Gobryas) is the one who entered Babylon without a battle on the sixteenth of the same month. On the third of the month Mardchesvan (October 29, 539 B.C.), Cyrus himself entered Babylon and was welcomed with "green twigs" spread before him, and later the same month, the "?" of the king died.

The corrupted text might be "son," "wife," "commander" or something else. It cannot refer to Belshazzar since Daniel recorded "that very night Belshazzar, king of the Babylonians, was slain." Xenophon says that Belshazzar was slain by two lords, Gadatas and Gobrias, who joined Cyrus to avenge themselves of certain wrongs, which he had done them.

All accounts agree that the city of Babylon was conquered with little loss of life. It took three days for many to discover they were citizens of a new empire.

Applications and Typical Prophecies of Chapter Five

Liberal scholars insist that this chapter is a made-up tale based on Genesis (Genesis 37, 39-41). Conservative scholars see God repeating history. Repetition of events is one way of showing that He overrules adverse circumstances to accomplish His plans and purposes. There are interesting parallels that exist between Joseph and Daniel, such as both are:

Taken into captivity
Handsome as a youth
Given dreams of the future
Able to interpret dreams
Become a prime minister of a Gentile kingdom
Possessors of the Holy Spirit
Told what will happen by God
Downcast and distressed by what will happen
Given a gold chain for the neck

As in the lineage of Israel's kings, Belshazzar manifested the fact that a godly heritage does not ensure a godly descent. It is each individual's responsibility to fear the LORD and submit to His will (cf. Ezekiel 18). A chain of good or a chain of evil can be broken at any time by faithfulness or unfaithfulness to God. This principle is illustrated by Daniel's closing of this chapter with the judgment of profane Belshazzar, and the introduction of the pious Darius the Mede.

In 168 B.C., Antiochus IV Epiphanes launched a full-scale persecution against the Jews because of their unwillingness to adopt Hellenism. This chapter assured the Jews that Antiochus, who desecrated the holy vessels of the Temple of Jerusalem (1 Maccabees 1:20-28; 2 Maccabees 5:16), would suffer a destiny similar to Belshazzar's.

Four lines that God draws are apparent in this chapter:

1. God's deadline for His patience
2. God's line on blasphemy
3. God's line for judgment
4. God's finish line for a person and nation

Belshazzar crossed all four lines in one night. Christians have another line to cross as modeled by the apostle Paul.

I have fought the good fight, I have finished the race, I have kept the faith. Now there is in store for me the crown of righteousness, which the Lord, the righteous Judge, will award to me on that day—and not only to me, but also to all who have longed for his appearing (2 Timothy 4:7-8).

If God is for us, who can be against us? If we set ourselves up against God, who can be for us? If God writes "finished" across our record and "doomed" across our destiny, we cannot win, no matter how well fortified and protected we may be.

Profaning the sacred is blasphemy. All who draw breath are to praise and glorify God alone. Man is to keep sacred the things Yahweh sanctifies as holy; for example, Yahweh told Aaron in Leviticus 10:11-12:

> You must distinguish between the holy and the common, between the unclean and the clean, and you must teach the Israelites all the decrees the LORD has given them through Moses.

The suddenness of disaster is a wakeup call for repentance (cf. Luke 13:1-5). In a single night, the Babylonian Empire ceased. It is predicted that the Revived Roman Empire ("Babylon the Great") will come to a sudden end. Chapter 18 of Revelation provides a vivid forecast of its fall; a parallel to that dramatic October night of 539 B.C.

> When the kings of the earth who committed adultery with her and shared her luxury see the smoke of her burning, they will weep and mourn over her. Terrified at her torment, they will stand far off and cry: "Woe! Woe, O great city, O Babylon, city of power! In one hour your doom has come!" (Revelation 18:9-10).

As with the end of the original Babylon, there will be an immediate and sudden change of governments for the world. The fall of Babylon the Great is followed by the KING OF KINGS AND LORD OF LORDS coming from heaven with His army to rule the world for one thousand years (Revelation 19-20).

Prior to Christ's return, the condition of this world will be like the blasphemous feast of Belshazzar and the days of Noah.

> As it was in the days of Noah, so it will be at the coming of the Son of Man. For in the days before the flood, people were eating and drinking, marrying and giving in marriage, up to the day Noah entered the ark; and they knew nothing about what would happen until the flood came and took them all away. That is how it will be at the coming of the Son of Man (Matthew 24:37-39).

Intoxicated with drink and pleasure, humanity will have lost their senses. People will ignore "the handwriting on the wall" as God rains His judgments from heaven. Though terrified, they will not believe the end is near. Like Belshazzar, who made Daniel the third highest ruler, they believe there will be a tomorrow. They should fall to their knees, repenting and crying to God for mercy. Instead, their actions may be likened to shaking one's fist in the face of God as they attempt to hide from His wrath (cf. Revelation 6:15-17). The king believed he was safe and well protected behind the walls of Babylon, and so will the lost in the end times.

As God numbered the days of the Babylonian Empire, He also has determined the number of days of the end time empire—seven years from the Antichrist's confirmation of the covenant (Daniel 9:27)—and not a day longer!

Sir John Glubb in *The Fate of Empires and Search for Survival*, identified seven cycles, which empires have in common:

1. The Age of Outburst (or Pioneers)
2. The Age of Conquests
3. The Age of Commerce
4. The Age of Affluence
5. The Age of Intellect
6. The Age of Decadence
7. The Age of Decline and Collapse

In his seventeen-volume classic, *The Decline and Fall of the Roman Empire*, Edward Gibbon concluded that there were five significant factors in the collapse of the Roman Empire:

1. A rapid increase in divorce
2. A craze for pleasure
3. The building of gigantic armaments while the enemy was within
4. An increase in violence
5. The decline of religion

Throughout history, empires and nations have fallen for much the same reasons as Babylon and Rome: drunkenness, pleasure, madness, immorality, idolatry, blasphemy, willful rejection of God, greed, impure motives, materialism, confidence in human society and armaments, corrupt leadership, decline of the family, pride, and refusal to repent.

Past empires are microcosms of the world at the end of this present age. After a period of rise and prosperity, empires decline, so it will be in the end times. Therefore, we should not be surprised to read in 2 Timothy 3:1-5:

> But mark this: There will be terrible times in the last days. People will be lovers of themselves, lovers of money, boastful, proud, abusive, disobedient to their parents, ungrateful, unholy, without love, unforgiving, slanderous, without self-control, brutal, not lovers of the good, treacherous, rash, conceited, lovers of pleasure rather than lovers of God— having a form of godliness but denying its power. Have nothing to do with them.

The spirit of Babylon continues from the Tower of Babel to Babylon the Great. Then its end will occur in one great event, the coming of the stone cut out without hands. The finger of God has written, the handwriting is on the wall!

A poem from an unknown poet applies the fifth chapter of Daniel to us.

> At the feast of Belshazzar and a thousand of his lords,
> While they drank from golden vessels, as the Book of Truth records,
> In the night as they revelled in the royal palace hall,
> They were seized with consternation at the hand upon the wall.

> See the brave captive Daniel as he stood before the throng,
> And rebuked the haughty monarch for his mighty deeds of wrong;
> As he read out the writing, 'Twas the doom of one and all,
> For the kingdom was now finished said the hand upon the wall.

> See the faith, zeal, and courage that would dare to do the right,
> Which the Spirit gave to Daniel this the secret of his might.
> In his home in Judea, a captive in its hall,
> He still understood the writing of his God upon the wall.

> So our deeds are recorded; there is a hand that's writing now.
> Sinner, give your heart to Jesus, to His royal mandate bow;
> For the day is approaching, it must come to one and all,
> When a sinner's condemnation will be written on the wall.

Darius' Den of Lions and Decree
(Daniel 6)

Time Line

YEAR B.C.	539	538
MEDO-PERSIA	Cyrus II	
BABYLON	Darius the Mede	
EVENTS	Daniel's Prayer & Seventy Weeks	Cyrus' Decree

Outline of Chapter Six

Advancement of Daniel, 1-3

Adversaries of Daniel, 4-9

Attitude of Daniel, 10

Accusation against Daniel, 11-13

Anxiety of Darius, 14-20

Assurance of Darius, 21-23

Avenging of Darius, 24

Announcement of Darius, 25-27

Achievement of Daniel, 28

Background of Chapter Six

Darius, son of Xerxes (a Mede by descent), was made ruler over the Babylonian kingdom (Daniel 9:1). This Xerxes should not be confused with the Persian ruler in the time of Esther. It was common for rulers to have two names in Ancient Near Eastern history. Daniel 6:28 may be translated: "So Daniel prospered during the reign of Darius, even the reign of Cyrus the Persian." Some scholars, therefore, believe Cyrus is Darius. Darius could have been a localized name for Cyrus. It also is possible that Darius is a title since at least five Persian kings are called by that name.

The Nabonidus Chronicle states that Cyrus made Gubaru (Gobryas) governor over Babylonia and Gubaru installed sub-governors in Babylon. Darius did not conquer Babylon, but was placed in power by Cyrus the Persian, and therefore was a subordinate to Cyrus. Another possibility is that Gubaru was both governor of Gutium, who conquered Babylon, and the man Cyrus appointed to rule over Babylon. "Darius the Mede took over the kingdom, at age sixty-two," and "was made ruler over the Babylonian kingdom" (Daniel 9:1) fits the circumstances.

Gubaru is frequently mentioned in cuneiform documents during the subsequent fourteen years as "Governor of Babylon and the Region Beyond the River," a description indicating the entire Fertile Crescent. The designation of "king" is accurate since the term was used of any ruler with this much power.

Recent archeological discoveries and inscriptions from Babylon and Persia confirm that the former empire used fire for their executions and the latter empire used lions, just as recorded by Daniel. Only a writer from those times would have known these two distinct methods of execution. The liberal critics, who assigned this book to the second century B.C., are mistaken again.

Chapter six of Daniel is like the book of Jonah. Both men are preserved and delivered by God from the jaws of death. Both men are a prophetic preview of Christ.

The flow of this chapter is: (1) Daniel is despised; (2) Darius is deceived, distressed, delighted; (3) Deceivers are destroyed; and (4) Daniel prospered.

God Preserves Daniel in the Lions' Den

ADVANCEMENT OF DANIEL (6:1-3). Darius' skills were in administration. He appointed 120 satraps to rule throughout the kingdom, along with three administrators, one of whom was Daniel. The satraps (governors of Persian provinces) were made accountable to Daniel so that the king might not suffer loss. Greed and corruption were rampant, but Daniel stood in the gap.

The prophet was about eighty-one years old in the year 539 B.C. He had distinguished himself by his extraordinary spirit (gifted, filled and led by the Holy Spirit) in the golden empire, and again in this silver empire. Through Daniel, Yahweh was able to demonstrate that He, as the God of the exiled Jews, is really the sovereign God of the nations. Whether or not the king recognized this fact, Darius planned to set Daniel over the whole kingdom.

ADVERSARIES OF DANIEL (6:4-9). Envy and jealousy, probably because Daniel was a Jew, soared from the hearts of administrators and satraps as they conspired to circumvent the king's plans. However, they could find no grounds for an attack on Daniel's integrity. In all his years of service, there was not one blemish on Daniel's record. He was not corrupt; he was trustworthy and diligent in discharging his responsibilities. If the adversaries were to be successful in blocking Daniel's appointment with an accusation, it must arise from the law of his God. Indeed, Satan is the mastermind behind their plan as can be seen in Jesus' depiction of the adversary.

> He was a murderer from the beginning, not holding to the truth, for there is no truth in him. When he lies, he speaks his native language, for he is a liar and the father of lies (John 8:44).

The conspirators took their cleverly devised plot to the king. "The royal administrators, prefects, satraps, advisers and governors have all agreed"—liars! Daniel never would have agreed that the king should issue an edict and enforce a decree that would result in deifying Darius. Their intent is to murder Daniel. Truly, the conspirators belong to their father the Devil. In order to insure the success of their plan, they asked for an irrevocable decree.

> Now, O king, issue the decree and put it in writing so that it cannot be altered—in accordance with the laws of the Medes and Persians, which cannot be repealed (Daniel 6:8).

Drunk, not on wine, but on flattery and the anticipated adulation he would receive, Darius consented to the plot and signed it into law, which according to Medo-Persian custom was irrevocable. It is noteworthy that the power of the monarchs of the silver empire had diminished from the golden empire. A king was subject to the laws that he passed; they could not be changed. Bewitched by lies and flattery, King Darius put the decree in writing.

ATTITUDE OF DANIEL (6:10). Daniel's uncompromising faithfulness to God sparkled. He was a light to the world, which Jesus desires of all believers. When Daniel learned of the decree, he did what was his long established practice. He went home to his upstairs room where the windows opened towards Jerusalem. Three times a day he got down on his knees and prayed, giving thanks to his God, just as he had done before.

The practice of prayer develops perfection! Prayer is the secret of Daniel's boldness, courage, wisdom, and elevation in two empires. God rewards the thankful and dependent heart. Before his conversion, Nebuchadnezzar had praised himself for success but Daniel always thanked Yahweh for his success. Unfortunately, Darius was duped into having the prayers of the people offered to him.

Praying towards Jerusalem was the custom among the Israelites when away from the Holy City (1 Kings 8:44-51; 2 Chronicles 6:34; Psalm 5:7; 28:2; 138:2; Jonah 2:4). The faithful prayed privately at three intervals during the day, possibly on their knees (Psalm 55:17; 95:6). The morning and evening prayers correspond with the times of the morning and evening sacrifices; the halfway prayer was the one at noon.

Tests, trials, and temptations continued to come to this aged saint. Daniel was either absent or not required to bow before the golden image erected on the plain of Dura. Ironically, everyone now was standing and Daniel was bowing in prayer before his God. Yahweh now gave Daniel the test that he had missed fifty years earlier.

One almost can hear the Devil whispering to the prophet: "Daniel, do not be foolish! God understands; He knows your heart. Close the windows and enter into your closet—and pray in secret!" It would have been easy to close the windows and draw the curtains but not for one who dares to be a Daniel; he lets God's light shine through him.

Daniel is a man of courage. He prays and thanks God in the open. Do you give thanks to God for your food in restaurants or before unsaved family? Dare to be a Daniel!

ACCUSATION AGAINST DANIEL (6:11-13). To no one's surprise, the conspirators found Daniel praying to his God. To ensure the king would not renege on his decree, they asked him about it. Unaware that Daniel is the intended victim of their devious plot, Darius assured the conspirators that the laws of the Medes and Persians could not be repealed.

The trap had been sprung—the accusation against Daniel is made. Unquestionably, they had caused Darius to act foolishly—not a very wise thing to do to an Ancient Near Eastern monarch. Jealousy, envy and hatred always blur rational thinking.

ANXIETY OF DARIUS (6:14-20). When conspirators accused Daniel's three friends of not bowing down to Nebuchadnezzar's golden image, he grew intensely angry and threw the three Jews into the fiery furnace. Darius' reaction is the exact opposite.

> When the king heard this, he was greatly distressed; he was determined to rescue Daniel and made every effort until sundown to save him (Daniel 6:14).

One is wise to stand in awe of God and not make rash decrees or oaths. Under Medo-Persian law, Darius could not plead that it was a mistake and neither can anyone who makes vows and oaths to God (Ecclesiastes 5:1-7). All of Darius' efforts had failed to change the outcome.

There is a spark of faith in Darius' words. God will blow on the spark until it bursts into flames.

> So the king gave the order, and they brought Daniel and threw him into the lions' den. The king said to Daniel, "May your God, whom you serve continually, rescue you!" (Daniel 6:16).

The Aramaic "may rescue you" (יְשֵׁיזְבִנָּךְ *shezab*) is an imperfect passive intensive construction. Some translations follow the LXX's interpretation, which reads, "he will deliver you." Eugene Peterson's rendering of this verse, in *THE MESSAGE: The Bible in Contemporary Language,* reflects the confidence of Darius in most translations.

> The king caved in and ordered Daniel brought and thrown into the lions' den. But he said to Daniel, "Your God, to whom you are so loyal, is going to get you out of this (Daniel 6:16 MSG).

Darius exhibits a greater degree of faith than Daniel's three friends, who were saying, "It's not a matter of whether God is able to deliver us, but rather, if He is willing to deliver us."

Bound by His own decree and the law of the Medes and Persians, Darius was powerless to deliver Daniel from the lions' den. Interestingly, God also was powerless to deliver His Son from the cross being bound by His own prophecies of the Messiah and the law of holiness and love which permeates His being.

In Psalm 22, David foretold what Christ thought and said on the Cross. Jesus saw His enemies as "roaring lions tearing their prey open their mouths wide against me" (Psalms 22:13). Jesus felt like He had been thrown into the lions' den. Daniel was thrown literally into the lions' den and it was sealed but so were the mouths of the lions.

Daniel in the den of lions foreshadows Christ in the tomb. In his Pentecost message, Peter quoted what David said about Christ in Psalm 16:8-11. Through the psalmist, God had promised that His Holy One would not be abandoned to Sheol nor would His body see decay; He would be resurrected to life. Daniel much like Isaac, was as good as dead, but figuratively speaking, was received back from the dead (cf. Hebrews 11:17-19). Darius' faith compares favorably with Abraham's faith.

Darius spent a sleepless night on his bed alone with his thoughts. "Without eating" and "without any entertainment" might be a way of saying that the king was fasting and praying without any distractions. If his faith in the living God was not fanned into flames during the night, then he is one of the most foolish and ridiculous men who ever lived.

At the first light of dawn, the king got up and hurried to the lions' den. When he came near the den, he called to Daniel in an anguished voice, "Daniel, servant of the living God, has your God, whom you serve continually, been able to rescue you from the lions?" (Daniel 6:19).

Ironically, none of Christ's disciples, at the first light of dawn on the third day, hurried to the tomb of Jesus and called out, "Are you alive!" Repeatedly, Jesus told them that He would rise the third day, but their faith did not measure up to Darius' faith. Had they believed that God is able to rescue from the dead, they would have been there. If Darius lacked faith, he would never have called Daniel the "servant of the living God" and uttered his cry to the prophet. Obviously, the light of Daniel's witness had led Darius to belief in the living God.

ASSURANCE OF DARIUS (6:21-23). The wisdom of God is wiser than the foolishness of this world!

> Daniel answered, "O king, live forever! My God sent his angel, and he shut the mouths of the lions. They have not hurt me, because I was found innocent in his sight. Nor have I ever done any wrong before you, O king" (Daniel 6:12).

The prophet's words, "O king, live forever," are not an empty platitude, for Darius believed in the Living God, and consequently, his inheritance is eternal life.

Who was with Daniel in the lions' den? Possibly, it was a theophany of the Second Person of the Trinity or "his angel" could refer to an angel assigned to protect Daniel (cf. Hebrews 1:14). Some angelic ministries occur without people knowing it (Hebrews 13:2). Daniel was aware of the presence and power of this angel.

Critics who deny miracles maintain that the lions were toothless, or so gorged with choice meats, that they were not hungry.

AVENGING OF DARIUS (6:24). What happens next manifests a fundamental law of God.

> Do not be deceived: God cannot be mocked. A man reaps what he

sows. The one who sows to please his sinful nature, from that nature will reap destruction; the one who sows to please the Spirit, from the Spirit will reap eternal life (Galatians 6:7-8).

The fate of the officials who conspired against Daniel is one of the numerous illustrations of the axiom "What goes around comes around."

> At the king's command, the men who had falsely accused Daniel were brought in and thrown into the lions' den, along with their wives and children. And before they reached the floor of the den, the lions overpowered them and crushed all their bones (Daniel 6:24).

Was Daniel too old and tough for the lions to chew? No! The immediate and swift attack of the lions on the conspirators proves that Daniel had been miraculously delivered. The prophet was a living miracle.

The practice in the Ancient Near East was to punish the families of those who committed crimes. For instance, under the instructions of Yahweh, Joshua did the same with Achan and his family (Joshua 7:14-26). There is corporate solidarity in mankind. All are condemned and die because of Adam's one trespass and we are saved and live through Christ's one act of righteousness (Romans 5:17-18). So, was Darius just and righteous in his actions, when he cast the families of the conspirators into the lions' den? See Deuteronomy 5:8-10; 7:9-10; and Ezekiel 18.

ANNOUNCEMENT OF DARIUS (6:25-27). King Darius has become the servant of God. His words are recorded forever in Scripture. His decree exalting the living God is sevenfold.

1. All people must fear and reverence the God of Daniel.
2. He is the living God.
3. He endures forever.
4. His kingdom is eternal.
5. He rescues and saves.
6. He performs signs and wonders.
7. He has delivered Daniel from lions.

ACHIEVEMENT OF DANIEL (6:28). It is uncertain whether Daniel prospered during the reign of two different kings of Medo-Persia, or one. In either case, God continued to bless His tried and proven servant.

Applications and Prophetic Types of Chapter Six

The NT is straightforward; God expects every Christian to be holy; to be a Daniel in this crooked and perverse world.

> Do everything without complaining or arguing, so that you may become blameless and pure, children of God without fault in a crooked and depraved generation, in which you shine like stars in the universe as you hold out the word of life—in order that I may boast on the day of Christ that I did not run or labor for nothing (Philippians 2:14-16).

> But you are a chosen people, a royal priesthood, a holy nation, a people belonging to God, that you may declare the praises of him who called you out of darkness into his wonderful light (1 Peter 2:9).

> Live such good lives among the pagans that, though they accuse you of doing wrong, they may see your good deeds and glorify God on the day he visits us (1 Peter 2:12).

> So then, dear friends, since you are looking forward to this, make every effort to be found spotless, blameless and at peace with him (2 Peter 3:14).

Daniel was an overcomer until the end of his life. He had overcome the depraved, debased ways of the world, and God rewarded His faithful servant with authority and power in two empires. In these ways, Daniel foreshadows all overcomers.

> To him who overcomes and does my will to the end, I will give authority over the nations—"He will rule them with an iron scepter; he will dash them to pieces like pottery"—just as I have received authority from my Father (Revelation 2:26-27).

Who is it that overcomes the world? Only he who believes that Jesus is the Son of God (1 John 5:5).

In the time of Esther, King Ahasuerus (Xerxes) of Persia (486-465 B.C.) repeated Darius' mistake. Captivated by Haman's flattery, Xerxes unwittingly decreed in writing to destroy all Jews. In the case of Xerxes' decree for the slaughter of the Jews (Esther 3:13), he could not reverse it, but at the request of his queen, the king issued another edict which neutralized the first one (Esther 8:5-11). Daniel's deliverance from the lions may have foreshadowed the deliverance of the Jews from the jaws of death in 474 B.C.

The conspirators were against Daniel because he was Jewish. It can be heard in their voices, "Daniel, who is one of the exiles from Judah, pays no attention to you, O King." Such anti-Jewish sentiments will prevail in the end times. The Antichrist and his army will attempt to kill the Jews, and consequently, they will suffer similar results. The conspirators and their families, who were cast into the lions' den by Darius, foreshadow God's treatment of Israel's enemies in the end times. Yahweh will keep His promise to Abraham.

> I will bless those who bless you, and whoever curses you I will curse; and all peoples on earth will be blessed through you (Genesis 12:3).

Like Daniel, the remnant of the nation of Israel will be miraculously delivered by Christ. At Armageddon, the nations will conspire and gather to do battle (Revelation 16:16). However, their destruction will be as swift as that of the conspirators who were thrown alive into the lions' den. The two conspirators of the end times, the False Prophet and the Antichrist, will be thrown alive into the lake of fire (Revelation 19:17-21). At the second resurrection, the unsaved will be cast alive into hell (Revelation 20:14-15). Observe what the prophet wrote in Daniel 6:24:

> At the king's command, the men who had falsely accused Daniel were brought in and thrown into the lions' den, along with their wives and children. And before they reached the floor of the den, the lions overpowered them and crushed all their bones.

There is no mention of the conspirators and families being consumed by the lions. When God paints a type, He is accurate down to the finest details. Those who are cast into the Lake of Fire will be overpowered and crushed but never consumed (cf. Isaiah 66:24; Mark 9:47-48).

Paradoxically, the imagery of a lion represents Christ as well as the Devil in the Scriptures.

> See, the Lion of the tribe of Judah, the Root of David, has triumphed. He is able to open the scroll and its seven seals (Revelation 5:5).

> Your enemy the devil prowls around like a roaring lion looking for someone to devour (1 Peter 5:8).

We should not be surprised that God uses dual imagery and types. The first identified type in Scripture is Adam, who was a pattern (type) of Christ, as well as the human race (Romans 5:14). As this chapter ends, Darius is a man of faith, but earlier in this chapter, he prefigured the Antichrist. The same is true of Nebuchadnezzar before his conversion, when he ordered that the golden image be worshiped. Darius went a step further. His decree stated that he was to be prayed to exclusively for thirty days. Thus, Darius foreshadows the Antichrist as well as a man of faith.

> Don't let anyone deceive you in any way, for that day will not come until the rebellion occurs and the man of lawlessness is revealed, the man doomed to destruction. He will oppose and will exalt himself over everything that is called God or is worshiped, so that he sets himself up in God's temple, proclaiming himself to be God (2 Thessalonians 2:3-4).

Nebuchadnezzar, Darius and the Antichrist are types of every person who rejects the rule of God in their life. They worship themselves by doing what is right in their own eyes, setting themselves up as God. Those who exchange truth for a lie see truth as relative, applying it as they please to their own situation or circumstances.

Imagine the laughter and scoffing of the conspirators that night. They had deceived Darius; they believed that the prophet of God had been

143

delivered over to death, just as they had plotted. Hear the laughter—it is in heaven!

> Why do the nations conspire and the peoples plot in vain? The kings of the earth take their stand and the rulers gather together against the LORD and against his Anointed One. "Let us break their chains," they say, "and throw off their fetters." The One enthroned in heaven laughs; the Lord scoffs at them. Then he rebukes them in his anger and terrifies them in his wrath, saying, "I have installed my King on Zion, my holy hill" (Psalm 2:1-6).

Yahweh has warned, "Do not touch my anointed ones; do my prophets no harm" (1 Chronicles 16:22). Daniel was a servant of the Most High God. Thus, the fate of the conspirators foreshadows the fate of those who touch and harm God's servants, whether Gentiles or Jews (Matthew 21:33-46).

This chapter, along with other parts of Daniel, illustrates great prophetic truths concerning God's plan for the world and the Anointed One who will rule it. In this prophecy, the reader stands on the vista and looks with prophetic vision across the ages to see God's Anointed One, Christ Jesus our Lord.

To "allegorize" the Scriptures is to take historical events, people, or things and apply to them a meaning not originally intended. For instance, in Galatians 4:21-31, Paul allegorizes the account of Sarah and Hagar to illustrate the difference between the Old Covenant and New Covenant. A "type" in Scripture is an intended foreshadowing of a future event, person, or thing.

The events of this chapter parallel many events in the Passion Week of Christ as recorded in the four Gospels by Matthew, Mark, Luke and John. The four Gospel writers recorded the events surrounding Christ' after the fact. Daniel had the privilege of writing, beforehand, the Gospel in the typical events of his life that foreshadow Christ.

The following chart is a comparison of the thirty-four events in chapter six of Daniel with the events surrounding the death and resurrection of Christ in the Gospels.

The Gospel According to Daniel

Daniel blocked corruption
Christ overturned the tables of corruption
Daniel was to be set over the whole kingdom
Christ is to be set over the Kingdom of God
Daniel was hated as the chosen one of the king
Christ is hated as the Chosen One of God
Daniel was rejected by the officials
Christ was rejected by the elders of Israel
Leaders conspired and plotted to kill Daniel
Leaders conspired and plotted to kill Christ
Daniel declared innocent of any wrongdoing
Christ declared innocent of any wrongdoing
Daniel obeyed the Law of God
Christ fulfilled the Law of God
Daniel was found to be without fault or error
Christ was found to be without fault or error
Daniel was tested and tempted
Christ was tested and tempted
Daniel accused after praying
Christ accused after praying
Daniel was despised because he was of Judah
Christ was despised because He was of Nazareth
Darius trapped by his decree and law
Pilate trapped by his past actions and fear
Darius distressed but ordered the execution
Pilate distressed but ordered the crucifixion
Darius made every effort to release Daniel
Pilate made every effort to release Christ
Darius was powerless to save Daniel
God was powerless to save Christ
Darius could not break his word and law
God could not break His Word and Law
Daniel was thrown into the lions' den
Christ was thrown to the roaring lions

Daniel was delivered by God's angel
Christ refused to call angels to deliver Him
Decree and law of Darius were satisfied
Decree and Law of God were satisfied
Stone was placed over the entrance of the den
Stone was placed over the entrance of the tomb
Seal was placed on the stone of the lion's den
Seal was placed on the stone of the tomb
Darius at first light went to the lions' den
Women at first light arrived at Christ's tomb
Darius came anguished to the lions' den
Women came anguished to Christ's tomb
Daniel was delivered from death and was alive
Christ was delivered out of death and is alive
Daniel's body was untouched by the lions
Christ's glorified body is untouched by death
Daniel's innocence proven by his being alive
Christ's innocence proven by His being alive
Daniel was trustworthy
Christ is trustworthy
Darius was overjoyed that Daniel was alive
The women were overjoyed that Christ was alive
Darius' faith in the living God was bolstered
Disciples' faith in the living God was bolstered
Conspirators and families were thrown to the lions
Conspirators and families were killed in A.D. 70
Darius proclaimed the living God of Daniel
Disciples proclaimed Christ the living God
Daniel was delivered from death to rule
Christ was delivered out of death to rule
Darius installed Daniel as ruler as planned
God will install Christ as King as planned
Daniel prospered in the silver kingdom
Christ will prosper in His Kingdom

Daniel's Dream of the Four Beasts
(Daniel 7)

Time Line

YEAR B.C.	553	551	539
MONARCHS	Belshazzar		Darius the Mede
DANIEL	Visions of Four Beasts & Son of Man	Visions of Ram & Goat	Prayer & Gabriel's "Seventy-Sevens"

Outline of Chapter Seven

Vision and Dream of the Three Beasts, 1-6
Vision of the Fourth Beast, 7-8
Vision of God's Throne, 9-12
Vision of the Son of Man, 13-14
Visions and Dream Interpreted, 15-28

Background of Chapter Seven

Chapter seven begins the second part of the book and is a flashback. The dream and visions, which Daniel had in one night during the first year (553 B.C.) of King Belshazzar's reign, are recorded here. From this point forward, apocalyptic genre expands and narrative dwindles. Thus, the prophet's visions are dominated by symbols and images that forecast the future.

In this chapter, Daniel was about seventy years old and apparently was no longer an active official of Belshazzar's court. The king might have retired the interpreter of dreams and visions, but not God! In this second part of the book, Daniel's dream and visions arise from his profound experiences with the supernatural that leave the prophet shaken. Chronologically, this dream and the visions occur between chapters four and five.

This chapter will end the Aramaic section. It is linguistically joined to what has preceded, and logically related to what follows. It is the heart of the book of Daniel. Here Daniel introduces two coming princes: "The Little Horn" and "The Son of Man." He presents a panorama of history from Nebuchadnezzar's kingdom to Messiah's kingdom, along with a vision that takes place at the throne in heaven.

Daniel's dream and his visions of four beasts fill in the sketch of prophetic history, which had been revealed in Nebuchadnezzar's dream of the great image. Each of the four beasts corresponds to the four parts of that image.

The vision in heaven unveils the King of the everlasting kingdom. With phenomenal accuracy, the dream and visions cover the "times of the Gentiles" until Christ's kingdom fills the whole earth. Like the books of Kings record history from man's perspective and the books of Chronicles record history from God's perspective, chapter two depicts world dominion from man's perspective and chapter seven from the divine view.

Man sees the kingdoms of the world as great human nobility, which is symbolized by the image of the dream of dreams. On the other hand, God sees the kingdoms of the world as wild and brutal beasts, which crush and devour humanity. While deterioration in the quality of the kingdoms is depicted in the metals of the image, there is a heightened degree of terror and fright depicted in each successive beast.

God Judges Four World Empires

VISION AND DREAM OF THE THREE BEASTS (7:1-6). Daniel wrote down the substance of his dream prior to it fading and being forgotten. It is always a good practice to write down insights revealed by God's Spirit when reading the Bible.

There are visions within the dream that link it to Nebuchadnezzar's dream of dreams.

Daniel said: "In my vision at night I looked, and there before me were the four winds of heaven churning up the great sea. Four great beasts, each different from the others, came up out of the sea (Daniel 7:3).

Literally, חֲזֵה הֲוֵית ("I was looking" or "I was watching") is an Aramaic participle, indicating continuation of action. This expression occurs ten times in this chapter. In other words, Daniel's attention was deeply fixed on his five visions—the four great beasts and the one like a son of man, coming in the clouds.

"The substance of his dream" indicates Daniel wrote down the essential features and details of the vision. Being carried along by the Holy Spirit, the prophet left out the unessential details. Around A.D. 95, the Revelation of Jesus Christ to the apostle John would provide additional details of the end times.

The Four Winds of Heaven

What are the Four Winds of Heaven? The Jews held that the winds from due north, south, east, and west to be favorable, while those from the angles were unfavorable. Many commentators identify these winds as the "powers of the air" or "spiritual forces of evil" of which the apostle Paul wrote in Ephesians 6:12:

> For our struggle is not against flesh and blood, but against the rulers, against the authorities, against the powers of this dark world and against the spiritual forces of evil in the heavenly realms.

In Revelation 7:1, the four winds of the earth can be taken as literal or symbolic, representing the destructive forces of either God or evil.

> After this I saw four angels standing at the four corners of the earth, holding back the four winds of the earth to prevent any wind from blowing on the land or on the sea or on any tree.

The LORD announced in Jeremiah 49:36:

> I will bring against Elam the four winds from the four quarters of the heavens; I will scatter them to the four winds, and there will not be a nation where Elam's exiles do not go.

Elam is the Hebrew name of a region lying east of Babylonia and extending to the mountains of Media in the northeast, and along the Persian Gulf to the borders of ancient Persia in the south. Its two divisions were Elam proper in the north and Anshan in the south, the latter being an independent kingdom until it was annexed by Persia around 600 B.C.

Elam assisted in the overthrow of Babylon and was absorbed by the Persian Empire. The four winds do not represent four nations coming against Elam; they symbolize the widespread scattering of the people of Elam by God.

In three passages, the four winds symbolize the scattering or gathering of the elect to or from the ends of the earth (Zechariah 2:6; Matthew 24:31; Mark 13:27). In Ezekiel's vision of the Valley of the Dry Bones, the four winds symbolize the Holy Spirit's breath of salvation, breathed into Israel.

> Then he said to me, "Prophesy to the breath; prophesy, son of man, and say to it, "This is what the Sovereign LORD says: 'Come from the four winds, O breath, and breathe into these slain, that they may live'" (Ezekiel 37:9).

In the figurative language of Scripture, the blowing of the four winds of heaven has either positive or negative ramifications. The Aramaic does not indicate whether the four winds blew at the same time, or followed each other in sequence. A separate and sequential churning of the Great Sea by each wind matches the historical fulfillment of this passage. In verses 6 and 7, the phrase "after that" points to the sequential blowing of the winds.

Of the 192 references to "wind" in the Bible, 60 relate to events and ideas that involve the power and sovereignty of God.

The Great Sea

What is the Great Sea? The Mediterranean Sea is normally called the Great Sea (Numbers 34:6). Geographically, prophecy is centered around Palestine, which sits on the banks of the Mediterranean Sea. Unlike the

Unlike the

Greek and Roman empires, the Babylonian and Medo-Persian empires were not situated on the shores of the Mediterranean Sea. Therefore, another explanation should be sought for this symbolism.

According to ancient mythology, the Great Sea is the circumambient ocean. It goes all around and underneath the earth and is the antitheses of heaven. This sea is "the Nammu" of the Sumerians and "the Tiamat" of the Babylonians. The waters and the deep of Genesis 1:2 and Amos 7:4 are cosmically the opposite of the heaven above. The Babylonian creation epic, *Enuma Elish*, tells of the battle fought between Marduk and the dragon of chaos, Tiamat. A few elements of Daniel's vision parallel that Babylonian poem.

The mythological idea of the Great Sea would have been readily understood in Daniel's day, much as Americans recognize donkeys and elephants to be symbols of democrats and republicans today. Hence, the Great Sea is not the Mediterranean, but rather the ancient sea that represented the powers of disorder, powers that must be subdued. This becomes clearer as the great conflict is unfolded in the book of Daniel.

By obvious analogy, the churning of the sea came to symbolize the raging of many nations upon the earth. Throughout the Bible, the sea is usually a symbol of chaos.

> Oh, the raging of many nations—they rage like the raging sea! Oh, the uproar of the peoples—they roar like the roaring of great waters! Although the peoples roar like the roar of surging waters, when he rebukes them they flee far away, driven before the wind like chaff on the hills, like tumbleweed before a gale (Isaiah 17:12-13).

Out of the bubbling, swirling waters of chaos, there arose three great beasts, followed by the fourth monstrous beast. The book of Revelation sees the beast (the Antichrist) coming out of the sea—that part of the world, which surrounds the Mediterranean Sea.

> And the dragon stood on the shore of the sea. And I saw a beast coming out of the sea. He had ten horns and seven heads, with ten crowns on his horns, and on each head a blasphemous name.

> Then the angel said to me, "The waters you saw, where the prostitute sits, are peoples, multitudes, nations and languages. The beast and the ten horns you saw will hate the prostitute (Revelation 17:15-16).

The sea and waters represent that part of the world symbolized in the beasts and image of Nebuchadnezzar's dream. It will cease to exist with the coming of the everlasting kingdom. However, after a thousand years, the dragon (Satan, the Devil) will be released from the bottomless pit in order to deceive the nations in the four corners of the earth. Then God will devour with fire from heaven those who march across the earth to do battle with the holy city. Finally, the Devil will be cast into the lake of fire (Revelation 20:7-10). The apostle John reveals what comes next.

> Then I saw a new heaven and a new earth, for the first heaven and the first earth had passed away, and there was no longer any sea (Revelation 21:1).

This verse literally reads, "and the sea is no longer"—not many seas, just one! The sea—the world—that the Devil ruled as prince (John 14:30; 16:11; Ephesians 2:2) is no more!

What are the Four Beasts? In succession, each pictures the empires of Babylon, Medo-Persia, Greece, and Rome. Each of the four winds of heaven sequentially produces an empire by churning up the sea. From the human perspective, each empire will arise because of war and conquest. In reality, each exists by the power and authority of heaven.

The First Beast

The four winds of heaven churned up the Great Sea and out came four beasts, each different from the others. "The first was like a lion, and it had the wings of an eagle." The lion-eagle, or winged lion, represents the Babylonian Empire. It is composed of the noblest of beasts and the noblest of birds, just as this empire was symbolized by gold, the noblest of metals, in the dream of dreams. Archaeology has uncovered great winged lions that adorned Mesopotamian temples and palaces. Nebuchadnezzar compared himself to a lion and his armies to eagles, as does the Bible.

> A lion has come out of his lair; a destroyer of nations has set out. He has left his place to lay waste your land. Your towns will lie in ruins without inhabitant (Jeremiah 4:7).

Israel was a scattered flock that lions had chased away. The first to devour Israel was the king of Assyria; the last to crush Judah's bones was Nebuchadnezzar king of Babylon (cf. Jeremiah 50:17).

> The word of the LORD came to me: "Son of man, set forth an allegory and tell the house of Israel a parable. Say to them, 'This is what the Sovereign LORD says: A great eagle with powerful wings, long feathers and full plumage of varied colors came to Lebanon. Taking hold of the top of a cedar, he broke off its topmost shoot and carried it away to a land of merchants, where he planted it in a city of traders'" (Ezekiel 17:1-4).

In this parable, the great winged eagle is King Nebuchadnezzar. The top of a cedar is the House of David. The topmost shoot is King Jehoiachin of Judah. A land of merchants and a city of traders is Babylon. Therefore, what happens in Daniel's vision to the lion-eagle would not have shocked the prophet.

> I watched until its wings were torn off and it was lifted from the ground so that it stood on two feet like a man, and the heart of a man was given to it (Daniel 7:14).

Interestingly, Mesopotamian art depicts animals standing up and acting as men. However, this vision pictures the conversion of a king that God viewed as a beast! When the king humbled himself and raised his eyes toward heaven, his sanity was restored, and he praised God (Daniel 4:34). At that moment, the eagle wings (feathers and claws) were plucked, and the king stood like a man and was given the heart of a man—a saved man. This vision confirmed to Daniel that his prayers were truly answered; he would see his potentate, Nebuchadnezzar, in heaven.

The eagle wings denote the swiftness displayed by Babylon in conquering the nations around it. The lion is the king of beasts and the eagle is the king of birds; God already had identified Nebuchadnezzar as "the king of kings" (Daniel 2:37).

The plucking of the eagle wings from the lion and the standing to its feet with a human heart pictures the king turning from his former beastly treatment of his subjects to a humane treatment at the end of his reign. Of course, such action is attributable to his conversion.

The Second Beast

> And there before me was a second beast, which looked like a bear. It was raised up on one of its sides, and it had three ribs in its mouth between its teeth. It was told, "Get up and eat your fill of flesh!" (Daniel 7:5).

The Medo-Persian Empire followed the Babylonian Empire. It was like a huge lumbering bear with its enormous movements of troops. This is an apt description of the military under Cyrus and Cambyses. Xerxes utilized two and half million fighting men against Greece. Medo-Persia's massive armies won due to their weight of numbers. The military of this empire devoured much flesh. It was a grisly and destructive force. However, the bear is less majestic and swift than either a lion or eagle. The Antichrist is depicted as a beast with "feet like those of a bear and a mouth like that of a lion" (Revelation 13:2).

Persia, the more powerful of the two nations, is represented by the higher side of the bear. This lopsidedness symbolizes the comparative strength of the Persians to the Medes.

The three ribs stand for three great powers that were overcome by the beast: *Lydia* in Asia Minor under King Croesus (546 B.C.); *Babylon* under Nabonidus and Belshazzar (539 B.C.); and *Egypt* under Psamitk III (525 B.C.). In addition, the three ribs typify the absorbing of their cultures into the Medo-Persian Empire.

Interestingly, the second beast is told to "get up and eat your fill of flesh" after conquering these three powers. Medo-Persia was noted for its insatiable desire for conquest.

The second beast has been called "the continental divide" between conservative scholars and rationalistic critics, who maintain that the second beast is Median, the third beast Persian, and the fourth beast Grecian. The rationalistic view denies predictions and holds that the prophecies of the book of Daniel were written after the fact. This view definitely clashes with the scope of the book as well as its other dreams and visions.

The Third Beast

> After that, I looked, and there before me was another beast, one that looked like a leopard. And on its back it had four wings like those of a bird. This beast had four heads, and it was given authority to rule (Daniel 7:6).

The third beast is Greece. Alexander the Great conquered the world, with a speed and swiftness characteristic of a leopard. Such speed and swiftness had been unprecedented in warfare. The imagery of the speed and swiftness of a leopard is enhanced by the four wings of a bird. However, the four wings of a bird on the leopard's back are inferior to the wings of an eagle on the lion.

Alexander's conquest was twice as swift as Nebuchadnezzar's. In ten years, Alexander conquered the world; his military was the opposite of the lumbering and devouring army of Medo-Persia.

Leopards, known for agility as well as speed, depict that which is terrifying (Jeremiah 5:6; Hosea 13:7; Habakkuk 1:8). Out of sheer terror, many cities like Jerusalem surrendered to Alexander the Great without a fight (*Antiquities of the Jews,* 11:8.6), Tyre being a notable exception (Ezekiel 26).

At the age of thirty-three, Alexander died in Babylon on June 13, 323 B.C. Following his death, Alexander's four generals divided the empire into four parts, as symbolized by the leopard's four heads (cf. Daniel 7:20-23; Revelation 17:9-11). *Lysimachus* ruled Thrace and Bithynia; *Cassander* ruled Macedonia and Greece; *Seleucus* ruled Syria, Babylonia and eastward to India; and *Ptolemy,* ruled Egypt, Palestine and Arabia

Petraea.

The Fourth Beast

VISION OF THE FOURTH BEAST (7:7-8). Daniel passes quickly over the first three beasts to get to the fourth, which captured his interest.

> After that, in my vision at night I looked, and there before me was a fourth beast—terrifying and frightening and very powerful. It had large iron teeth; it crushed and devoured its victims and trampled underfoot whatever was left. It was different from all the former beasts, and it had ten horns (Daniel 7:7).

Nothing in nature compares to the fourth beast; it is perverse and vicious. The apostle John described this beast as a hybrid of the previous three beasts.

> The beast I saw resembled a leopard, but had feet like those of a bear and a mouth like that of a lion. The dragon gave the beast his power and his throne and great authority (Revelation 13:2).

The Roman Empire followed the Greek Empire. Rome boasted that it did not destroy the cultures of the nations it conquered but incorporated them into itself, which is symbolized by "it crushed and devoured its victims." The teeth of Rome were like iron as its army conquered and ruled with an iron hand until the empire eventually faded from power. The great iron teeth correspond to the legs of iron on the image in the dream of dreams (Daniel 2:33, 40-43).

The fourth beast is dreadful, terrible, and exceedingly strong since its power and great authority will come from Satan. The unholy trinity that directs this beast will be judged by God.

> In that day, the LORD will punish with his sword, his fierce, great and powerful sword, Leviathan the gliding serpent, Leviathan the coiling serpent; he will slay the monster of the sea (Isaiah 27:1).

Most likely, the gliding serpent epitomizes Satan; the coiling serpent is the False Prophet; and the monster of the sea is the Antichrist.

Prophetically, the time of the fourth beast is not completed. The ten horns are the same as the ten toes of Daniel 2:41 and ten horns of Revelation 13:1:

> And the dragon stood on the shore of the sea. And I saw a beast coming out of the sea. He had ten horns and seven heads, with ten crowns on his horns, and on each head a blasphemous name.

Horns are emblems of power, dominion, glory, and fierceness, just as they are the chief means of attack and defense for the animals endowed with them. Horns are symbolic of kings and their kingdoms in Scripture. Zechariah, the father of John the Baptist, identified Christ Jesus as a horn, announcing, "He has raised up a horn of salvation for us in the house of his servant David" (Luke 1:69). In other words, the Messiah is a strong and powerful Savior, who is the King of Israel.

Each horn of the fourth beast represents a future king and kingdom. All ten horns are present at once; therefore, they are a ten-kingdom confederacy. There is no period in history that comes close to fitting Daniel's vision of the ten horns; it remains future to this day.

Today, the *European Union* is united under *The Treaty of Rome*, signed on March 25, 1957. Initially, the European Union consisted of just six countries: Belgium, Germany, France, Italy, Luxembourg and the Netherlands. Denmark, Ireland and the United Kingdom joined in 1973, Greece in 1981, Spain and Portugal in 1986, Austria, Finland and Sweden in 1995. In 2004, the biggest ever enlargement took place with 10 new countries joining it.

The Treaty of Rome, as amended by subsequent treaties, deals with goods, capital, persons, services, and significantly, its associations with overseas nations and territories. Since 1999, passports are no longer required for travel between twelve European countries and the Eurodollar has been replacing national currencies and gaining economic strength in world markets.

Southern Europe, Western Asia and Northern Africa were part of the Ancient Roman Empire, but are not part of the European Union at this time. It seems unlikely that the ten kings of the Revived Roman Empire will be limited to Western Europe. It is possible that the foundation for the ten kings is being laid in the European Union. Nevertheless, any configuration of this ten-kingdom confederation at this time would be speculation—we will need to wait for history to reveal prophecy.

The Little Horn of the Fourth Beast

A seemingly insignificant eleventh king rises to power during the time of this ten-kingdom confederacy.

> While I was thinking about the horns, there before me was another horn, a little one, which came up among them; and three of the first horns were uprooted before it. This horn had eyes like the eyes of a man and a mouth that spoke boastfully (Daniel 7:8).

A little horn came up בֵּין (*beyn*, between, among) the ten horns. "Eyes like the eyes of a man" suggests this king is an intellectual genius with penetrating insight and discernment. "A mouth that spoke boastfully" suggests persuasive oratory skills, which at the same time blasphemes God. This little horn is the Wilful King of Daniel 11:36-39, also known as "the Antichrist," and "the man of lawlessness" of 2 Thessalonians 2:3-4:

> Don't let anyone deceive you in any way, for that day will not come until the rebellion occurs and the man of lawlessness is revealed, the man doomed to destruction. He will oppose and will exalt himself over everything that is called God or is worshiped, so that he sets himself up in God's temple, proclaiming himself to be God.

The little horn will be satanically inspired, according to Revelation 13:4-6:

> Men worshiped the dragon because he had given authority to the beast, and they also worshiped the beast and asked, "Who is like the beast? Who can make war against him?" The beast was given a mouth to utter proud words and blasphemies and to exercise his authority for forty-two months. He opened his mouth to blaspheme God, and to slander his name and his dwelling-place and those who live in heaven.

The outlook for the future is pessimistic. Biblical prophecy forecasts no peace-loving world ruler until the Messiah establishes His kingdom. Ravenous commercialism and political imperialism accompanied by the most beastly warfare will dominate the world scene. Progressive evolution and social advancement are the fabrications of the Evil One. Over the horizon awaits the monstrosities of the fourth beast.

Daniel reveals a great deal more concerning "the little horn" in 7:19-27; 9:26-27; and 11:36-45. Critics identify this king as Antiochus IV Epiphanes and the kingdom as Greece. They assume that the foregoing passages depict the Seleucids and its ruler.

Critics generally agree that the ten horns upon the creature's head represent ten kings, not contemporaries, but successive rulers that begin with either Alexander the Great or with the Selucus Nicator, the founder of the Seleucid dynasty. Then the rulers continue, in the same line, down to the point at which Antiochus IV Epiphanes came to the throne.

There are three major difficulties with the critics' assumption. *First*, one cannot pinpoint ten successive kings in history. *Second*, Jesus announced, long after the death of Antiochus, that "the abomination that causes desolation" that Daniel attributes to the little horn is still future (Daniel 9:27; Matthew 24:15). *Third*, the kingdom of the little horn is to be replaced by Christ's kingdom (Daniel 7:26-27), which clearly did not happen in the middle of the second century B.C.

Uprooted (עֲקַר `aqar) may denote either a gradual process, where new growth pushes out the old, or where it is plucked up quickly. It is uncertain, whether "the little horn" will take control of all three areas at once or over time. In either case, he will be recognized as the ruler of the remaining horns.

Notably, the book of Daniel either reveals the name of, or details about, the initial rulers of the first three empires: Nebuchadnezzar of Babylon; Cyrus of Medo-Persia; Alexander the Great of Greece and its division by his four generals—Lysimachus, Cassander, Seleucus and Ptolemy. However, nothing is revealed about the initial ruler of the fourth empire of Ancient Rome. Instead, the prophecy focuses on the kings of the

Revived Roman Empire of the last days, especially its "little horn."

Instead of a king conquering territory and people, there was a gradual expansion of the Roman power, culminating in the establishment of a unified empire by Augustus (B.C. 30 to A.D. 14), who was emperor at the time of the Messiah's birth and during part of His lifetime. The Roman Empire was unique in regards to its predecessors.

The Empire bound together a variety of peoples and cultures, maintaining itself not only by military power but by efficient and generally lenient provincial administration. Another unifying factor was the nearly universal use of the Greek language and a general acceptance of Greek culture and values. In addition, a complex of major land and sea routes linked major cities of the Empire, permitting the easy movement of people and goods as well as armies.

Regarding freedom, while Roman law imposed harsh penalties for criminal acts and for any activity that might be considered treasonable, most national groups were permitted to follow their own customs and religions. Self-government by each national group, under its own laws and courts, was encouraged, although Roman laws and courts were supreme.

The Empire, which gave the varied peoples of Europe and the Mediterranean a common language and permitted free movement of persons and ideas, was essential to the spread of Christianity (abstracted from "Roman Empire," *The Revell Bible Dictionary*).

Parallels between the Roman Empire and the European Union are remarkable. The first phase of the Roman Empire paved the way for the coming of the Messiah and the spread of Christianity. The second phase (feet and ten toes) of the Roman Empire will pave the way for the Antichrist and the spread of his false religion.

The following charts demonstrate that the fourth is the Revived Roman Empire, which is the seventh and eighth empires of Revelation 17.

The Times of the Gentiles

The Future from God's Perspective
(Daniel 7)

FROM BEAST TO BEAST

Sovereignty of the King's Rule
Cursing and Devouring Conquests
Rapid Conquests of Alexander
Terrifying Power of Rome

Babylon (605-539 B.C.)

Winged Lion—Majesty
Eagle Wings–Swiftness to Conquer
Lion and Eagle—King of Beasts

Medo-Persia (539-330 B.C.)

Bear—More Destructive than Lion
Raised Up—Lopsided Dualism
Ribs—Absorbed Cultures

Greece (330–63 B.C.)

Winged Leopard—Great Swiftness
Four Heads—Alexander's Generals
 Seleucus—Babylon
 Ptolemy—Egypt
 Cassander—Macedonia & Greece
 Lysimachus—Trace & Asia Minor

Rome (63 B.C.–A.D. 1453)

Revived Roman Empire (?)

Ten Horns of Revelation 13 & 17
Little Horn—The Antichrist

Linking of Daniel 7:8, 23-25 and Revelation 17:8-11

While I was thinking about the horns, there before me was ANOTHER HORN, A LITTLE ONE, which came up among them; and THREE OF THE FIRST HORNS WERE UPROOTED before it. This horn had eyes like the eyes of a man and a mouth that spoke boastfully (Daniel 7:8, uppercase for emphasis).

The fourth beast is a fourth kingdom that will appear on earth. It will be different from all the other kingdoms and will devour the whole earth, trampling it down and crushing it. THE TEN HORNS ARE TEN KINGS who will come from this kingdom. After them ANOTHER KING will arise, different from the earlier ones; he will SUBDUE THREE KINGS. He will speak against the Most High and oppress his saints and try to change the set times and the laws. The saints will be handed over to him for a time, times and half a time (Daniel 7:23-25, uppercase for emphasis).

The beast, which you saw, ONCE WAS, NOW IS NOT, and WILL COME UP out of the Abyss and go to his destruction. The inhabitants of the earth whose names have not been written in the book of life from the creation of the world will be astonished when they see the beast, because HE ONCE WAS, NOW IS NOT, AND YET WILL COME. This calls for a mind with wisdom. The seven heads are seven hills on which the woman sits. They are also seven kings. FIVE HAVE FALLEN, ONE IS, THE OTHER HAS NOT YET COME; but when he does come, he must remain for a little while. The beast who once was, and now is not is an eighth king. He belongs to the seven and is going to destruction (Revelation 17:8-11, uppercase for emphasis).

ONCE WAS—FIVE HAVE FALLEN
- 1. Egypt
- 2. Assyria
- 1. 3. Babylon — Uprooted
- 2. 4. Medo-Persia — Uprooted
- 3. 5. Greece — Uprooted — Little Horn of Daniel 8 (Antiochus IV)

ONE IS
- 4. 6. Ancient Rome

WILL COME—OTHER HAS NOT YET COME
- 4. 7. Revived Rome (10 Kingdom Confederacy)
    Ten Horns initially but three horns subdued by the Little Horn (The Antichrist)

THE BEAST WHO ONCE WAS, AND NOW IS NOT
- 4. 8. Kingdom belongs to the seven — the Little Horn

162

The rise and fall of the Egyptian and Assyrian Empires occurred before Daniel's time, and therefore, they are passed over in his prophecy but are cited by John in the book of Revelation.

The Revived Roman Empire will be succeeded by the eighth empire, which will be ruled by "the little horn," the Antichrist. "The beast" will rise out of obscurity to uproot three nations of the ten-nation confederacy of the future as the Ancient Roman Empire had uprooted Babylon, Medo-Persia and Greece.

In one sense, the eighth king belongs to the seven because the cultures and people of each succeeding empire were integrated. This integration in the end times is symbolized by the toes, which are partly iron and partly clay (Daniel 2:42-43).

The Coming Judge

VISION OF GOD'S THRONE (7:9-12). The scene changes from the terrestrial to the celestial, from earth to heaven. This vision contains the most descriptive picture of the First Person of the Trinity in the Bible.

To distinguish Him from the Son, God the Father is identified as "the Ancient of Days." He is the eternal, self-existent One, the Creator of all things (Isaiah 43:10), and He has been viewing the activities of men and demons from His throne in Heaven.

His clothing as white as snow symbolizes His righteousness, justice, purity and holiness. Hair white as snow stands for wisdom. Fire symbolizes holiness, wrath and judgment (Psalm 50:3; 97:3-5) as well as God's presence (Exodus 13:21).

There is no escape from His judgment—a river of fire comes flowing out from before Him. He is the Lord of Hosts as thousands upon thousands (an infinite number of celestial beings, possibly included are the raptured saints) await His command to execute judgment.

His throne is flaming fire and its wheels are all ablaze. The wheels, on which the throne rests, are moving about and they are ringed with fire.

Such symbolism describes God's omnipotence, omnipresence, and omniscience in Ezekiel 1:12-18.

God is enthroned as the Great King and He sits in judgment of the kingdoms of the world. The first two to be judged in God's court will be the boastful little horn—the Antichrist and the False Prophet. Their eternal destiny is blazing fire, the Lake of Fire, in which they are thrown alive, bypassing Sheol/Hades (Revelation 19:20).

Daniel records that "the other beasts had been stripped of their authority, but were allowed to live for a period of time." This period falls between Armageddon and the Great White Throne Judgment. Then Satan, his demons and all his subjects will be judged (Revelation 20:1-15), when the books are opened. What books? The Lamb's Book of Life, the books of the deeds of men, and the Scriptures, especially the Law. If one's name is not recorded in the first, the other books become the basis of God's judgment as seen in Revelation 20:11-15. It appears that Daniel and John beheld the same scene.

There is no judgment for the animal kingdom, but for unsaved man "it is a dreadful thing to fall into the hands of the living God" (Hebrews 10:31). The rebellion of angels and men will be judged. This scene is also similar to the one in chapters 4-6 of Revelation, where the slain Lamb comes and takes the scroll (the title deed to the earth) from the right hand of Him who sat on the throne. After taking the scroll, He proceeds to break its seven seals, which commences God's judgment on the kingdom of the fourth beast.

VISION OF THE SON OF MAN (7:13-14). Next, Daniel beheld the Ancient of Days entrusting one "like a son of man" with all judgment.

> In my vision at night I looked, and there before me was one like a son of man, coming with the clouds of heaven. He approached the Ancient of Days and was led into his presence. He was given authority, glory and sovereign power; all peoples, nations and men of every language worshiped him. His dominion is an everlasting dominion that will not pass away, and his kingdom is one that will never be destroyed (Daniel 7:13-14).

Who is the one like a son of man? Eighty-one times Jesus referred to Himself as "the Son of Man" in the Gospels. Three titles associated with Christ's sonship appear in the Gospels:

1. Son of David, which points to His earthly throne
2. Son of God, which points to His eternity
3. Son of Man, which points to His relationship to the human race

Interestingly, Jesus did not refer directly to Himself by the first two titles. However, He had to become man in order to fulfill all three titles. Through the Son of Man's incarnation, the Second Person of the Trinity was able to fulfill the threefold role of the Kinsman-Redeemer. *First*, the kinsman-redeemer redeemed the land, which his brother had wasted away (Leviticus 25:25). *Second*, he redeemed his brother from his voluntary slavery (Leviticus 25:48). *Third*, he became the avenger of the blood of his brother, who was wrongly slain (Numbers 35:27).

This passage in Daniel is the only place in the OT where the title "Son of Man" is used clearly of a divine personage. It does appear in a verse in a Psalm of Asaph, where Israel is mistakenly imploring God Almighty to bless and restore the nation and then it would turn to Him!

> Let your hand rest on the man at your right hand, the son of man you have raised up for yourself (Psalm 80:17).

"The son of man" in this verse may apply to Israel instead of Christ since the pleas of the rest of the psalm have not been answered. It is very clear that Jesus took this title from Daniel 7:13 and applied it to Himself.

> At that time the sign of the Son of Man will appear in the sky, and all the nations of the earth will mourn. They will see the Son of Man coming on the clouds of the sky, with power and great glory (Matthew 24:30).

> In the future you will see the Son of Man sitting at the right hand of the Mighty One and coming on the clouds of heaven" (Matthew 26:64).

> At that time men will see the Son of Man coming in clouds with

great power and glory (Mark 13:26).

"Like a son of man" refers to Christ's incarnate nature. He is a true man as well as true God—100% man and 100% God. Through incarnation by virgin birth, He became the seed of the woman without being a son of man. The article ("the") as used in the title by Jesus points to the one Daniel saw in his night vision.

Significantly, Nebuchadnezzar saw one like "a son of the gods" with the three Hebrews in the fiery furnace (Daniel 3:25). Hence, the one who is "the Son of God" and "the Son of Man" is revealed in this book.

"The one like a son of man" is appointed absolute Lord and Judge by virtue of His propitiatory ministry as God incarnate. He is King of kings and Lord of lords; hence, *The Great Commission* begins by echoing Daniel 7:14.

> Then Jesus came to them and said, "All authority in heaven and on earth has been given to me (Matthew 28:18).

Christ does not usurp authority; He does not take honor for Himself; He receives the kingdom from God the Father—the Ancient of Days (Hebrews 1:1-14; Philippians 2:5-11). In contrast, the four beasts and their self-exaltations are doomed to destruction.

There are four proofs that the one identified as "a Son of Man" is deity in Daniel 7:13-14.

1. He was given what God will not give away—authority, glory and sovereign power.
2. He is worshiped—only God is to be worshiped.
3. He is given an everlasting kingdom—only God's kingdom is everlasting.
4. He is like a son of man—only through incarnation can "one be like a son of man" and not actually be so.

Compare John's vision of "someone like a son of man" in Revelation 1:12-18 with the Ancient of Days in Daniel. Keep in mind that "the Son is the radiance of God's glory and the exact representation of his being"

(Hebrews 1:3). John's vision confirms Christ's deity also.

Both the Ancient of Days and the Son of Man are seen as separate Persons by the same prophet at the same time and place, so there must be at least two Persons in the Godhead. Actually, there are three Persons in One: Father, Son and Spirit.

When Jesus called Himself "the Son of Man," every Jew should have known that He was referring to Daniel's prophecy. The Sanhedrin understood that this title denoted His deity; note their reaction.

> Again the high priest asked him, "Are you the Christ, the Son of the Blessed One?" "I am," said Jesus. "And you will see the Son of Man sitting at the right hand of the Mighty One and coming on the clouds of heaven." The high priest tore his clothes. "Why do we need any more witnesses?" he asked. "You have heard the blasphemy. What do you think?" They all condemned him as worthy of death (Mark 14:61-64).

"Coming with the clouds of heaven" might indicate Christ coming with the armies of heaven (Revelation 19:14) or His deity (Exodus 13:21-22; 19:9, 16). Conversely, at Christ's ascension into heaven, a cloud hid Him from the sight of the disciples and two men dressed in white told them that "He will come back in the same way you have seen Him go into heaven" (Acts 1:11). Whatever the case, the Son of Man will execute the judgment prescribed by the Ancient of Days. Jesus confirmed Daniel's vision when He said, "Moreover, the Father judges no one, but has entrusted all judgment to the Son" (John 5:22).

There is a significant contrast between the Son of Man coming from heaven and the beasts coming up out of the sea (the chaos of the world under the Evil One's dominion). The Antichrist comes to bring havoc on the earth while Christ comes to restore order to this world.

VISIONS AND DREAM INTERPRETED (7:15-28). Daniel was more than a casual observer; he became emotionally involved in the visions. It is assumed that the one the prophet approached is an angel, whom many call "the interpreting angel."

167

When Jesus asked His disciples whether they understood, they answered in the positive. Instead of asking Him questions, they went away lacking insight. Not Daniel, he asked questions.

> I approached one of those standing there and asked him the true meaning of all this. So he told me and gave me the interpretation of these things: "The four great beasts are four kingdoms that will rise from the earth. But the saints of the Most High will receive the kingdom and will possess it forever—yes, for ever and ever" (Daniel 7:16-18).

Five kingdoms appeared in Daniel's night vision: Babylonian, Medo-Persian, Grecian, Roman, and Christ's (7:2-14). The first four kingdoms are of the earth, the fifth is of heaven. Since there are only four kingdoms of the earth until Christ's kingdom, the implication is that the Roman Empire will be revived in the end times. This explains the meaning of "the beast, which you saw, once was, now is not, and will come up out of the Abyss and go to his destruction" (Revelation 17:8; see chart on page 162, *Linking of Daniel 7:8, 23-25 and Revelation 17:8-14*).

Daniel's interest was focused on the fourth beast, its ten horns and the boastful little horn that became more imposing than the other horns. Another feature of the fourth beast, which was not previously mentioned, is "bronze claws." The extent of the Antichrist's devouring with iron teeth and crushing with bronze claws is apparent from the books of Daniel and Revelation.

> As I watched, this horn was waging war against the saints and defeating them, until the Ancient of Days came and pronounced judgment in favor of the saints of the Most High, and the time came when they possessed the kingdom (Daniel 7:21-22).

> After this I looked and there before me was a great multitude that no one could count, from every nation, tribe, people and language, standing before the throne and in front of the Lamb (Revelation 7:9).

> I answered, "Sir, you know." And he said, "These are they who have come out of the great tribulation; they have washed their robes and

made them white in the blood of the Lamb (Revelation 7:14).

Of course, a great number of Israelites will be included in this multitude according to Zechariah 13:8:

"In the whole land," declares the LORD, "two-thirds will be struck down and perish; yet one-third will be left in it."

In this light, we can understand the interpreting angel's explanation.

The fourth beast is a fourth kingdom that will appear on earth. It will be different from all the other kingdoms and will devour the whole earth, trampling it down and crushing it. The ten horns are ten kings who will come from this kingdom. After them another king will arise, different from the earlier ones; he will subdue three kings. He will speak against the Most High and oppress his saints and try to change the set times and the laws. The saints will be handed over to him for a time, times and half a time (Daniel 7:23-25).

Daniel's prophecy has four descriptive titles for the one who wages war against the saints: *"a little horn"* (7:8; 8:9 cf. 7:20, 24); (2) *"a stern-faced King"* (8:23); (3) *"the ruler who will come"* (9:26); and (4) *"the king will do as he pleases"* (11:36). The condensed titles are "the Little Horn," "the Stern-faced King," "the Coming Prince," and "the Wilful King." All four titles are wrapped up in the title, "the Antichrist," which is the popular name employed by commentators.

The Antichrist's reign of terror will last three and one-half years. Satan will energize one of the horns (the Antichrist) of the fourth beast (the Revived Roman Empire). The Antichrist will pursue the survivors of Israel into the desert, but the earth will protect a remnant of Jews. Then the Antichrist will make war with all who obey God (Revelation 12). However, one hundred and forty-four thousand Israelites will be sealed by God and protected from the Antichrist in the Tribulation, but all others who are saved during this period will face the fury and oppression of this horn, who is energized by the Devil.

But woe to the earth and the sea, because the devil has gone down to you! He is filled with fury, because he knows that his time is short (Revelation 12:12).

According to the interpretation of Daniel's vision, the Antichrist will try to change the set times and the laws. The law he will intend to change will probably be the Law of God. Isaiah 5:20 is an example of the kinds of lies the man of lawlessness will speak:

> Woe to those who call evil good and good evil, who put darkness for light and light for darkness, who put bitter for sweet and sweet for bitter.

Today, relativism is supplanting truth in the religious, social and political arenas of the western world. If the United States of America and Europe are any indication, the world of the twenty-first century is ripe for the Antichrist.

Daniel 7:24-27 covers the entire Tribulation Period (Revelation 6:1-20:3). Verse 24 belongs to the first three and one half years and verse 25 to the second three and one half years. Verses 26-27 belong to the very end of the Tribulation when Christ comes as the crushing stone and His kingdom, the mountain, fills the whole earth.

The judgment of the Antichrist is unavoidable. "The court will sit, and his power will be taken away and destroyed completely forever." God's kingdom will come to earth and His will done as it is in heaven. Then the prayer that Jesus taught His disciples to pray is answered!

Overwhelmed by the conflict between good and evil, light and darkness, the prophet kept the matter to himself. Apparently, Daniel did not reveal these visions for some time.

Applications of Chapter Seven

The enthronement of the Son of Man is reflected in this chapter, as well as in Genesis 1:28, Psalms 2 and 8. He has been given royal authority over creation. Therefore, we should be living in anticipation of the one like a son of man coming with the clouds of heaven.

In Daniel's time, this chapter served as a polemic against the annual re-enthronement of the king when he was presented to Marduk in the New Year Festival. In contrast, Christ's power will never be taken away or destroyed like the four beasts. His kingdom will be an everlasting kingdom and re-enthronement will never occur.

The book of Daniel provides, to the exiles in Babylon and to us, the prophetic answer to the question," How long, O God?" This chapter contains many clues to the duration and depth of Israel's subjugation when it is compared with other Scriptures. The kingdom will not be restored to Israel until the Son of Man comes with the clouds of heaven.

The visions that passed through Daniel's mind deeply troubled his thoughts, and his face turned pale. How are you affected when you ponder the awesomeness of the Ancient of Days and God's plans for the future? The Scriptures that make known the wrathful nature of God and His predictions of a turbulent future should deeply frighten and alarm us. Undoubtedly, Daniel was deeply troubled about what would happen to his own people in the future—how about you?

GOD'S SOVEREIGNTY IN THE RISE OF PRINCES

Daniel's Vision of the Ram, the Male Goat, and the Little Horn
(Daniel 8)

Time Line

YEAR B.C.	553	551	539
MONARCHS	Belshazzar		Darius the Mede
DANIEL	Visions of Four Beasts & Son of Man	Visions of Ram & Goat	Prayer & Gabriel's "Seventy-Sevens"

Outline of Chapter Eight

The Vision of the Ram, 1-4
The Vision of the Goat, 5-8
The Vision of the Little Horn, 9-12
The Time-span of the Host Trampling the Sanctuary, 13-14
The Interpretation of the Vision by Gabriel, 15-27

Background of Chapter Eight

The chronological order of the chapters of the book of Daniel is 1, 2, 3, 4, 7, 8, 5, 9, 6, 10, 11, and 12.

The time of the vision in this chapter was the third year of the reign of Belshazzar (551 B.C.), twelve years before the fall of Babylon. Daniel was about seventy years old that year. In 539 B.C., Daniel could interpret the handwriting on the wall because he already knew the future course of the world empires. But, there is much for the prophet and his readers to learn of the future. The vision in this chapter reveals details about the rulers of the Medo-Persian and Greek empires.

This chapter begins with a switch from Aramaic back to Hebrew, indicating that Israel is back in the prophetic picture and is the intended audience for the last five chapters of this book. These five chapters are intended to show Israel its place in prophetic history and to prepare the Jews for the terrible persecutions that lie ahead. The bad news is that persecution is coming, but the good news is that it will end at God's set time.

Chapter eight elaborates and expands certain features of the dream and visions in chapter seven. Chapter seven was a sweep of history, while chapter eight deals with specifics of the second and third kingdoms, focusing on another "little horn" who foreshadows the Antichrist.

Here Daniel becomes a time traveler. He is projected into the future and to a different location, somewhat like the prophet Ezekiel and the apostle John.

This chapter contains a vision, apocalyptic symbolism, history told in veiled terms, angels, persecution, prediction, and the interpretation of the vision. It has three parts:

1. A vision of a ram and a goat (1-12)
2. An introduction of heavenly interpreters (13-19)
3. An interpretation of the vision (20-27)

Nabonidus' policy toward Cyrus was friendly and cooperative until the Persian merger with the Medes. Then Nabonidus made secret overtures with Lydia and Egypt, hoping to forge a triple alliance against the dangerous and aggressive Cyrus the Great. The great sea is churning; a new world empire is coming out of the sea.

Israel's Persecution

THE VISION OF THE RAM (8:1-4). "I Daniel had a vision, after that one that had already appeared to me" indicates that the previously recorded visions of the four beasts (chapter 7) were recorded before this vision (Chapter 8). This was done for prophetic and literary purposes.

Daniel was not physically in the citadel of Susa (שׁוּשַׁן *Shuwshan,*

Shushan), but transported there in his vision. The prophet Ezekiel had a similar experience in which he was transported in a vision to Jerusalem (Ezekiel 8-10). The fortress of Susa was 230 miles east of Babylon and 120 miles north of the Persian Gulf. It became the royal city of Cyrus and so continued in the time of Xerxes and Esther. Now the city is famous for the *Hammurabi Code,* a sophisticated ethical and moral law that predated Moses.

The first Babylonian kingdom had seized Susa, the capital of Elam. Susa was destroyed during the Neo-Babylonian Empire by Ashurbanipal in 640 B.C., rebuilt in 521 B.C., and later restored to its greatness by Darius Hystaspis. Susa's existence as a city is doubtful in 551 B.C. Therefore, Daniel is transported in the vision to the future.

The nine hundred foot-wide artificial Ulai Canal passed near Susa and flowed from the Choaspes (modern Kerkha River). Standing by the Ulai Canal, Daniel sees the vision unfold before him.

> I looked up, and there before me was a ram with two horns, standing beside the canal, and the horns were long. One of the horns was longer than the other but grew up later. I watched the ram as he charged towards the west and the north and the south. No animal could stand against him, and none could rescue from his power. He did as he pleased and became great (Daniel 8:3-4).

The ram symbolizes the Medo-Persian alliance. The smaller horn is Media, the longer and later horn is Persia. The detail is similar to the beast that looked like a bear raised up on one side. Persia would become stronger than Media. Cyrus and his Persians came later than Cyaxeres and Astyages of Media. Herodotus relates some blood curdling accounts of Cyrus' acquirement of the kingdom of the Medes (*Histories,* Book I, 113-130).

The ram was the guardian spirit of Persia. The ram is frequently found on Persian seals and when the king of Persia led his army, he wore the head of a ram instead of a crown. A zodiacal document from the Persian period shows each country represented by an animal. Persia appeared under the ram and Syria under Capricorn, symbolized by a goat. In addition, Babylonian astrological charts show Persia represented by the constellation of the ram and Syria as the goat. In Daniel's vision, the goat represents Greece.

The three directions the ram charged were the three areas of Medo-Persian expansion: *West* (Lydia, Ionia, Thrace, and Macedonia); *North* (Caspians of the Caucasus Range and the Scythians east of the Caspian Sea and the Oxus Valley to the Aral Sea); and *South* (Babylon and Egypt). Medo-Persian troops were nearly invincible and Cyrus II became arrogant over his universal success. He became known as Cyrus the Great.

THE VISION OF THE GOAT (8:5-8). Another conqueror would be given the title, "the Great," which Cyrus had held. This conqueror was depicted by a prominent horn between the eyes of a male goat (הָעֵזִים-צָפִיר *`ez tsaphiyim*). Normally, a goat has two horns but not this one. The goat is Greece and this horn is Alexander the Great.

The national emblem of Macedonia (Greece) was a "goat," and the goat is found on the coins of that country. Its ancient capital was called Aegae, or the "Goat City," while the adjacent waters were called the Aegean or "Goat-Sea." Hence, the son of Alexander the Great by Roxana was called Aegus, the "Son of a Goat."

Alexander the Great was born in 356 B.C., and educated under Aristotle. His father, Philip of Macedonia, was a great conqueror. When he was murdered, Alexander took over a powerful military.

In 334 B.C., Alexander the Great came from the region of Macedonia and Greece, striking a fatal blow to Medo-Persia. Like a giant goat, he leaped over the Hellespont with his army of 30,000 infantry and 5,000 cavalry, and he completely crushed a Persian army on the banks of the Granicus. He then swiftly advanced eastward and a year later defeated a Persian army of 600,000 in a battle at Issus. By 331 B.C., Alexander was on the banks of the Tigris River, where he defeated an enormous army led by King Darius.

Between the years 330 B.C. and 327 B.C., Alexander captured the outlying provinces of the Persian Empire. He invaded and conquered the entire Near East and Middle East within three years. His rapid conquest is symbolized by the goat crossing the whole earth without touching the ground. To this day, Alexander's rapid conquest remains unique in military history. Despite the Persian forces' immense numbers and commanding military equipment (including war elephants), young Alexander's tactical genius and disciplined Macedonian army won the day.

At the height of Alexander's power in 323 B.C., the goat's prominent horn was broken off. At age 33, the world conqueror died at Babylon, in his vomit from a drunken stupor or from poison given by Cassander or complications from malaria. His early demise is a demonstration of God's sovereignty over the rise and fall of empires and of great leaders.

> And in its place four prominent horns grew up towards the four winds of heaven (Daniel 8:8).

As indicated earlier by the four heads of the third beast (7:6), Alexander's four generals divided the empire into four parts: *Lysimachus* ruled Thrace and Bithynia; *Cassander* ruled Macedonia and Greece; *Seleucus* ruled Syria, Babylonia and eastward to India; and *Ptolemy,* ruled Egypt, Palestine and Arabia Petraea. This division occurred after twenty-one years of intense fighting to gain rule following the death of Alexander. *Antigonus* was a fifth general who was defeated and shoved out, leaving only four. If Antigonus had gotten in as the fifth ruler, the reader could throw away the book of Daniel!

THE VISION OF THE LITTLE HORN (8:9-12). Out of one of them (Seleucus) came another horn (Antiochus IV Epiphanes), who started small but grew in power to the south (Egypt) and to the east (Arabia Petraea) and towards the Beautiful Land (Palestine). Antiochus IV was one of twenty-six kings who ruled Syria. He continued as king from 175 B.C. until 164 B.C., ruling from Antioch.

The name "Antiochus" means "opposer" or "withstander." Antiochus II was known as "theos," meaning "God" and Antiochus III, was known as "the Great." Descending from such lineage, Antiochus IV developed an exalted view of himself. He assumed the title "Theos Epiphanes," meaning "the Manifest God." However, he was known by his enemies as Epiphames ("madman" or "insane"), which required a change of one letter ("n" to "m") in the Greek spelling of his title. This change in his title occurred after he had slaughtered one hundred thousand Jews (1 Maccabees 1:24, 37, 57-64; 2 Maccabees 5:11-14, 23-26). Centuries before it happened, Daniel witnessed this trepidation in his vision.

This "little horn" of the goat is not to be confused with the "little horn" of the fourth beast (7:8). The little horn of the goat rises out the Greek Empire, while the other rises from the Revived Roman Empire. Both "little horns" oppose God, magnify themselves to the level of deity and persecute the people of God. Both are energized by Satan. Both rulers demonstrate fallen man's extreme obsession to rule the world apart from God. There are strong similarities between the two "little horns" since the one of the goat foreshadows the one of the beast in the end times. And both the typical little horn (Antiochus IV Epiphanes) and the antitypical little horn (the Antichrist) appear in succession in chapter eleven.

Comparison of the Little Horns

LITTLE HORN OF CHAPTER 7 BEAST	LITTLE HORN OF CHAPTER 8 GOAT
From Rome (Fourth kingdom)	From Greece (Third Kingdom)
Eleventh horn, rooting up three horns	Fifth horn, coming out of one of four horns
Persecutes God's people for 42 months or 3 1/2 years	Persecutes God's people for 2,300 days or over 6 years
Is the Antichrist	Is Antiochus IV Epiphanes

Antiochus IV ascended to the throne by intrigue. Following the murder of his brother Demetrius, the rightful heir, who was being held hostage in Rome, Antiochus seized the throne and became the eighth ruler of the Seleucid dynasty. This little horn grew "until it reached the host of the heavens, and it threw some of the starry host down to the earth and trampled on them." The starry host is the promised offspring of Abraham (Genesis 12:3; 15:5; Jeremiah 33:22).

How did Antiochus throw to the earth some of the faithful Jews (the starry host) and trample on them? Antiochus was a tyrant, a ruthless dictator, who suppressed the Biblical faith and the worship of the one true God during the time of the Maccabees. He expelled Israel's godly high priest Onias III from his office at the beginning of his reign in 175 B.C., and he assassinated the priest in 171 B.C. Thereafter, he pursued his evil policy of securing control of the high priesthood and bringing increasing pressure on the Jewish hierarchy to surrender their religious loyalties in the interest of conformity to Greek culture and idolatry as predicted.

> It set itself [Antiochus] up to be as great as the Prince of the host [High Priest]; it took away the daily sacrifice from him (High Priest), and the place of his sanctuary [Temple] was brought low [statue of Zeus erected and a pig sacrificed on the altar]. Because of rebellion [Maccabean Revolt], the host of the saints [Israel] and the daily sacrifice were given over to it. It prospered in everything it did, and truth was thrown to the ground [all copies of Torah burned].

In 169 B.C., Antiochus arrogantly entered God's sanctuary and took the golden altar and the lampstand. Two years later, he sent letters by messengers to Jerusalem to profane the Sabbath and feasts, to defile the sanctuary and the priests, to build altars and sacred precincts and shrines for idols, to sacrifice swine and unclean animals, and to forget the law and change all the ordinances (1 Maccabees 1:41-49). Outside the Most Holy Place of the Temple, Greek games were held. Since participants of these games were naked, this led to the Jews' compromise of circumcision.

On top of everything else, these games were dedicated to Zeus, whose statue was erected in the Temple. Apollo, the historic deity of the dynasty, disappeared almost entirely from the Seleucid coinage after the reign of Antiochus, and Apollo was replaced by Zeus.

Antiochus (and Satan) knew that the uniqueness of Israel depended on its sacrificial system and the truth written in the Torah.

> The books of the law which they found they tore in pieces and burned with fire. Where the book of the covenant was found in the

possession of anyone, or if anyone adhered to the law, the decree of the king condemned them to death (1 Maccabees 1:56-57).

It is possible that this decree could have led to the Essenes hiding their scrolls or the Jewish priests hiding the Temple scrolls in the caves of Qumran. Discovered in A.D. 1947, the writings are known as the Dead Sea Scrolls.

THE TIME-SPAN OF THE HOSTS TRAMPLING THE SANCTUARY (8:13-14). The holy ones may refer to angels or saints. The important mystery the angels or saints want answered is "How long will it take for the vision to be fulfilled?" The answer is directed to Daniel.

> He said to me, "It will take 2,300 evenings and mornings; then the sanctuary will be reconsecrated" (Daniel 8:14).

Since "evenings and mornings" are associated with the daily sacrifices at the Temple, some commentators interpret the number as 1,150 days, while others hold to 2,300 days.

According to 1 Maccabees 4:52-59 and Wentzel's *A Chronology of Biblical Christianity*, the Holy Place was properly restored on Kislev (December) 25, 165 B.C. On this date, the first *Hanukkah* was celebrated. Working backwards, 2,300 days from this restoration date, we arrive at September 6, 171 B.C. Around this time, Onias III was assassinated by Antiochus. In Mid-September 171 B.C., Lysimachus, brother of the corrupt High Priest Menelaus, desecrated the Temple by stealing its sacred vessels (2 Maccabees 4:31-59).

If 1,150 days are used, the starting time is Kislev (December) 15, 168 B.C., the precise date the Temple was desecrated by Antiochus (1 Maccabees 1:54; 4:52). Is it possible that this prophecy was fulfilled twice?

THE INTERPRETATION OF THE VISION BY GABRIEL (8:15-27). Gabriel (גבריאל Gabriy'el) means "warrior of God" or "man of God." Gabriel is the archangel that Yahweh employed to send messages of great importance to Daniel, Zechariah, and Mary. This angelic being took the appearance of a man.

The man's voice that Daniel heard could have been Enoch, Elijah, an angel or God Himself. Terrified by the presence of Gabriel, Daniel fell, prostrate, in a deep sleep. The archangel touched Daniel and raised him to his feet.

Gabriel began the interpretation by declaring that the vision pertained to "the time of the end," "the appointed time," and "the time of wrath." These three times describe the same period—the period of history during God's indignation or anger with Israel because of its rebellion against Him. Gentile domination and mistreatment of the Jews began with the northern kingdom of Israel being dispersed by Assyria. It continued with the southern kingdom of Judah being exiled to Babylon, and it will continue until the second coming of Christ. Yet, the times announced by Gabriel point to "the time of the end" or "the times of the Gentiles," which Jesus calls "the time of punishment."

> When you see Jerusalem being surrounded by armies, you will know that its desolation is near. Then let those who are in Judea flee to the mountains, let those in the city get out, and let those in the country not enter the city. For this is the time of punishment in fulfillment of all that has been written. How dreadful it will be in those days for pregnant women and nursing mothers! There will be great distress in the land and wrath against this people. They will fall by the sword and will be taken as prisoners to all the nations. Jerusalem will be trampled on by the Gentiles until the times of the Gentiles are fulfilled (Luke 21:20-24).

This is "the appointed time," and "the time of wrath." Gabriel's interpretation of the vision, therefore, skips rapidly over Medo-Persia and Greece to predict events at the end of this age—"what will happen later in the time of wrath."

Hence, the vision concerning the "little horn" has a double fulfillment. Antiochus IV Epiphanes is a type of the Antichrist. With the rise of both "little horns," God judges Israel as a rebel because the people have become completely wicked. Wickedness is the primary reason for God's wrath (cf. Genesis 6:5-7). The first part of Gabriel's prediction fits Antiochus as well as the Antichrist.

> A stern-faced king, a master of intrigue, will arise. He will become very strong, but not by his own power. He will cause astounding devastation and will succeed in whatever he does. He will destroy the mighty men and the holy people. He will cause deceit to prosper, and he will consider himself superior (Daniel 8:23-25).

Was Antiochus a man energized by the power of Satan? It is definitely predicted that the Antichrist will be empowered by Satan. "The dragon gave the beast his power and his throne and great authority" (Revelation 13:2). We are told that Satan entered into Judas Iscariot (John 13:27) and undoubtedly, he has entered others in history. Possibly, Adolph Hitler, who was involved with the occult, was possessed by Satan in his attempt to rule the world before "the appointed time of the end."

How the stern-faced king, a master of intrigue, rises to power and becomes very strong is predicted in chapter eleven. This ruler will arrive upon the scene riding a white horse; he will have a bow in his hand, but no arrow. He will present himself as the prince of peace (Revelation 6:2). He will announce himself as the savior of the world and God will assist him with the deception.

> The coming of the lawless one will be in accordance with the work of Satan displayed in all kinds of counterfeit miracles, signs and wonders, and in every sort of evil that deceives those who are perishing. They perish because they refused to love the truth and so be saved. For this reason God sends them a powerful delusion so that they will believe the lie (2 Thessalonians 2:9-11).

The second part of Gabriel's prediction applies only to the Antichrist.

> When they feel secure, he will destroy many and take his stand against the Prince of princes. Yet he will be destroyed, but not by human power (Daniel 8:25).

This prediction cannot apply to Antiochus IV. Judas Maccabeus drove out the Syrian army in 165 B.C., at which time the Temple was cleansed from its pollution and rededicated. The death of Antiochus IV Epiphanes in 163 B.C. is described in 1 Maccabees 6:8-13. When the king heard the news that the Jews tore down the abomination he had erected, he became downhearted and a deep grief overcame him unto death. His death was not supernatural.

It is the Antichrist, who "will take his stand against the Prince of princes." The Prince of princes is Christ Jesus. The stern-faced king will be no match for Him. Christ will destroy the Antichrist by His divine power as predicted; the Seed of the Woman will crush the serpent's head (Genesis 3:15).

The time involved in Gabriel's interpretation needs to be decoded.

> The vision of the evenings and mornings that has been given you is true, but seal up the vision, for it concerns the distant future (Daniel 8:26).

How long is "the distant future" from Daniel's time—several hundred years, twenty-six hundred years, or more? Is this prediction a double reference prophecy? How long is it to be sealed up? Certainly, those who have attempted to make the 2,300 evenings and mornings equal 2.300 years have turned out to be very foolish.

We can be a little foolish and make some educated guesses at the fulfillment of this prediction if we do not take them too seriously. If "2,300 evenings and mornings" represent 2,300 days, the period must extend beyond the Tribulation since the ending of the daily sacrifice and setting up of the image of the beast does not occur until the middle of the Tribulation. The 2,300 days might refer to the time it will take to build or reconsecrate the Temple (Ezekiel 40:1-44:31).

If evenings and mornings each represent sacrifices instead of days, the 2,300 equals 1,150 days (3 years, 2 months, and 10 days based on the 360-day prophetic year). Thus, the image of the beast might stand on the wing of the Temple for that amount of time. On the 1,150th day from its erection, "the abomination of desolation" will come down. On the other hand, this image might be destroyed by the end time earthquake that causes the cities of the nations to collapse (Revelation 16:18).

One needs to add 110 days (3 months and 20 days) to 1,150 days before reaching 1,260 days or 42 months or 3 1/2 years—God's predetermined time for the second half of the Tribulation Period (Daniel 9:27; 12:7; Revelation 12:4; 13:5).

When the Jews see the abomination of desolation spoken of through the prophet Daniel, they are told to flee into the mountains (Matthew 24:16-21). They will flee for the whole 1,260 days according to Revelation 12:6-14. Will those who remain in Jerusalem reconsecrate the sanctuary 110 days before the end of the Tribulation? That could be the catalyst that brings the kings together at Armageddon (Revelation 16:16).

It also is possible that Christ's statement on days cut short affects any calculation.

> For then there will be great distress, unequaled from the beginning of the world until now—and never to be equaled again. If those days had not been cut short, no one would survive, but for the sake of the elect those days will be shortened (Matthew 24:21-22).

The time of the end is stated in Daniel 8:25 as being when the little horn stands up against the Prince of princes—Christ.

The vision of chapter seven deeply troubled Daniel and his face turned pale. This vision had a greater effect on him.

> I, Daniel, was exhausted and lay ill for several days. Then I got up and went about the king's business. I was appalled by the vision; it was beyond understanding (Daniel 8:27).

The strain on the aged prophet was more than he could bear physically, mentally and spiritually, yet after several days he went to his work. The prophet had the same concern for his people as the apostle Paul (Romans 9:1-3). Overwhelmed by what the future held for his people, Daniel was appalled by the vision.

There are two ways to take "it was beyond understanding:" (1) certain aspects of the vision were beyond understanding; or (2) God's future wrath upon His people was beyond understanding. There is always a sense of awe and mystery in the ways of God.

Applications of Chapter Eight

The persecution under Antiochus IV Epiphanes is a preview of the Tribulation Period. Just as the terror of Antiochus' reign ended according to God's timetable so will the reign of the Antichrist cease on schedule. There is a light at the end of the tunnel.

A remnant of Jews returned to Palestine after the Babylonian captivity, but the succeeding generations of Jews turned their back on God. Therefore, Antiochus was permitted to persecute Israel. Today, the nation's spiritual status in the Promised Land is far worse than in the second century B.C. It cries out to God for another madman!

Man is without excuse; God has warned the world of the coming prince. Antiochus was a living preview of this madman, who was possessed or controlled by Satan. The Antichrist will be more profane and brutal than Antiochus.

If the Antichrist is alive today, he is unrecognizable. Antiochus IV Epiphanes rose out of obscurity as did men like Napoleon Bonaparte and Adolph Hitler and so will the end times' ruler.

The speed and power of Alexander the Great foreshadow the rapidness of the Antichrist's attempt to dominate the world. He will ride out on the white horse at the beginning of the Tribulation; three and one-half years later the Antichrist will control the Revived Roman Empire; and then he will set out to rule the world. At the height of his power, his horn will be broken off also. The Antichrist's kingdom will not be divided among generals; Christ will smash it and it will be gone with the wind.

If Alexander the Great died in a drunken stupor, he was defeated by his own sinfulness. Certainly, Antiochus IV Epiphanes died because of his lust for power, prestige and a desire to play God. Such men stand as a warning that unchecked sin destroys like a cancer.

Iran, Iraq will [handwritten]
Syria, the will come from one of these [handwritten]
Antichrist [handwritten]

The mere touch of the archangel Gabriel strengthened Daniel. The NT manifests that fallen angels (demons) have the power to make a person physically impaired and weak (cf. Matthew 4:24; 8:16-17; 9:32; 12:22). Does God send the holy angels to strengthen His people today?

Gabriel's interpretation of the vision, if anything, complicates it. Daniel could not fully understand it, even with angelic help. We also need to be careful not to be too dogmatic concerning the details of the future. The overall thrust of prophecy can be understood in any age, but those who live through its literal fulfillment will see it unsealed before their eyes.

It is evident that superpowers come and go in history. The military that any nation depends upon fails, no matter how large or efficient. When God says it is over, it is over!

Since God has outlined history so graphically, He wants us to be alert, ready and waiting for the coming of Christ. He will come for His Church before the Tribulation and return to the earth with the armies of heaven at the very end of it. Christians do not have to look forward with dread to the rise of "the little horn"—"the coming prince"—because the Prince of princes will save all born-again believers from the time of wrath (1 Thessalonians 5:9).

The next upcoming event on God's prophetic calendar is either the invasion of Israel as predicted in Ezekiel 38-39 or the Rapture of the Church (1 Thessalonians 4:16-17). Those left behind will see the rise of "the little horn." His lawlessness and tyranny will plunge the world into absolute chaos. The majority of those who turn to God in the time of wrath will be martyred during the Antichrist's reign of terror (Revelation 7:9-14).

Today is the day of salvation from wrath. The final three and one-half years (the Great Tribulation) and its horror goes beyond our imagination as both Satan and the Lamb pour out wrath upon the earth and upon its inhabitants. Though multitudes will be saved in the Tribulation Period, they will experience the terrors of the Antichrist's reign as well as the seal, bowl, and trumpet judgments that are predicted in Revelation 6-19.

As God's fellow-workers we urge you not to receive God's grace in vain. For he says, "In the time of my favor I heard you, and in the day of salvation I helped you." I tell you, now is the time of God's favor, now is the day of salvation (2 Corinthians 6:1-2).

Like Daniel, we should be appalled at what is coming, and warn the lost to get ready before it is too late. The unsaved should be given a chance to hear the Gospel at least once. Without Christ, there is no hope!

Here is an easy presentation of the Gospel that you can share with your family, friends, neighbors, and co-workers.

The Gospel

The GOSPEL is simple as A - B - C.

A. Admit you are a sinner in need of God's grace.

   1. As it is written: There is no one righteous, not even one (Romans 3:10).
   2. For all have sinned and fall short of the glory of God (Romans 3:23).
   3. For the wages of sin is death, but the gift of God is eternal life in Christ Jesus our Lord (Romans 6:23).

B. Believe in your heart that Jesus died for your sins and rose from the dead so that God can declare you righteous.

   1. He was delivered over to death for our sins and was raised to life for our justification (Romans 4:25).

   2. But God demonstrates his own love for us in this: While we were still sinners, Christ died for us (Romans 5:8).

C. Confess that Jesus is Lord and call on Him.

   1. That if you confess with your mouth, "Jesus is Lord," and believe in your heart that God raised him from the dead, you will be saved. For it is with your heart that you believe and are justified, and it is with your mouth that you confess and are saved (Romans 10:9-10).

   2. For, "Everyone who calls on the name of the Lord will be saved" (Romans 10:13).

   3. For it is by grace you have been saved, through faith—and this not from yourselves, it is the gift of God—not by works, so that no one can boast (Ephesians 2:8-9)

Daniel's Prayer and
Vision of the Seventy Sevens
(Daniel 9)

70 AD
Temple destroyed

Time Line

YEAR B.C.	551	539
MONARCHS	Belshazzar	Darius the Mede
DANIEL	Vision of Ram & Goat	Prayer & Gabriel's "Seventy Sevens"

Outline of Chapter Nine

Prayer of Daniel
    Its Prompting, 1-3
    Its Particulars, 4-15
    Its Petition, 16-19
    Its Power, 20-23
Prophecy of Gabriel
    Its Mathematics, 24
    Its Message, 25-27

Background of Chapter Nine

Sixty-six years have passed since Daniel had been exiled. The prophet is about eighty years old in 539 B.C. The golden empire has been replaced by the silver empire of Medo-Persia. Nebuchadnezzar's own dream of having his empire continue forever, as seen in his golden image, has fallen by the wayside.

Nebuchadnezzar's dream of the great image, Daniel's dream of the four beasts and his vision of a ram and a goat point to an extended period before Israel takes its coveted place in the world. Consequently, the purpose of this chapter is to elaborate on the predictions of chapters seven and eight, as well as to reveal God's timetable for His future dealings with Israel.

There is no symbolic imagery in this chapter. The archangel Gabriel may have actually come to Daniel and presented his most important message with a vision. Gabriel outlines the future in terms of time as it relates to the coming of two prominent princes and an abomination that causes desolation. This chapter is a significant part of the framework or skeleton upon which all prophecy is built or fleshed out during the times of the Gentiles.

Daniel 9, Ezra 9 and Nehemiah 9 contain three of the great intercessory prayers of the Scriptures. Here Daniel pours out his heart to God on behalf of Israel. His prayer is one of the most sublime, touching, burning and effective prayers in the Word of God.

The events of chapter nine occur in 539 B.C., the first year of Darius' reign, when change was the order of the day. How would the change of empires affect God's people in captivity? Undoubtedly, the answer to this pressing question prompted Daniel to search the Scriptures for the answer.

Prayer of Daniel

ITS PROMPTING (9:1-3). The overthrow of Babylon by Medo-Persia was a momentous event. The handwriting on the wall, the first part of the dream of dreams, and the predictions that Daniel had conveyed to the first and last kings of Babylon have been fulfilled before his own eyes. The liberation of the exiled Jews was next on God's calendar. When would it occur?

> In the first year of his reign, I, Daniel, understood from the Scriptures, according to the word of the LORD given to Jeremiah the prophet, that the desolation of Jerusalem would last seventy years (Daniel 9:1-2).

Jeremiah 25:1-14 predicted that the desolation and exile would last seventy years. The prophet had sent a letter (Jeremiah 29:1-14) to the exiles with seven instructions for living in Babylon, telling them:

1. To build houses and settle down
2. To plant gardens and eat what they produce
3. To marry and have families—increase in numbers
4. To seek the peace and prosperity of Babylon
5. To pray to Yahweh for Babylon so they would prosper
6. To not be deceived by the prophets and diviners among them
7. To wait for the completion of the seventy years

Nebuchadnezzar's first invasion of Jerusalem occurred in 605 B.C., when he took to Babylon some exiles and articles from the Temple. The desolation of Jerusalem began at that time. Daniel's heart must have started beating faster as he read the words of the prophet Jeremiah.

> This whole country will become a desolate wasteland, and these nations will serve the king of Babylon for seventy years. But when the seventy years are fulfilled, I will punish the king of Babylon and his nation, the land of the Babylonians, for their guilt," declares the LORD, "and will make it desolate forever. I will bring upon that land all the things I have spoken against it, all that are written in this book and prophesied by Jeremiah against all the nations (Jeremiah 25:11-13).

Less than fifty years had elapsed since the fall of Jerusalem in 586 B.C. However, the earliest *terminus a quo* for the seventy years could be the time of Daniel's own captivity. Jews often counted part of a day or a year as whole days or years. Hence, the length of time from the first exile of 605 B.C. to Cyrus' decree issued in his first official year (spring of 538 to spring 537 B.C.) could be rounded to seventy years. Daniel understood the prophecy. He knew that the end of the seventy years and the return of his people to their land were fast approaching if God marked the exile from 605 B.C.

Note that Daniel recognized the writings of Jeremiah as being inspired by God, long before they would become part of the Hebrew canon. Interestingly, Daniel does not mention Cyrus even though he knew all about him, for Yahweh had revealed his name through the prophet Isaiah in the seventh century B.C.

Who says of Cyrus, "He is my shepherd and will accomplish all that I please; he will say of Jerusalem, "Let it be rebuilt," and of the temple, "Let its foundations be laid" (Isaiah 44:28).

I will raise up Cyrus in my righteousness: I will make all his ways straight. He will rebuild my city and set my exiles free, but not for a price or reward, says the LORD Almighty (Isaiah 45:13).

Daniel's heart must have been stirred when he first heard reports of the young King Cyrus of Ashan, Persia. Cyrus had brilliantly overthrown his uncle Astyages in battle and had made himself ruler of the entire Medo-Persian domain.

There are two significant hermeneutical lessons about prophecy here. *First*, Daniel believed in the literal fulfillment of prophecy—should not also the modern interpreter? *Second*, the closer the fulfillment of prophetic events become, the more the student of the Bible is able to discern the times. Those who are lazy when studying the Scriptures have a tendency to brush prophecy aside and say, "In the end it will all pan out." Not with Daniel, he wanted to understand what God was doing in his time! He wanted to make a difference.

Like Daniel, a diligent student of the Bible builds his prayer life on the Word of God. The Scriptures and prayer go hand in hand. Serious prayer always begins with God's will, not man's will. We are to submit ourselves to God's plans, not vice versa. Twice Jesus taught a model prayer to His disciples on how to pray; according to His teaching, our attitude should be that of subordinate (child, subject) to Superior (parent, sovereign), desiring His will.

Our Father in heaven, hallowed be your name, your kingdom come, your will be done on earth as it is in heaven (Matthew 6:9-10; cf. Luke 11:2).

Jesus echoed His model prayer in the Garden of Gethsemane as the Son yielded to the Father's will.

Father, if you are willing, take this cup from me; yet not my will, but yours be done (Luke 22:42).

191

The apostle John reinforces this manner of praying.

> This is the confidence we have in approaching God: that if we ask anything according to his will, he hears us (1 John 5:14).

Once Daniel understood the will of God, knowledge and understanding of the prophecy did not puff up the prophet, but humbled him. He turned to the Lord God and pleaded with Him in prayer, while fasting in sackcloth and ashes. Fasting is a sign of mourning and distress. Sackcloth and ashes show outwardly the inward reality of being a penitent sinner. Prayer has been described as ACTS:

Adoration
Confession
Thanks
Supplication

Supplication is to ask humbly and earnestly. Daniel's prayer moves back and forth between adoration, confession and supplication. The giving of thanks is missing from it.

ITS PARTICULARS (9:4-15). Daniel models the powerful prayer of a humble person. He reveals how a true man of God approaches the Sovereign God of the Universe on behalf of his nation. His prayer should be read and studied in light of 2 Chronicles 7:14:

> If my people, who are called by my name, will humble themselves and pray and seek my face and turn from their wicked ways, then will I hear from heaven and will forgive their sin and will heal their land.

God gave specific instructions on praying for one's nation in the time of Solomon. Daniel followed God's instructions in his intercessory prayer, praying on behalf of his people and their land. In 2 Chronicles 7:14 and Daniel 9:4-19, two sides to prayer are present, man's part and God's part as illustrated by the following chart.

Intercession for One's Nation

Man's Part

COVENANT RELATIONSHIP: *"If my people, who are called by my name"* indicates there must be a covenant relationship with God (cf. Daniel 9:4b).

CONTRITE HEART: *"Will humble themselves"* is to approach the Lord with a repentant spirit (cf. Daniel 9:3).

CONSULT GOD: *"And pray"* is to beseech God first and foremost (cf. Daniel 9:4a).

CONFESSION OF SIN: *"Seek my face"* requires confession (cf. Daniel 9:4c-16).

CHANGE OF WAYS: *"And turn from their wicked ways"* is the act of repentance (cf. Daniel 9:11).

God's Part

COMMUNICATION CONNECTION: *"Then will I hear from heaven"* is the assurance that God will give ear to prayer and hear it (cf. Daniel 9:17-18a).

COMPASSIONATE RESPONSE: *"And will forgive their sin"* indicates that God will be merciful (cf. Daniel 9:18b).

COVENANT ACTION: *"And will heal their land"* indicates God is obligated under His covenant promises to act when His people respond this way (cf. Daniel 9:19).

Daniel combines covenant and love in "His covenant of love" to define why God is great and awesome. Love (חֶסֶד *hesed*) is best translated as "steadfast-loving-kindness." The combination of *Hesed* and His covenant is equivalent to saying, "God is faithful," a fact that saturates this prayer from its beginning to its end. Certainly, Daniel's heart was beating in tune with Jeremiah 29:12-14 and 2 Chronicles 7:14.

I prayed to the LORD my God and confessed: "O Lord, the great and awesome God, who keeps his covenant of love with all who love him and obey his commands, we have sinned and done wrong (Daniel 9:4-5).

It is a theological error to believe that God unconditionally loves us and will keep His promises of blessing, no matter what we do. The blessings of the Adamic, Noahic, Abrahamic, Mosaic, Palestinian, Davidic and New Covenants each carry the obligation of love, which Jesus has defined, "If you love me, you will obey what I command" (John 14:15).

While God's greatness exalts Him above man, it also brings Him near to those who love (אהב *'ahab*) and obey Him.

There are at least seven truths about God in Daniel's prayer.

1. He is a great God.
2. He is an awesome God to be feared.
3. He keeps His covenants with steadfast-loving-kindness to those loving Him.
4. He is a righteous God.
5. He is a God of judgment.
6. He is a God of mercy and forgiveness.
7. He is a God who acts.

Daniel's prayer manifests three steps to receiving the blessing of God:

1. Prayer and confession of sin
2. Turning from iniquity
3. Understanding and obeying truth

Daniel records that "I prayed to יהוה (*Yahweh*) my אלהים (*'elohiym*, God)," yet he began his prayer "O אדני (*adonai*, Lord);" thereby he has utilized the three primary Hebrew words for the Divine. The prophet recognized his own covenant relationship with God when he said, "Yahweh's my God." When he prayed on behalf of his people, he did not begin with the covenant Name of Yahweh since the Jews were outside the covenant relationship at that time. Therefore, confession of sin immediately followed the hallowing of God's name.

With the exception of Christ, Joseph and Daniel are the most spotless (purest) characters of the Bible. Yet, Daniel identifies himself with the sin of his people. The solidarity of the nation is all-inclusive—the righteous and the unrighteous—have sinned and done wrong. Consider the verbs that Daniel employed to describe their woeful condition.

Sinned (חטא *chata'*)	To miss the mark of God's glory
Done Wrong (עוה *`avah*)	To distort, act perversely
Wicked (רשע *rasha`*)	To do known wrong
Rebelled (מרד *marad*)	To defy authority
Turned Away (סור *cuwr*)	To satisfy self
Not Listened (לא שמע *lo shama`*)	To reject truth

He acknowledged what Yahweh had said about Israel through the prophets. The Biblical meaning of the word "confess" is to agree with God. That is the way to understand the term "confess" in 1 John 1:9:

> If we confess our sins, he is faithful and just and will forgive us our sins and purify us from all unrighteousness.

No excuses, no skirting the facts, just an outright declared recognition of iniquity and trespasses, which is what God requires to forgive sin. Hence, a large portion of Daniel's prayer contains specific acknowledgments of unrighteousness. He confessed sins of commission and omission, not by the rulers alone but by all Israel. He acknowledged the nation's failure to obey the Scriptures and its failure to seek the favor of Yahweh in prayer—the two things that had ultimately brought the disaster upon them (verses 13-14).

He acknowledged that sin is wrongdoing, wickedness, rebellion, and a turning away from God's commands and law. Sin is the outcome of not listening to God and obeying Him. Like Paul, Daniel discovered from reading the Law of Moses and the prophets that all fall short of the glory of God.

As it is written: "There is no one righteous, not even one; there is no one who understands, no one who seeks God. All have turned away, they have together become worthless; there is no one who does good, not even one" (Romans 3:10-12; cf. Isaiah 53:6).

God's law exposes the fact that all are sinners (cf. Romans 7:12-13). Therefore, Daniel confessed that the nation of Israel is one hundred percent at fault. There were no complaints like in Job. God is right and just in His actions. The nation's rebellion had compelled God to bring the promised curses on His people and His land (Deuteronomy 28:15-68; Leviticus 26:39-45). For instance, Yahweh had predicted through Moses in Leviticus 26:33-34:

> I will scatter you among the nations and will draw out my sword and pursue you. Your land will be laid waste, and your cities will lie in ruins. Then the land will enjoy its sabbath years all the time that it lies desolate and you are in the country of your enemies; then the land will rest and enjoy its sabbaths.

Consequently, the writer of Chronicles recorded that the Babylonian captivity was a result of the Israelites not observing the sabbath rests. Over a period of 490 years, the land had missed 70 rests as the Israelites continuously cultivated the land. Significantly, the time marker of the vision that follows Daniel's prayer is "seventy sevens" or 490 years. Counting back 490 years from 586 B.C., one arrives at a time prior to the monarchy, known as the period of the Judges. It appears that the kings did not enforce the sabbath rests for the land; so God took what was due His land.

> The land enjoyed its sabbath rests; all the time of its desolation it rested, until the seventy years were completed in fulfillment of the word of the LORD spoken by Jeremiah (2 Chronicles 36:21).

Daniel acknowledged in His prayer that the destruction of Jerusalem and the captivity were of God.

> You have fulfilled the words spoken against us and against our rulers by bringing upon us great disaster. Under the whole heaven nothing has ever been done like what has been done to Jerusalem (Daniel 9:12).

What had been done to Jerusalem? Thirty months (two and one-half years) of siege by the Babylonians had brought starvation, cannibalism, and then the total destruction of Jerusalem. It was a great disaster!

Daniel believed in God's sovereignty, yet he understood the free will of man. He did not sit back on his recliner and wait for the completion of the seventy years. It might be four years off or even twenty years depending upon when God began counting. He immediately did something about it—he prayed for God to act and not to delay!

ITS PETITION (9:16-19). Daniel's prayer contains ten pleas presented to the Lord.

1. Turn Your anger and wrath away from Jerusalem and Your Holy Hill.
2. Hear my prayers.
3. Hear my petitions.
4. Look with favor on Your sanctuary.
5. Incline Your ear to hear.
6. Open Your eyes.
7. See the desolations of the city that bears Your Name.
8. Forgive our sins.
9. Listen and act.
10. Do not delay.

"Our Father in heaven, hallowed be your name, your kingdom come" permeates Daniel's petition. It is Your sanctuary, Your city, Your people, Your Name that are at stake, God! This is like the intercessory prayer Moses prayed on behalf of Israel, the one that so moved God, He relented from destroying His people (Exodus 32:11-14).

Daniel also reminded the Lord of His reputation—not that God needs reminding! The chief end of man is to glorify God and enjoy Him forever. The prophet's prayer revealed his desire to see God's name hallowed; this should be our prime objective in life.

> So whether you eat or drink or whatever you do, do it all for the glory of God (1 Corinthians 10:31).

Daniel and his three friends began the exile with this objective. The prophet hallowed God's name with his entire life in both word and deed. His prayer was not hollow words but a sincere petition from the heart. His plea was for compassion, not justice; and it was urgent.

> O Lord, listen! O Lord, forgive! O Lord, hear and act! For your sake, O my God, do not delay, because your city and your people bear your Name (Daniel 9:19).

Notice the verbs: *listen, forgive, hear, act,* and *do not delay.* Daniel wanted God's kingdom to come to His people as soon as possible. The burden of his prayer was for the return and restoration of the nation. Therefore, he confessed the sin of the people and sought God's mercy so that His Name would be hallowed.

ITS POWER (9:20-23). Does God answer this kind of prayer? Absolutely! Look at what the brother of Jesus wrote.

> Therefore confess your sins to each other and pray for each other so that you may be healed. The prayer of a righteous man is powerful and effective (James 5:16).

Daniel had not even finished praying when the answer arrived. Now that is powerful and effective praying! Judging by the length of Daniel's prayer, it took less than five minutes for Gabriel to come from God's throne in heaven. The moment we pray, the Spirit intercedes for us in accordance with God's will (Romans 8:26-27).

Daniel was given a taste of millennial blessing: "Before they call I will answer; while they are still speaking I will hear" (Isaiah 65:24). Gabriel arrives to give understanding to Daniel because the prophet was held in high esteem by God.

Prophecy of Gabriel

The Seventy Sevens

ITS MATHEMATICS (9:24). There are seven predictions within Gabriel's prophecy. These seven predictions have to do with Israel and the events that will take place in its holy city, Jerusalem.

1. Seventy sevens are decreed for your people and your holy city
2. To finish transgression
3. To put an end to sin
4. To atone for wickedness
5. To bring in everlasting righteousness
6. To seal up the vision and prophecy
7. To anoint the most holy

The Church is not the focal point of this prophecy. To spiritualize these prophecies concerning Israel's future by applying them to the Church is wrongly dividing the Word of God.

Israel's transgression is still transpiring; their sin has not ended. Through His blood, Christ's propitiating sacrifice provided man with the redemption he needs in order to be reconciled to God and to receive righteousness from God (Romans 3:22-26). However, the nation of Israel continues to be estranged from God. Everlasting righteousness does not mark God's people or their holy city. The nation of Israel has not perceived the message of this vision and prophecy. The ancient location of the Most Holy Place on Mount Moriah is covered today by the Muslim's Dome of the Rock.

All seven predictions of this vision still belong to the future. Each awaits fulfillment when Israel enters the New Covenant (Deuteronomy 30:6-10; Isaiah 59:20-21; Jeremiah 31:31-34; Ezekiel 36:24-38) prior to Christ's second coming (Zechariah 12:1-13:6).

How long is the decreed seventy sevens (שבעים שבעים *shib'iym* or שבוע *shabua*)? The latter Hebrew expression indicates a unit of sevens (days, weeks or years), a "heptad," just as we would use the word "dozen" to designate a collection of twelve things.

Liberals attempt to make the seventy sevens either seventy days or 490 days. Amillennialists symbolize the seventy sevens as indefinite periods. The answer is to be found in the Bible as the OT employs "sevens" for days, years and weeks of years.

1. *A week of days*—from one sabbath to another (Exodus 20:8-11).
2. *A week of years*—from one sabbatical year to another (Leviticus 25:3-7).
3. A *week of seven times seven years*, or forty-nine years—from one Jubilee to another (Leviticus 25:8-18).

The Jews had been removed from the land in order that it might rest for seventy years, since the sabbatical year had been violated for 490 years, or exactly seventy sevens. A week of years was just as familiar to the Jew as the week of da

> For six years sow your fields, and for six years prune your vineyards and gather their crops. But in the seventh year the land is to have a sabbath of rest, a sabbath to the LORD. Do not sow your fields or prune your vineyards (Leviticus 25:3-4).

The seventy sevens cannot be understood as days or weeks in light of the events predicted, such as the persecution of God's people at the hands of the Coming Prince. The Jews would be under the protection of Media-Persia for two hundred years.

Daniel 7:24-25 speaks of the same coming prince and the same persecution, fixing the duration as "a time and times and dividing of time" or "three and a half times." Revelation 13:4-7 refers to the same persecution, stating the duration in the exact terms of Daniel 7:25. This period is further defined in Revelation 12:6 as 1,260 days, and elsewhere as 3 1/2 years or 42 months (Revelation 13:5). Therefore, the phrase must speak of years, not days or weeks.

The prophetic year of Scripture is composed of 360 days, or twelve months of thirty days. The earliest biblical history of the length of a month is recorded with the Flood that began on the seventeenth day of the second month (Genesis 7:11), and ended on the seventeenth day of the seventh month (8:4). This period is stated in terms of days as "one hundred and fifty days" (7:24; 8:3), which is five months of thirty days.

Various calendars of the nations have used years of different lengths, correcting the error by the addition of days from time to time. Our own year of 365 days is not exact, the shortage being a little less than one day in four years.

The Coming of Two Princes

ITS MESSAGE (9:25-27). Once the period of seventy sevens had been introduced, Gabriel spoke of the two key persons of the future and their positioning in the seventy sevens.

> Know and understand this: From the issuing of the decree to restore and rebuild Jerusalem until the Anointed One, the ruler, comes, there will be seven 'sevens', and sixty-two 'sevens'. It will be rebuilt with streets and a trench, but in times of trouble. After the sixty-two 'sevens', the Anointed One will be cut off and will have nothing (Daniel 9:25-26).

Here is the most significant title attached to the name of Jesus: מָשִׁיחַ (*mashiyach,* "Messiah," literally "the Anointed One"). In the Greek, this title is translated χριστος (*christos*), which is "Christ" in English. The Messiah is Prince or Ruler. When Pilate had the placard placed on the cross, he got it right—for there hung the King—the Prince of Peace.

> Above his head they placed the written charge against him: THIS IS JESUS, THE KING OF THE JEWS (Matthew 27:37).

> But he was pierced for our transgressions, he was crushed for our iniquities; the punishment that brought us peace was upon him, and by his wounds we are healed (Isaiah 53:5).

The Anointed One's peace rules in the believer's heart during this present age, and in the age to come. His reign on the earth will be characterized by peace.

> Let the peace of Christ rule in your hearts, since as members of one body you were called to peace (Colossians 3:15).

> For to us a child is born, to us a son is given, and the government will be on his shoulders. And he will be called Wonderful Counselor, Mighty God, Everlasting Father, Prince of Peace. Of the

increase of his government and peace there will be no end. He will reign on David's throne and over his kingdom, establishing and upholding it with justice and righteousness from that time on and forever. The zeal of the LORD Almighty will accomplish this (Isaiah 9:6-8).

The Decoding of the Seventy Sevens

Around the turn of the twentieth century, Sir Robert Anderson of Scotland Yard, in *The Coming Prince,* decoded Daniel's "Seventy Sevens." In a chronological diagram of the history of Judah, Anderson observed three eras of seventy weeks. He dated Israel's entrance into Canaan as 1585 B.C., the kingdom established under Saul as 1096 B.C., Judah's servitude to Babylon as 606 B.C., and the Mystic Era beginning with the restoration of Jerusalem as 445 B.C.

490 years From Canaan to Kingdom
490 years From the Kingdom to Servitude
490 years Mystic Era of Seventy Weeks

This writer dates Israel's entrance into Canaan as 1406 B.C., the kingdom established under Saul as 1050 B.C., Judah's servitude to Babylon as 605 B.C., and the Mystical Era beginning with the restoration of Jerusalem as 444 B.C. Anderson's three eras of seventy weeks are questionable, but his calculation from the restoration of Jerusalem to the Messiah being cut off is extremely helpful.

Gabriel's prediction is concerned with the seventy weeks that begin in 444 B.C., and the exact time that the Anointed One (Messiah) would be cut off (His rejection by Israel and crucifixion on the cross). Consequently, Christ would not acquire the messianic kingdom envisioned in the OT during His first advent. Hence, the seventy sevens are "weeks" (seven-year periods), totaling 490 years of prophetic time for the Jews. Gabriel divided this time into three parts:

1. Seven sevens (7 x 7 = 49 years)
2. Sixty-two sevens (62 x 7 = 434 years)
3. One seven (7 years)

It took 49 years to rebuild Jerusalem, which occurred in troublesome times according to the book of Nehemiah. Then 434 years later, the Messiah, the Ruler, was cut off. The total is 483 years. Using a solar year to calculate when the Messiah would be cut off, one arrives at A.D. 38. By all reckoning, Christ died before A.D. 38. Thus, there must be a different way of making this calculation.

Verse 25 predicts that the event, which triggers the 490 years, would be a decree permitting the Jews to restore and rebuilt Jerusalem. History tells us there were four different decrees relating to Jerusalem. *Cyrus* (Ezra 1:2-4), *Darius* (Ezra 6:3-12), and *Artaxerxes* (Ezra 7:12-26) issued decrees concerning the rebuilding of the Temple (Ezra 1, 6, 7); and *Artaxerxes* decreed that Nehemiah could return to rebuild the walls (Nehemiah 2:8, 13-15). Gabriel's indicator as to which decree is the starting point for counting the 483 years is that "it will be rebuilt with streets and a trench, but in times of trouble." Chapters 3-6 of Nehemiah are about the rebuilding of the walls and Jerusalem in "times of trouble."

The date of Artaxerxes' decree to rebuild Jerusalem is given in the biblical record as "in the month of Nisan in the twentieth year of King Artaxerxes," which is March/April of 444 B.C. (Nehemiah 2:1).

Christ's death occurred on Friday, Nisan 14 in A.D. 33 (Friday, April 3, A.D. 33, on the Gregorian calendar). The common Jewish practice was to reckon from the first day of the month. Nisan 1 was March 5, 444 B.C., and from this date to Monday, March 30, A.D. 33 (the day of the Triumphal Entry on Nisan 10, A.D. 33, the day the Passover lambs were selected) is 173,880 days. When the period between these two dates is calculated, using the prophetic year of 360 days, one arrives at 173,880 days.

> 69 x 7 x 360 = 173,880 days
> March 5, 444 B.C. to March 30, A.D. 33 = 173,880 days

See *Chronological Aspects of the Life of Christ* for a more detailed explanation of this calculation.

Sir Robert Anderson used the older dating system and calculated from

March 14, 445 B.C. to April 6, 32 A.D., which was also the Tenth of Nisan that year, the day Christ might have presented Himself at Jerusalem.

Some conservative scholars use the earlier decree of Cyrus and arrive at the possible time of Christ's birth in 5/4 B.C. Others use the decree of Darius and arrive at the possible date of Christ's baptism in A.D. 26.

Liberal scholars, who claim that Daniel was written in the bitter days of the Jews' persecution by Antiochus IV Epiphanes, have proposed various starting dates. One begins the 490 years on the day Jeremiah announced the future restoration of Jerusalem. This one counts seven sevens (49 years) from 586 B.C. to 538 B.C., and arrives at an anointed one, a prince, who is Cyrus the Great. Then the sixty-two sevens (434 years) represent the period during which Jerusalem was to be rebuilt while experiencing many troubles. At the end of that time, the anointed one that is cut off is the beloved and honored High Priest Onias III, an event of great significance to the Jews (2 Maccabees 3:1, 3-40; 4:7ff., 23ff.).

Overall, liberal scholars reject any application of the prophecy to the Messiah of the NT. Note that 483 years from 586 B.C. is 103 B.C., and the date Onias was murdered is 171 B.C. Such erroneous calculations often occur in calculations that attempt to keep "the anointed one" from being Christ Jesus.

This writer believes Artaxerxes' decree to rebuild Jerusalem triggers the counting of the 483 years, which ends on the date of the Triumphal Entry, March 30, A.D. 33. Why? Because on this day, the outcomes of Christ's first advent and of the nation were fixed, just as Gabriel predicted.

> As he approached Jerusalem and saw the city, he wept over it and said, "If you, even you, had only known on this day what would bring you peace—but now it is hidden from your eyes. The days will come upon you when your enemies will build an embankment against you and encircle you and hem you in on every side. They will dash you to the ground, you and the children within your walls.

They will not leave one stone on another, because you did not recognize the time of God's coming to you" (Luke 19:41-44).

Jesus expected the Jews to know the day of His bringing peace, for it was predicted to the very day in the prophecy of the seventy sevens. The Jew's failure to study prophecy was tragic!

Jesus was declared Israel's King on the day of the triumphal entry as the crowds shouted, "Hosanna!" "Blessed is he who comes in the name of the Lord!" "Blessed is the King of Israel!" (John 12:13).

However, Jesus would receive no crown, except a crown of thorns! He was cut off from David's throne and the kingdom was not restored to Israel at that time.

Early the next day, Jesus cursed the fig tree (symbolic of Israel) for not bearing fruit (cf. Matthew 21:18-20; Mark 11:14) and made His way to the Temple, where He drove out the merchandisers, while quoting Jeremiah 7:11:

> "It is written," he said to them, "'My house will be called a house of prayer,' but you are making it a 'den of robbers'" (Matthew 21:13).

Significantly, Jesus had quoted only a portion of the prophecy in Jeremiah; the Jews should have known what followed and should have repented on the spot.

> But I have been watching! declares the LORD. Go now to the place in Shiloh where I first made a dwelling for my Name, and see what I did to it because of the wickedness of my people Israel. While you were doing all these things, declares the LORD, I spoke to you again and again, but you did not listen; I called you, but you did not answer. Therefore, what I did to Shiloh I will now do to the house that bears my Name, the temple you trust in, the place I gave to you and your fathers. I will thrust you from my presence, just as I did all your brothers, the people of Ephraim (Jeremiah 7:11-15).

The destruction of God's dwelling place (at Shiloh by the Philistines in the days of Samuel) and the destruction of the Temple (at Jerusalem in

586 B.C.) foreshadowed the destruction of the Temple in A.D. 70. On the evening of the day following His triumphal entry, Jesus sat on the Mount of Olives overlooking Jerusalem and foretold its destruction.

> When you see Jerusalem being surrounded by armies, you will know that its desolation is near. Then let those who are in Judea flee to the mountains, let those in the city get out, and let those in the country not enter the city. For this is the time of punishment in fulfillment of all that has been written. How dreadful it will be in those days for pregnant women and nursing mothers! There will be great distress in the land and wrath against this people. They will fall by the sword and will be taken as prisoners to all the nations. Jerusalem will be trampled on by the Gentiles until the times of the Gentiles are fulfilled (Luke 21:20-24).

"For this is the time of punishment in fulfillment of all that has been written" applies specifically to Gabriel's prophecy, and generally to other predictions in the OT. The cited events during the Passion Week clearly establish that the Jews had rejected Jesus as their King and He had rejected Israel before the morning of the day after the Triumphal Entry (Nisan 11). He had been cut off, and left with nothing, before His crucifixion on Friday (Nisan 14). He had been selected as the Passover Lamb by the people on the tenth of Nisan according to the Scriptures (Exodus 12:1-11).

Verse 26 reads, "After the sixty-two "sevens," the Anointed One will be cut off and will have nothing." The Hebrew כרת (*karath*) translated "cut off" usually denotes a violent kind of death or separation (Genesis 9:11; Psalm 37:9; Proverbs 2:23). Hence, our Passover Lamb had been selected (cut off) on Monday. He would be violently crucified on Friday, at the exact time the Passover lambs were being killed at the Temple.

Ironically, כרת (*karath*, cut off) is the same word translated "made" in Genesis 15:18:

> On that day the LORD made [cut] a covenant with Abram and said, "To your descendants I give this land, from the river of Egypt to the great river, the Euphrates."

When the Anointed One was cut off, those promises of the Abrahamic Covenant regarding the land were cut off with Him until the Second Advent.

What followed Christ's death? Except for a remnant, the Jews lied about Him, persecuted His messengers, and refused to acknowledge His kingship. So what happened? The next part of Gabriel's prophecy was fulfilled.

> The people of the ruler who will come will destroy the city and the sanctuary (Daniel 9:26).

Notice that the prophecy reads "the people of the ruler (נָגִיד *nagiyd*, prince) who will come." "The people" refers to the Romans who destroyed Jerusalem in A.D. 70. Hence, the coming prince of the end times appears to be Roman! Some insist this ruler must be Jewish, saying Israel enters into a seven-year covenant with him.

> He will confirm a covenant with many for one "seven." In the middle of the "seven" he will put an end to sacrifice and offering. And on a wing *of the temple* he will set up an abomination that causes desolation, until the end that is decreed is poured out on him (Daniel 9:27).

Technically, the Hiphel perfect of גָבַר (*gabar*) indicates that the covenant is confirmed or strengthened by this prince "with many." Israel might not even enter into its negotiation. Although current events show that Israel appears willing to enter into peace agreements with those opposed to its existence, we cannot assume it is party to this covenant. That the coming ruler must be Jewish is a mute issue. The coming prince is "the little horn" of Daniel 7:8, "the stern-faced king" in 8:23, and "the king who does as he pleases" in 11:36. See chapter 11 for details.

In A.D. 70, the Romans under Titus fulfilled the prediction of the destruction of the city and sanctuary. According to, eleven hundred thousand Jews perished in the siege of Jerusalem, and ninety-seven thousand were sold for slaves (*The Works of Josephus: War of the Jews*, 6:9:3). This prophecy was atrociously fulfilled! Gabriel and Jesus were correct.

> They will fall by the sword and will be taken as prisoners to all the
> nations. Jerusalem will be trampled on by the Gentiles until the
> times of the Gentiles are fulfilled (Luke 21:24).

"Trampled" (וּתְרֵאֹמ *pateo*) indicates Jerusalem would be treated with
insult, contempt and be desecrated. John Wesley describes the trampling
of A.D. 70.

> The land was sold, and no Jew suffered even to come within sight of
> Jerusalem. The very foundations of the city were ploughed up, and a
> heathen temple built where the temple of God had stood (*Notes on
> the Old and New Testaments*, Luke 21:24).

In Luke 21:24, Jesus introduced new terminology, "the times of the
Gentiles," to cover the predictions in the book of Daniel. The times of
the Gentiles run from the Fall of Jerusalem in 586 B.C. to the Fall of
Babylon the Great at the end of the Tribulation.

The surviving Jews were scattered among the nations in A.D. 70. Not
only had the nation "cut off" Jesus Christ, He had "cut off" fruitless
Israel and they would not become a sovereign nation until May 14, 1948.

Additionally, the prophecy of the seventy sevens reveals what it will be
like during the times of the Gentiles.

> The end will come like a flood: War will continue until the end, and
> desolations have been decreed.

The world is not going to improve during the Church age—anything but!
There will be wars and rumors of war on earth among men until the Lord
returns (cf. Matthew 24:6). There will be no permanent peace until the
Prince of Peace arrives. Desolations (ravages) have been decreed—
whether we like it or not—God has spoken!

Gabriel's prediction contains an unstated time of turmoil, especially for
the Jews, between the sixty-ninth and seventieth seven. When Israel
crucified the Messiah, the "prophetic clock" stopped ticking. It will

begin ticking again when the ruler who will come (the Antichrist) confirms a covenant with many for one seven. Jesus predicts that the Jews will be deceived by the Antichrist.

> I have come in my Father's name, and you do not accept me; but if someone else comes in his own name, you will accept him (John 5:43).

Between the death of Christ and the Antichrist's confirmation of this covenant stretches the entire Church Age. There is "a great parenthesis" or "a gap" in God's program for Israel.

Liberal scholars and Amillennialists insist there is no gap in the seventy sevens, which can only mean that Jerusalem should have been destroyed by A.D. 35, instead of A.D. 70. That one detail alone demands a gap between the 69th and 70th sevens. And certainly, the end has not come like a flood to this day.

Biblical prophecy contains many gaps that are not always obvious. For instance, Jesus read the prophecy of Isaiah 61:1-2 and said, "Today this scripture is fulfilled in your hearing" (Luke 4:16-20). However, Jesus finished reading the prophecy in the middle of a sentence and rolled up the scroll. Why did He stop so abruptly? Why did He not continue to read "the day of vengeance of our God"? Those words belong to His second coming. Hence, there is a gap of almost two thousand or more years in Isaiah's prophecy. This gap could not be recognized until the first part of the prophecy was fulfilled. The very same principle is true of the seventy sevens. Another familiar prophecy that has a gap between the first and second advents of Christ is Isaiah 9:6.

For to us a child is born	Christmas
to us a son is given	Good Friday
and the government will be on his shoulders	Second Advent

Many read this passage every December and think little of it. Little wonder that the apostle wrote:

> Concerning this salvation, the prophets, who spoke of the grace that was to come to you, searched intently and with the greatest care,

trying to find out the time and circumstances to which the Spirit of Christ in them was pointing when he predicted the sufferings of Christ and the glories that would follow (1 Peter 1:10-11).

All prophecy that sees together what history must unfold as separate is complex. Here history has unfolded, separating the seventieth seven from the sixty-ninth seven.

The time marker for when the seventieth seven starts is given as "he will confirm a covenant with many for one "seven." Nothing in history remotely resembles such a covenant. Certainly, "he" does not refer to the Messiah as some suggest from Galatians 3:15-18. Furthermore, Jesus never sat on David's throne and He was not received by His own people.

"Many" appears to indicate more than Israel will enter into a covenant with the coming prince. Most likely, this covenant looms as an intricate part of the Antichrist's peaceful rise to power (Revelation 6:2). The "many" of this covenant could refer to the ten nations of the Revived Roman Empire, especially, since the term "confirm" (גבר *gabar*) denotes "to strengthen." If so, the coming Roman prince will strengthen the European Union or some other confederation of ten nations when he rises to power.

On the other hand, there is a prediction in Isaiah that is remarkably similar to the seventy sevens.

> So this is what the Sovereign LORD says: "See, I lay a stone in Zion, a tested stone, a precious cornerstone for a sure foundation; the one who trusts will never be dismayed. I will make justice the measuring line and righteousness the plumb-line; hail will sweep away your refuge, the lie, and water will overflow your hiding-place. Your covenant with death will be annulled; your agreement with the grave will not stand. When the overwhelming scourge sweeps by, you will be beaten down by it (Isaiah 28:16-18).

This prophecy contains three sections: (1) Christ the tested stone is crucified and resurrected; (2) desolations upon Israel follow; and (3) the arrival of the covenant with death, which appears to leap into the distant future to the time when apostate Israel enters into the seven-year covenant with the Antichrist, who breaks it halfway through the Tribulation Period.

The seventieth seven of Gabriel's prophecy is known as the Tribulation Period, or the Time of Jacob's Trouble. Revelation 6-19 describes it in detail. Gabriel assigned a time marker that divides the seventieth seven; the second half is known as "the Great Tribulation."

> In the middle of the "seven" he will put an end to sacrifice and offering. And on a wing of the temple he will set up an abomination that causes desolation, until the end that is decreed is poured out on him (Daniel 9:27).

Many assume that three and one-half years into the covenant, the coming Roman prince breaks the covenant. That is true only if the covenant involves Israel. "The temple" is properly supplied in the NIV translation in light of Jesus' interpretation of this prediction in Matthew 24:15 and the Septuagint's translation "upon the temple."

Christ places "the abomination that causes desolation" at the end of the age just prior to His return in power and glory (Matthew 24:15-30). Daniel 9:24 predicts great blessings that will come after the seventy sevens, specifically "to bring everlasting righteousness" and "to anoint the most holy." The latter most likely refers to the dedication of the Millennial Temple (Ezekiel 40-44).

The Antichrist will stop all worship at Israel's Temple when he exalts himself "above" or "over" (επι *epi*) everything that is called God (2 Thessalonians 2:4) and forces the world to worship him and his image. The abomination that causes desolation will end when Christ returns to earth to meet the rebel armies at Armageddon and defeat them (Revelation 19:11-21).

Applications of Chapter Nine

Daniel's prayer provides many insights on how we can intercede on behalf of God's people, the Church and Israel, as well as our nation. Praying for the coming of God's kingdom to earth should permeate our prayer life.

God outlined throughout Scripture His plan and program for the world. We err greatly if we do not give considerable time to the study of His revelations. We should be as determined as Daniel to know what God is doing in our time, especially as we observe many of the things predicted so long ago beginning to take shape. Daniel's example speaks to us today: "Study the Scriptures and pray!"

The key to spiritual and God-honoring prayer begins with a clear grasp of the holiness of God and His attributes of truth and love. Daniel, Job and Isaiah saw God clearly and confessed their sinfulness.

> We have sinned and done wrong. We have been wicked and have rebelled; we have turned away from your commands and laws. We have not listened to your servants the prophets, who spoke in your name to our kings, our princes and our fathers, and to all the people of the land (Daniel 9:5-6).

> My ears had heard of you but now my eyes have seen you. Therefore I despise myself and repent in dust and ashes (Job 42:5-6).

> "Woe to me!" I cried. "I am ruined! For I am a man of unclean lips, and I live among a people of unclean lips, and my eyes have seen the King, the LORD Almighty" (Isaiah 6:5).

Job and Isaiah saw God with their eyes; up to this point, Daniel had only seen Him in the prophetic Scriptures! The more of God we see and understand, the more we will see ourselves as being woeful and ruined by sin.

Praying in harmony with the Scriptures is a prerequisite for obtaining a proper understanding of prophecy. May Daniel's experience and blessing in prayer become ours as we seek to understand God's Word.

It is noteworthy that the Temple at Jerusalem was rebuilt seventy years after it was destroyed. Its construction had been stopped by the opposition of the people who already lived in the land (Ezra 4:1-5, 24). This delay partially fulfilled the prophecy of troublesome times as well as God's time schedule. The Second Temple, which replaced the one destroyed in 586 B.C., was completed, and dedicated in 515 B.C., the decreed seventy years! From a human standpoint, it was delayed; from a divine standpoint, it was on time.

The Jews possessed God's prophetic calendar! They should have recognized the day and time of His coming; how tragic also for those who miss His coming the second time. Christ's *Parable of the Ten Virgins* is about those prepared and unprepared for His second coming. The parable closes with an urgent entreaty.

> Therefore keep watch, because you do not know the day or the hour (Matthew 25:1-13).

Unlike at His first coming, this date is presently unknown. Nevertheless, Christ is coming again! Be ready, waiting, and watching!

The prophets of the Bible deliver common messages of confrontation and consolation, curses and blessings, despair and hope, and storm before calm. Such is the message of the vision of the seventy sevens.

In light of Gabriel's prophecy, Israel's present independence and partial possession of Jerusalem is only a temporary lull prior to the worst storm that Israel will ever face. Israel rejected the Messiah Prince and He was cut off with nothing, but Israel will receive the coming prince of the Revived Roman Empire and that spells "Trouble" with a capital "T".

The chart, *God's Time Table,* on the next page shows some of the terminology employed in the book of Daniel and in this commentary, and the way these terms are applied to the past, the present and the future.

God's Time Table

ETERNITY ——————— H I S T O R Y ——————— ETERNITY

CREATION ————————————————————— RECREATION
Heavens & Earth   New Heaven & New Earth

ANTEDILUVIAN AGE————THIS PRESENT AGE————THE AGE TO COME

The Flood   *Tribulation*

Day of Salvation ——————————— *Millennial Kingdom*

Old Covenant   New Covenant Blessings   New Covenant Fulfilled
Grace, Law & Israel   Grace, Spirit & Church   Israel & Saved Nations

Times of the Gentiles ———————]   *All Israel Saved*

Babylon, Medo-Persia, Greece, Rome   *Everlasting Kingdom*

Fall of   Fall of   Second Advent
Jerusalem   Babylon   of Christ &
586 B.C.   the Great   Israel Restored

69 Sevens *(Church Age)* 70th Seven
                                  End Times

444 B.C.   A.D. 33   A.D. ?

Restoration   *The Last Days*   *The Day of*   *Millen-*   *The Day*
of Jerusalem   *the Lord*   *nium*   *of God*

               Messiah &   The Lamb   Christ   The Son
               Israel   Opens the   Reigns   hands the
               Cut Off   Seven Seals   on Earth   Kingdom
                                                  over to
                                                    the
                                                    Father

Daniel's Vision of the Latter Days (Daniel 10)

Time Line

YEAR B.C.	539	536
MONARCHS	Darius the Mede in Babylon	Cyrus in Persia
DANIEL	Prayer & Seventy Sevens	Vision of a Man

Outline of Chapter Ten

The Preparation for the Vision, 1-3

The Appearance of the Man, 4-6

The Paralyzing Effect of the Man, 7-9

The Invigorating Touch of the Man, 10-11

The Adversary of the Man, 12-13

The Purpose of the Man, 14

The Veneration of the Man, 15-17

The Energizing Touch of the Man, 18-19

The Warfare of the Man, 20

Background of Chapter Ten

Chapters 10-12 form a single vision of the Latter Days. Daniel is invigorated in chapter ten; he receives the vision's predictions in chapter eleven; and responds to them in chapter twelve. These three chapter breaks are somewhat artificial.

The year of this section is 536 B.C. Assuming Daniel was fourteen in 605 B.C., his age was eighty-three years. The statesman had continued in office until the first year of Cyrus (538 B.C.) and then retired (Daniel 1:21). After Cyrus' decree allowing the Jews to return to Palestine, Daniel's lofty position in the two empires had served its final purpose. Nevertheless, as the prophet of God's plan for the world and His people Israel, his task was not complete. One more vision was forthcoming!

Israel would get little pleasure from its new freedom under the Persian rulers. Jerusalem and the Temple would be rebuilt in troublesome times. There is more bad news— "the Greeks are coming!" The Hellenists would invade Palestine militarily as well as culturally.

This chapter reveals a great conflict between the forces of good and evil within the spiritual realm. Here is a glimpse of the invisible warfare that is taking place between the organized dominion of darkness and the organized kingdom of light. It is essential to keep in mind that all gods of the nations are idols, and that behind every idol are demons (Psalm 96:5; 1 Corinthians 10:20). Considering the multitude of false gods worshiped during this period, Satan and his angels were extremely active. Israel's times of distress, difficulty and suffering center on the great conflict between God and Satan.

At the very sight of the glorious man in Daniel's vision of 536 B.C., the prophet's strength is sapped. This vision is breathtaking in many ways. Daniel required several touches before he was ready to receive the revelation. Three of the five touches received by the prophet are recorded in chapter ten (8:18; 9:21; 10:10, 16, 18). That Daniel is made strong, when weak. foreshadows what God will do for Israel after a time of distress.

Invigorated for the Prophecy

THE PREPARATION FOR THE VISION (10:1-3). The dates of Cyrus' third year extend from 536 into 535 B.C. Too aged for the difficult travel back to the land of his birth and the hardships of rebuilding the ruins of Jerusalem, the prophet remained behind. Since the Tigris flows between the two cities, Daniel would have remained either at Babylon or at Susa, the capital of Persia.

Daniel called Cyrus by the Hebrew title of מֶלֶךְ (*melek*, king) and he lets his readers know that he is still called Belteshazzar by the Persians. Daniel ("God is Judge") would have been an unpopular name among the Babylonians, Medes and Persians. Even to this day people only want to hear about the love and grace of God, not about His wrath and judgment. Appropriately, the book of Daniel embodies both aspects of God's

216

righteousness—love and wrath.

The prophet employed the terms "revelation," "message" and "vision" to what follows. He emphasized the veracity of the message and said it concerned צבא גדול (*saka gadowl*, "a great warfare," or "a great conflict").

It appears that the revelation came first, followed by three weeks of fasting by Daniel, and then the understanding of its message was given in a vision.

Daniel's fast was a result of mourning or lamenting; the revelation had been dreadful and grievous. The prophet himself illustrates what Jesus promises, "Blessed are those who mourn, for they will be comforted" (Matthew 5:4). Comfort means to strengthen, which is the underlying theme of this chapter. Fasting is not done to solicit the favor of God; fasting arises from sincere expressions of being poor in spirit. This fast indicates that Daniel was praying, seeking understanding and wisdom from heaven.

Daniel's fast was not a complete one. It involved a limited diet, possibly like the one in 605 B.C. Prior to the fast, Daniel had been enjoying meat, wine and lotions, indications of luxurious living, without compromising God's dietary laws. Endowed with wisdom from above, Daniel certainly lived 1 Corinthians 10:23-33 and Romans 14 within the boundaries of the Mosaic Law.

THE APPEARANCE OF THE MAN (10:4-6). Daniel sets the time and place of the vision. It occurred on the twenty-fourth day of the first month (April 4, 536 B.C.), on the bank of the great river, the Tigris. That other men (verse 7) were with Daniel indicates he was already physically near the banks of the Tigris and not carried to this place by the vision.

This date falls three days after the completion of Passover and the Feast of Unleavened Bread, which were celebrations of Israel's deliverance from Egypt. Daniel's fast took place at a time set aside for celebration.

The revelations concerning the great conflict for God's people had pierced the prophet's heart. Instead of joy and celebration, Daniel lamented. It was time to invigorate the seer.

> I looked up and there before me was a man dressed in linen, with a belt of the finest gold round his waist. His body was like chrysolite, his face like lightning, his eyes like flaming torches, his arms and legs like the gleam of burnished bronze, and his voice like the sound of a multitude (Daniel 10:5-6).

Who is this man? The archangel Gabriel? A mighty angel? Neither! It is the preincarnate Christ—the Anointed One, who is cut off in the previous vision! How can we be certain it is the Messiah?

First, Daniel's description of the man resembles Ezekiel's vision of the Second Person of the Trinity.

> Above the expanse over their heads was what looked like a throne of sapphire, and high above on the throne was a figure like that of a man. I saw that from what appeared to be his waist up he looked like glowing metal, as if full of fire, and that from there down he looked like fire; and brilliant light surrounded him. Like the appearance of a rainbow in the clouds on a rainy day, so was the radiance around him. This was the appearance of the likeness of the glory of the LORD (Ezekiel 1:26-28).

Second, Daniel's description parallels the Apostle John's portraiture of Christ.

> Someone "like a son of man," dressed in a robe reaching down to his feet and with a golden sash round his chest. His head and hair were white like wool, as white as snow, and his eyes were like blazing fire. His feet were like bronze glowing in a furnace, and his voice was like the sound of rushing waters. In his right hand he held seven stars, and out of his mouth came a sharp double-edged sword. His face was like the sun shining in all its brilliance (Revelation 1:13-16).

218

The man's clothing, head, hair, eyes, hand and feet, and voice equate to Christ. As we would expect from eyewitnesses, the prophet and the apostle employ different terms to describe the same person. The man of Daniel's vision was a theophany, which is the appearance of the preincarnate Christ in human form.

THE PARALYZING EFFECT OF THE MAN (10:7-9).

Daniel's encounter parallels Saul of Tarsus' encounter with Jesus on the road to Damascus (Acts 9:3-7). Neither the men with the apostle nor the men with the prophet saw Christ. Both Daniel and Paul fell to the ground at the sight of Christ, the apostle was blinded, and the prophet's strength was sapped.

How did the apostle John handle seeing the appearance of Jesus? "When I saw him, I fell at his feet as though dead" (Revelation 1:17). How did Daniel respond? "I fell into a deep sleep, my face to the ground." What happened when Ezekiel saw his vision of the Triune God?

> When I saw it, I fell face down, and I heard the voice of one speaking. He said to me, "Son of man, stand up on your feet and I will speak to you. " As he spoke, the Spirit came into me and raised me to my feet, and I heard him speaking to me (Ezekiel 1:28-2:2).

The pattern is obvious: vision, falling down, being raised up, speaking, and new revelations. Coincidence? No! It's Christ!

THE INVIGORATING TOUCH OF THE MAN (10:10-11).

This vision is more than an idea or image present in the mind. It is a concrete or objective reality, for a hand touched the prophet, and set him trembling on his hands and knees. We might ask if there was a second personage, a ministering angel, who touched the seer? It seems best to understand the touch as coming from the preincarnate Christ. This invigoration is a wonderful foreshadowing of the NT saint being strengthened by Christ (1 Corinthians 1:8; Philippians 4:13; 1 Thessalonians 3:13; 1 Timothy 1:12; 2 Timothy 2:1; 1 Peter 4:11; 5:10).

> He said, "Daniel, you who are highly esteemed, consider carefully the words I am about to speak to you, and stand up, for I have now been sent to you." And when he said this to me, I stood up trembling

(Daniel 10:11).

Daniel was highly esteemed at least two ways: (1) he beheld the preincarnate Lord; and (2) he would be taught the plans of God by the Messiah. We might also say that he had just received from his Master a "well done, good and faithful servant!" Daniel trembled in the fear of the LORD. He was ready to gain understanding and wisdom. Of course, this is another illustration of Proverbs 9:10!

THE ADVERSARY OF THE MAN (10:12-13). "Do not be afraid" is said many times by the LORD in the Bible. It is exactly what Jesus Christ said to John before He unfolded the visions of Revelation.

> Then he placed his right hand on me and said: "Do not be afraid. I am the First and the Last" (Revelation 1:17).

Our Lord affirms that the path to understanding is to humble oneself before God—humility is the attitude of one who fears the LORD.

In Chapter nine, Daniel's prayer was answered before he even finished praying, but here, a startling revelation is given by Christ.

> Since the first day that you set your mind to gain understanding and to humble yourself before your God, your words were heard, and I have come in response to them. But the prince of the Persian kingdom resisted me twenty-one days. Then Michael, one of the chief princes, came to help me, because I was detained there with the king of Persia (Daniel 10:12-13).

"Ah!" the skeptics say, "I told you the man was not Christ!" How can Christ be delayed by any resistance for twenty-one days and require help from the archangel Michael? Good question! Let's answer it with some questions.

> Did the LORD wrestle all night with Jacob?
> Did Satan tempt Jesus?
> Did angels attend to Jesus after Satan's temptations?
> Were twelve legions of angels at Jesus' disposal to rescue Him from the cross?

Does Satan come and take away the Word sown on the heart by Christ?

Did Jesus become hungry and tired while on earth?

Did Satan attempt to resist Christ through the apostle Peter?

Did Satan use the disciple Judas to betray Christ?

Was Jesus unsuccessful in releasing all the prisoners of Satan?

Was Christ cut off from Israel in His first advent?

The answer to each of these questions is YES! Remember Daniel said this vision concerns a great warfare or a great conflict. It is greater than we might have anticipated. Behind the scenes are invisible thrones, powers, rulers and authorities which have not been disarmed (Ephesians 3:10; 6:12; Colossians 1:16; 2:15). Satan the great counterfeiter has assigned positions of authority, power and dominion to fallen angels as God has to the holy angels.

When Christ took the very nature of a servant, being made in human likeness, the appearance of a man, He placed upon Himself the many limitations of being human. This vision is connected to the previous vision, which revealed, "The Anointed One will be cut off and will have nothing." His rejection by Israel was capped by His dying on the Cross. Hence, His limitations were so great that God in the flesh died both spiritually and physically on the Cross (Mark 15:34, 37).

We are not told exactly what limitations the Second Person placed upon Himself as a theophany in the OT economy. Certainly, they were such that Jacob could wrestle with Him all night (Genesis 32:24). How much resistance might a powerful cherub offer? In light of the fact that Yahweh had earlier associated the Guardian Cherub with the king of Tyre (Ezekiel 28:11-19), the prince (שׂר *sar*) of the Persian kingdom might be Satan.

We might ask, "Why doesn't Christ just swat Satan like a fly and be done with him?" God has foreordained to leave evil run its course before He brings about the final judgment. In the meantime, God overrules evil for good and limits Himself in this great conflict for reasons that are beyond our understanding.

God is allowing evil to run its course till God's final judgment

"For my thoughts are not your thoughts, neither are your ways my ways," declares the LORD. "As the heavens are higher than the earth, so are my ways higher than your ways and my thoughts than your thoughts" (Isaiah 55:8-9).

It does not help to say this glorious man was one of the holy angels—God's power would still be in question. Whenever God limits Himself, it is for His plans and purposes according to His infinite and ultimate wisdom (cf. Isaiah 46:10-11; 48:9-11).

Satan has been hindering God and His people throughout the history of the world. It began with Satan's fall, which was accompanied by one-third of the angels in heaven; then the rebellion moved to earth in the Garden of Eden with Adam and Eve. God could have prevented or put an end to all rebellion when it raised its ugly head but He didn't. Suffice it to say, God has His reasons for allowing evil, which He has not revealed to man.

Note that Michael (מיכאל *Miyka'el*, "who is like God") is one of the chief princes; there are others. Michael is an archangel according to Jude 9 as well as the prince of Israel in Daniel 11:1. The term "princes" applies to rulers among men as well as to powerful angelic beings, whether holy or evil, who rule in the invisible realm.

Chronologically, this was not the first time Michael and Satan engaged in conflict according to Jude 9:

> But even the archangel Michael, when he was disputing with the devil about the body of Moses, did not dare to bring a slanderous accusation against him, but said, "The Lord rebuke you!"

Neither will it be the last time according to Revelation 12:7-9:

> And there was war in heaven. Michael and his angels fought against the dragon, and the dragon and his angels fought back. But he was not strong enough, and they lost their place in heaven. The great dragon was hurled down—that ancient serpent called the devil, or Satan, who leads the whole world astray. He was hurled to the earth, and his angels with him.

Sometimes God starts wars on the earth to hinder Satan according to Isaiah 45; sometimes the Lamb and Satan begin wars, as seen in the predictions of the end times; and at other times wars are started by man to satisfy the evil desires of the sinful nature. All rebellion and wars will cease after the final battle of Gog and Magog (Revelation 20:7-15).

THE PURPOSE OF THE MAN (10:14). "Now I have come to explain to you what will happen to your people in the הימים (*tyrxa*, end or latter) days for the vision concerns a time yet to come." It is a mistake to try to interpret this vision as ending in the days of Antiochus IV Epiphanes since it reaches to the time of Christ's second advent.

THE VENERATION OF THE MAN (10:15-17).

> While he was saying this to me, I bowed with my face towards the ground and was speechless. Then one who looked like a man touched my lips, and I opened my mouth and began to speak. I said to the one standing before me, "I am overcome with anguish because of the vision, my lord, and I am helpless. How can I, your servant, talk with you, my lord? My strength is gone and I can hardly breathe" (Daniel 10:15-17).

Daniel silently bowed with his face towards the ground in an act of worship before the Lord. He was so excited that he could not catch his breath. What was so breathtaking? The prophet had identified who was speaking to him.

The phrase עֲדֹנִי-אֲ (*am-'adown*, my lord) also appears in Genesis 24:12, 14; 2 Samuel 19:37; and 1 Kings 1:37. Each of these occurrences is addressed to someone other than deity and is translated as a title of respect, something like "sir." Hence, the translators have not capitalized "lord."

However, אֲדֹנִי is capitalized numerous times when it obviously refers to deity, in passages like "the priests who carry the ark of the LORD—the Lord (אֲדֹנִי) of all the earth" (Joshua 3:13). Daniel uses "My Lord" as Thomas did when he recognized the risen Christ: "My Lord and my

God!" (John 20:28). Daniel's, "My Lord" is an expression of veneration or worship.

Observe Joshua's reaction and worship of the Lord when the preincarnate Christ appeared to him.

> Now when Joshua was near Jericho, he looked up and saw a man standing in front of him with a drawn sword in his hand. Joshua went up to him and asked, "Are you for us or for our enemies?" "Neither," he replied, "but as commander of the army of the LORD I have now come." Then Joshua fell face down to the ground in reverence, and asked him, "What message does my Lord have for his servant?" The commander of the LORD's army replied, "Take off your sandals, for the place where you are standing is holy." And Joshua did so (Joshua 5:13-15).

It is only fitting that Christ, the Commander of the Army of Yahweh, appeared to Daniel since this conflict is far greater than the battle of Jericho. It is unlikely that the prophet would identify himself as a servant of an angelic being any more than Mary would have (Luke 1:38).

The Lord touching Daniel's lips is similar to Isaiah's experience before the throne of God.

> Then one of the seraphs flew to me with a live coal in his hand, which he had taken with tongs from the altar. With it he touched my mouth and said, "See, this has touched your lips; your guilt is taken away and your sin atoned for" (Isaiah 6:6-7)

THE ENERGIZING TOUCH OF THE MAN (10:18-19). For the third time, Christ touches Daniel and speaks words to strengthen him. "Do not be afraid, O man highly esteemed," he said. "Peace! Be strong now; be strong." "Peace" is the result of sin being atoned, of guilt being taken away, and all fear being removed. The cleansed sinner, who is strengthened by the Lord, is qualified to hear Him speak and to speak for Him.

THE WARFARE OF THE MAN (10:20). The man answers his own rhetorical question, "Do you know why I have come to you?"

Soon I will return to fight against the prince of Persia, and when I go, the prince of Greece will come; but first I will tell you what is written in the Book of Truth. (No one supports me against them except Michael, your prince" (Daniel 10:20).

When Christ returned, accompanied by Michael, to fight on Israel's behalf against the prince of Persia and his forces, the prince of Greece came. This prince is either Alexander the Great or an evil angelic being. Insight into this invisible war provides the background of the book of Esther, where the great conflict over the preservation of God's people is apparent.

What is the Book of Truth? It cannot be the Bible since Daniel has not written down the prophecy at this point. Could it be God's Plan of the Ages, recorded in one of the books in heaven?

Applications of Chapter Ten

Here we are taught the triumph of persistent and humble prayer. We are given insight into the supernatural forces involved when a believer engages in protracted and earnest prayer. Mighty forces are unleashed when righteous people devote themselves to prayer. Delayed responses to prayer may result from a great conflict between good and evil.

Jesus stated that angels in heaven are assigned to believers (Matthew 18:10). Hebrews 1:14 asks, "Are not all angels ministering spirits sent to serve those who will inherit salvation?" Based on the Lord's revelation to Daniel, these angels run into resistance from demonic powers. It is clear that every Christian is involved in a great conflict.

Put on the full armor of God so that you can take your stand against the devil's schemes. For our struggle is not against flesh and blood, but against the rulers, against the authorities, against the powers of this dark world and against the spiritual forces of evil in the heavenly realms (Ephesians 6:11-12).

The only offensive weapon the believer has against the Devil is the Word of God. Look at the effort Satan exerted to keep Christ from delivering the understanding of His revelation to Daniel. What do you think the

Adversary and his forces do to keep Christians from reading and studying the Scriptures?

The Scriptures cannot be understood by an unregenerate person (1 Corinthians 2:6-9). Unconfessed and uncleansed sin produces guilt that hinders the believer's understanding. The believer needs the mind of Christ to comprehend the deep things of God (1 Corinthians 2:10-19) as illustrated by Daniel's experience.

Daniel prevailed in persistent prayer; though Satan's resistance delayed the answer, it came. Keep praying—we cannot see what is going on behind the scenes in the invisible realm. Might our prayers strengthen the side of good in the great conflict?

There is a close relationship of demonic rulers with world leaders of nations and governments. But these principalities and powers will be overthrown when Christ returns.

The sight of Christ in His glory will be breathtaking. Some will fall in adoration to their hands and knees, face down and confess that He is Lord; others will fall down in absolute terror before Him!

> Therefore God exalted him to the highest place and gave him the name that is above every name, that at the name of Jesus every knee should bow, in heaven and on earth and under the earth, and every tongue confess that Jesus Christ is Lord, to the glory of God the Father (Philippians 2:9-11).

Israel's Foreordained History
(Daniel 11:1-12:3)

Outline of Chapter Eleven

Two Empires
  Medo-Persia, 1-4
  Egypt and Syria, 5-20
Two Princes
  Antiochus IV Epiphanes, 21-35
  The Wilful King, 36-39
Two Events
  Mid-Tribulation Crisis, 40-45
  Final Deliverance of Israel, 12:1-3

Background of Chapter Eleven

The great unseen conflict between the forces of light and darkness introduced in chapter ten supplies the background for chapter eleven. Israel's disobedience, rebellion, and immorality have been weighed on the scales of God's justice, and the nation's chastisement is chronicled in foreordained history.

Chapter eleven divides easily into two parts: (1) fulfilled prophecies; and (2) yet to be fulfilled prophecies. Verses 1-35 describe the people and events of the first sixty-nine sevens that were revealed in the ninth chapter. Verses 36-45 cover events that take will place during the seventieth seven, including Israel's tribulation and the reign of the Antichrist.

From our perspective, the first part of this chapter shows history revealing prophecy and the second part shows prophecy revealing history. For Daniel, the latter was the case for both parts. He died before any of the prophecies in this vision were fulfilled.

Why does the Bible contain so many prophecies? One reason is to show that God controls history before it ever happens. Among many other reasons, prophecy (1) authenticates God's Word as Truth; (2) demonstrates that Yahweh is the Most High God of heaven; (3) validates that the coming Messiah is Lord and God; and (4) strengthens God's people for the future.

Prophetic truth is history written in advance. This chapter is a "light shining in a dark place" (2 Peter 1:19-21). In the first thirty-five verses, there are at least 135 prophecies, which have been literally fulfilled, a fact that can be corroborated by studying the history of this period. Even the liberal critics agree that the book of Daniel accurately details this period. That makes this one of the most unusual and controversial portions of Scripture, not due to any difficulty in understanding the details, but because the details themselves are so accurate. Hence, the liberal critics, who deny that "all Scripture is God breathed (2 Timothy 3:16), hold that Daniel was written after the fact. Otherwise, they would have to bow to the Most High God who is sovereign over the affairs of men.

The detailed fulfillments of this chapter's prophecies are covered in many commentaries on Daniel. Not all writers agree, of course, at every point. The following broad-brush presentation of the events predicted in this chapter has been compiled from many of the sources listed at the end of this book.

Two Empires

MEDO-PERSIA (11:1-4). The first empire seen in the vision is Medo-Persia. The man in the vision is the preincarnate Christ and the vision begins with Medo-Persia's first year as a world empire. The man rapidly moves through its future to arrive at the vision's second world empire, which is Greece. Keep in mind the great conflict over the dominion of Israel, which is taking place in the background of this vision. In this part of the vision, only the visible, earthly events are revealed.

Verse 1: Interestingly, Christ reveals that He supported and protected Darius the Mede in 539 B.C. The rapid and smooth transfer of Babylon to Persia was God's doing, not man's. This revelation is a reminder that

God controls what follows in the rise of these two empires.

Verse 2: This vision occurred during the reign of Cyrus the Great and three more kings who were Cambyses, Pseudo-Smerdis, and Darius Hystaspis. The fourth monarch was Xerxes, also known as Ahasuerus. The opening chapters of the book of Esther record King Xerxes' fabulous wealth and the great banquet that he employed, as a pretext, to stir up his guests against Greece.

Xerxes' expedition against Greece failed miserably in 480 B.C., and apparently, the king's attendants proposed that a search be made for beautiful young virgins to soothe the king's anger and depression. Esther was chosen queen as God worked behind the scenes. Interestingly, Mordecai said to his niece when the genocide of the Jews was decreed, "And who knows but that you have come to a royal position for such a time as this?" (Esther 3:14). God knows, and He orchestrates, the rise and fall of rulers for His purposes and that is the way we are to view these prophecies.

Verses 3-4: Since this prophecy touches on major events and characters, it jumps over nearly 150 years to the time of the Ram and the Goat. The mighty king who does as he pleases is Alexander the Great. In 336 B.C., Alexander came to the throne of Greece and Macedonia. He had only 35,000 soldiers to start the war with Persia, while the Persian king had hundreds of thousands of soldiers besides a great navy. Nevertheless, in thirteen years Alexander conquered the whole of the Persian Empire and beyond. He literally did "as he pleased," fulfilling this prophecy.

Alexander's empire was parceled out toward the four winds, and to four generals who were not his descendants: Ptolemy (Egypt); Antigonus (Babylon, North Syria); Lysimachus (Thrace, Bithynia); and Cassander (Macedonia). Naturally, the divided Greek Empire resulted in diminished power, but division did not diminish its influence on the society and culture over the next three hundred years.

EGYPT AND SYRIA (11:5-20). At this point, prophecy narrows its scope, from the four divisions of Alexander the Great's empire, down to two. Egypt (South) appears first, then Syria (North).

The Ptolemy and the Seleucid Princes in Daniel 11:5-32

Rulers of the Ptolemies (South/Egypt)		Rulers of the Seleucids (North/Syria)	
5	Ptolemy I Lagus "Soter" (323-280)	5	Seleucus I Nicator (312-281)
			Antiochus I Soter (281-262 skipped)
6	Ptolemy II Philadelphus (280-247)	6	Antiochus II Theos (261-246)
7-8	Ptolemy III Euergetes (246-222)	7-9	Seleucus II Callinicus (246-226)
10	Ptolemy Philopator (222-205)	10	Seleucus III Caraunus (226-224)
11-15	Ptolemy V Epiphanes (204-181)	10-19	Antiochus III The Great (224-187)
		20	Seleucus IV Philopator (187-176)
25	Ptolemy VI Philometer (181-145)	21-32	Antiochus IV Epiphanes (175-163)

Historically, the division ruled by the Ptolemies was headquartered in Egypt, and the division ruled by the Seleucids was headquartered in Syria. These two proved to be the most significant divisions of the Greek Empire. However, that is not the only reason the vision focuses on Egypt and Syria. These two divisions of the Greek Empire were involved in a great conflict for dominion over Israel. The land between Asia Minor, Africa and Arabia became the marching ground of armies. Behind the scenes of this great conflict for the land of Israel, God's sovereignty ruled over the rise of princes (rulers), as demonstrated by His foretelling of the future.

Verse 5: The first King of the South was Ptolemy Lagus, called "Soter," who ruled Egypt from 323 to 280 B.C. General Seleucus Nicator, who was the stronger than Soter, defeated Antigonus at Gaza in 312 B.C. Seleucus Nicator built the Seleucid Empire of Syria (North), which greatly exceeded that of the Ptolemies, reaching from Phrygia to India.

Verse 6: Berenice, daughter of Ptolemy Philadelphus (King of South (KS) from 280-247 B.C.), married Antiochus II (King of the North (KN), who ruled from 261-246). This was a political marriage. Antiochus II was forced by Ptolemy to divorce his wife Laodicea in order to marry Berenice. Two years later, Ptolemy died. After his death, Laodicea, a powerful and influential woman, poisoned Antiochus II, and managed to have Berenice and the couple's infant son assassinated. This alliance ended in complete failure.

Verses 7-8: Literally, out of a branch (run *netser*) of her roots (parents) rose Berenice's brother, Ptolemy Energetes III to become KS from 246-222. He succeeded Ptolemy Philadelphus. To avenge his sister's murder, Ptolemy invaded Syria. His invasion climaxed with great success against Seleucus Callinicus (KN 246-226). Jerome recorded that Ptolemy III took back to Egypt 40,000 talents of silver, 4,000 talents of gold and 2,000 costly idol statues.

Verses 9-10: Seleucus Callinicus (KN) invaded Egypt (c. 240), but was unsuccessful and returned home. His fleet perished in a storm. His two sons, Seleucus Caraunus (227-224) and Antiochus the Great III (224-187), stirred themselves to war. After Caraunus was killed in Asia Minor, Antiochus moved through Egypt and captured the Egyptian fortress at Gaza. Ptolemy Philopator (KS 222-205) offered no resistance at that time. By 219, Antiochus the Great had conquered parts of Israel and the Transjordan.

Verses 11-12: Ptolemy Philopator (KS) raised a large army of 73,000 soldiers, 5,000 cavalry, and 73 elephants. He overcame Antiochus the Great (KN) and destroyed his entire army of 70,000 at Raphia in 217. He did not press his victory but resumed his reprobate life.

Verses 13-14: In 203, Antiochus the Great (KN) raised an even greater army after his defeat at Raphia and came a second time against Egypt. Ptolemy Philopator and his wife had died that year. Ptolemy Epiphanes became the KS at age four or five. Realizing a weakness in Egypt, many rebelled against the KS, including Antiochus the Great who had formed a league with Philip of Macedonia. Even some Jews allied themselves with Antiochus, against Egypt, fulfilling the prediction: "The violent men among your own people will rebel in fulfillment of the vision, but without success." The Jews thought their alliance would aid Israel, but instead it brought their nation into Syria's grasp and made it subject to the horrors that Antiochus IV Epiphanes would bring upon it years later. God's prophets had consistently warned Israel against making alliances with other powers. Israel was to trust in God, not military might!

Verses 15-16: The Egyptian General Scopas was sent to offer a counteroffensive against Antiochus the Great (KN), but he was defeated when Antiochus captured the city of Sidon. Antiochus then turned his attention to Palestine ("the Beautiful Land"), but treated the Jews with favor because they were aiding him against the Egyptians.

Verse 17:   At this time, Rome began to exert its power in the eastern Mediterranean. This exertion prompted an alliance between Antiochus the Great and Ptolemy Epiphanes, which involved the marriage of Antiochus' daughter, Cleopatra to Ptolemy in 197. The marriage did not take place until 193 since Ptolemy was only ten years old in 197. Cleopatra is identified as הנשים ובת (*'ishshah bath*, "daughter of women"), an Aramaic idiom, possibly indicating she was still a child under the care of women. Antiochus' scheme to gain control of Egypt through his daughter backfired. Cleopatra loved her husband more than she loved her father; so when Antiochus engaged the Romans, Egypt aided Rome.

Verses 18-19:   Antiochus the Great turned his attention to the Mediterranean coastlands and islands, bringing him into conflict with the Romans. He invaded several Aegean Sea islands, portions of Asia Minor, and Trace, while Rome was seeking to control these areas. Antiochus boasted about what he was doing to Roman interests, so Rome sent General Lucius Cornelius Scipio to deal with him. Antiochus was defeated at Magnesia in 190 B.C.; his boasting came back upon his own head. Antiochus abandoned further conquests. In 188, Antiochus was compelled to sign the *Treaty of Apamea*, surrendering all claims to Europe, and the greater part of Asia Minor, and making his boundary the Taurus Range. The following year, Antiochus the Great was killed trying to plunder the temple of Belus in Elymais.

Verse 20:   Seleucus Philopator (KN 187-176), the eldest son of Antiochus succeeded his father and had the unpleasant task of being a raiser of taxes. Seleucus had inherited his father's tremendous debts and he was forced to pay the Romans an enormous, annual tribute of 1,000 talents.   He dispatched his foster brother and finance minister, Heliodorus, as a tax collector. Heliodorus seized the funds of the Temple treasury at Jerusalem (2 Maccabees 3:1-40). Shortly afterward in 176, Seleucus was mysteriously removed, probably poisoned by Heliodorus.

Two Princes

ANTIOCHUS IV EPIPHANES (11:21-35). Next, Daniel was told about the "little horn" of chapter eight, the one who foreshadows the Antichrist. The "little horn" is none other than Antiochus IV Epiphanes (175-163), the younger son of Antiochus the Great. Fifteen verses are dedicated to this detestable person. The ravages of the great conflict that flowed back and forth over the land of Palestine paved the way for the rise of this prince. His life and activities are typical of the Antichrist's in the end times.

Verse 21: Antiochus IV Epiphanes had no legitimate claim to the throne. It belonged to his nephew, Demetrius, the rightful heir. However, through various intrigues, political maneuverings and flatteries, he gained the throne. He was aided primarily by his brother Attalus and King Eumenes of Pergaumum.

Verse 22: Antiochus routed the forces of Egypt in battles that took place between Pelusium and the Caspian Mountains. "A Prince of Covenant," either refers to the Jewish High Priest Onias III, who was deposed, and later murdered in 170, or to a coconspirator prince, Ptolemy VI Philometer (181-145), who Antiochus befriended (verse 23), then defeated (verse 25).

Verse 23: Antiochus adopted a policy of artificial friendship with Egypt. He pretended to support his nephew Ptolemy Philometer against another nephew Ptolemy Euergetes. However, it was merely a cover to advance his interests. Some historians claim that Antiochus IV Epiphanes even managed to have himself crowned king at Memphis.

Verse 24: Antiochus greatly plundered his conquered lands, but differed from his predecessors by distributing the spoils lavishly to the people, thus winning friends for himself as an ancient Robin Hood. He used this maneuver to keep the strong fortress at Pelusium on the border of Egypt.

Verses 25-26: Antiochus made a second expedition against Egypt's Physcon. Some think Physcon was Philometor. It seems the two were brothers. Antiochus had a great army but was unsuccessful because

233

treason had broken out in his own camp. Some of his supporters deserted him.

Verse 27: When Physcon was proclaimed king, Antiochus entered into an alliance with Philometer on the pretense of taking his side. Philometer became suspicious that Antiochus entered the alliance to lay siege to the city of Alexandria. Philometer made overtures to Physcon, on the basis of a joint sovereignty, and was received into Alexandria. Both brothers then declared themselves to be against Antiochus.

Verse 28: In 169 B.C., Antiochus returned from Egypt with much plunder and marched through Judea. Hearing of the great rejoicing that took place in Jerusalem when the city heard a report of his death, Antiochus turned against the Jews. He put down an insurrection led by Jason and took the opportunity to plunder the Temple (1 Maccabees 1:20-40; 2 Maccabees 5).

Verse 29: In the spring of 168, Antiochus made a third expedition against Egypt, but it did not have the success of his previous invasions, because the Ptolemy brothers had reconciled.

Verse 30: The two Ptolemies sought the aid of the Romans, who responded by sending a fleet from the western coastlands (כתים Chittim, that is Cyprus and points west) to engage Antiochus at the siege of Alexandria. When the ships were within a few miles of the city of Alexandria, Antiochus went to salute the ships. Popilius Laenas, commander of the Roman fleet, delivered to Antiochus letters from the Roman Senate. The letters demanded, upon the threat of provoking a Roman attack, that Antiochus cease aggression. Popilius Laenas drew a circle with his staff in the sand around Antiochus, and commanded him to reach his decision before he stepped out. Antiochus lost heart and reluctantly accepted the Senate's demand to discontinue further aggression. He then returned home by way of Judea to gather information as to whether the apostate Jews would support him.

Then Antiochus came against Jerusalem, took it by storm and slaughtered 40,000 Jews. He sold many Jews as slaves. He committed many abominations, such as boiling swine's flesh and then sprinkling the broth in the Temple and on the altar.

> He arrogantly entered the sanctuary and took the golden altar, the lampstand for the light, and all its utensils. He took also the table for the bread of the Presence, the cups for drink offerings, the bowls, the golden censers, the curtain, the crowns, and the gold decoration on the front of the temple; he stripped it all off. He took the silver and the gold; and the costly vessels; he took also the hidden treasures that he found. Taking them all, he went into his own land. He shed much blood and spoke with great arrogance (1 Maccabees 1:21-24, NRSV).

He restored Menelaus to the office of High Priest and made Philip, a Phrygian, governor of Judea.

Verse 31: The armed forces of Antiochus stood on guard at the Temple and regular worship was discontinued. On the Sabbath day, the city was attacked, women and children were captured, and multitudes were slain. His army occupied the citadel overlooking the Temple. Heathen idolatry was made mandatory and Hellenic culture was made compulsory for the Jews. The climax of Antiochus' blasphemy was the erection of the image of Zeus on the Temple's altar of burnt offering (2 Maccabees 6).

Verse 32: Some Jews yielded to the demands of Antiochus and apostatized from the religion of Israel. Others firmly resisted, resulting in the Maccabean Revolt of 168-165 B.C.

Verses 33-35: Those who remained true to God refused to eat unclean things and many died for their faith. Times of tribulation are periods for refining, purifying and making spotless the wise. In verse 34, the term "fall" might refer to apostasy, or falling to the sword. Definitely, the Jews received little help in all their struggles against Antiochus IV Epiphanes, or other tyrants that persecuted them in history. Compromising with Antiochus turned out to be a deadly mistake for the Jews.

During the Maccabean Revolt, a group of godly persons called "Hasidaeans," was formed. This group was part of the many in Israel who stood up for the laws of God (cf. 1 Maccabees 1:62-64). Judas Maccabaeus, son of Mattathias, led a successful revolt against the Syrians and brought much relief from persecution. However, neither his successes, nor those of the rest of the Maccabean family, were permanent. There was still much suffering to endure. The Jewish apostates were treated with bloody severity by Judas Maccabaeus.

The predictions of verses 33-35 extend beyond the profanities and troublesome times under Antiochus IV Epiphanes. The time marker for the purification of Israel is "until the time of the end, for it [the seventieth seven] will still come at the appointed time." These predictions cover the huge time gap between Antiochus and the Antichrist. This madman, who committed detestable actions, foreshadows others like him until the type is ultimately fulfilled in the Antichrist—the Wilful King.

The following chart is a graphic portrayal of the first prince, Antiochus IV Epiphanes, drawn from chapters eight and eleven. In these chapters, Antiochus is identified as "the Little Horn" and "the King of the North."

Antiochus IV Epiphanes

Antiochus IV Epiphanes, "the Little Horn" of Daniel 8:23-25.

He is a stern-faced king, 23.
He is a master of intrigue, 23.
He is very strong, but not by his own power, 24.
He is the cause of astounding devastation, 24.
He is successful in whatever he does, 24.
He is the destroyer of mighty men and holy people, 24.
He is the successful promoter of deceit, 25.
He is one who considers himself superior, 25.
He is one who takes his stand against the Prince of princes, 25.
He is destroyed, but not by human power, 25.

Antiochus IV Epiphanes, "the King of the North" of Daniel 11:21-32.

He is a contemptible person, 21.
He is a master of intrigue, 21.

He is a military success, 22.

He is a deceitful person, 23.

He is an invader and overachiever, 24.

He is a plunderer and looter, 24.

He is a rewarder of his followers, 24.

He is a plotter, 24.

He is strong and courageous because of his military, 25.

He is a victim of losing heart, 29-30.

He is a furious enemy of the holy covenant, 30.

He is a rewarder of apostates, 30.

He is a desecrater of the Temple, 31.

He is an abolisher of the daily sacrifice, 31.

He is a corrupter, who flatters violators of the covenant, 32.

THE WILFUL KING (11:36-39). The second prince of Daniel's vision is the Wilful King ("the king will do as he pleases"). There will be no stopping the Wilful King once his rise to power begins. Much can be gleaned from the Scriptures concerning the Wilful King, who is popularly called the Antichrist.

The Wilful King

The Wilful King is none other than:

The Serpent's Seed of Genesis 3:15

The Wicked Man of Psalm 10

The Assyrian of Isaiah 10:5, 12

The King of Babylon of Isaiah 14:4-20

The Oppressor and the Aggressor of Isaiah 16:4

The Little Horn of Daniel 7:8

The Profane King of Daniel 7:25-27

The Stern-faced King of Daniel 8:23-25

The Coming Prince of Daniel 9:26-27

The Worthless Shepherd of Zechariah 11:11-16

The One who comes in His Own Name of John 5:43

The Man of Lawlessness of 2 Thessalonians 2:3-4, 8

The Antichrist of 1 John 2:18

The Beast of Revelation 13:18; 17:12-17; 19:19-21

First, as to the Wilful King's personality and genius:

He is a great orator and demagogue, Daniel 7:8.

He is a speaker with regal authority, Revelation 13:2.

He is a philosopher of distinction, who traffics in deception, Daniel 8:23.

He is a clever and persistent politician, Daniel 8:25.

He is a deceiver who will use the false religious system to gain power, Revelation 13:1-18.

He is a military genius, Daniel 7:8, 24; Revelation 6:1-2.

He is a man different from other men, Daniel 7:7, 19, 23; Revelation 13:4.

He is a highly intelligent man, Daniel 7:8.

He is a perfection of unholiness ("666"), Revelation 13:18.

He is a man who will look more imposing than other rulers, Daniel 7:20; Revelation 13:3-4; 17:8.

He is a last wonder of the world, Revelation 13:3-4.

Second, as to the moral character of the Wilful King:

He is the personification of selfish ambition, Daniel 11:36-37.

He is an absolute dictator, Daniel 11:36.

He is a blasphemer extraordinaire, Daniel 11:36; Revelation 13:1, 5-6; 2 Thessalonians 2:4.

He is the greatest antinomian (rejecting moral law), Daniel 11:36; 2 Thessalonians 2:7-8.

He is a rejecter of religion, Daniel 11:37.

He is an egotist, who exalts and magnifies himself above every god, Daniel 11:38.

He is a materialist, Daniel 11:38.

He is a worshiper and financier of military power, Daniel 11:38.

He is a rewarder of those who acknowledge him, Daniel 11:38.

Third, as to the origin of the Wilful King:

His economic origin is displayed in making prosperous the Revived Romans Empire, Revelation 17:1-5; 18:3.

His political origin is from the Revived Roman Empire, Daniel 2, 7- 8.

His national origin is Roman, Daniel 9:26.

His racial origin is Jewish according to some, Daniel 11:37; John 5:43.

His spiritual origin is of Satan, Genesis 3:15; Revelation 13:2; 16:3.

His providential origin is of God, Daniel 8:2, 8; Revelation 6:1-8.

Fourth, as to the steps in the rise to power of the Wilful King:

He will be the product of iniquity, 2 Thessalonians 2:3, 7-8.

He will have an inconspicuous beginning, Daniel 7:8; Revelation 6:1-2.

He will confirm a covenant with many, Daniel 9:27.

He will strengthen the Ten-Nation Confederacy, Revelation 7:8, 20, 24.

He will be the world power by the middle of the confirmed covenant, Revelation 17:12-13.

He will destroy the false religious system that helped him rise to power, Revelation 17:3, 16-17.

He will slay the Two Witnesses of God, Revelation 11:3-13.

He will persecute Israel and the Tribulation saints, Revelation 7:9, 14; 12:13-17.

Fifth, as to the Wilful King's rise to power, he will be aided by:

Chaotic world conditions, "Beginning of Birth Pains," Mark 13:5-13

False religion, Revelation 17:1-5

Satanic deception, 2 Thessalonians 2:9-10; Revelation 13:2

Divine permission and help, Psalm 75:6-7; Revelation 6:1-2; 2 Thessalonians 2:11

Economic and military sanctions, Revelation 13:15-17

Men who worship him and blaspheme God, Revelation 13:8; 16:10-11

Military might, Revelation 13:4

Sixth, as to the end of the Wilful King:

His campaign against the Lamb of God ends with the Battle of Armageddon, Revelation 16:12-16; 17:4; 19:17-19.

His capture takes place along with that of the False Prophet, Revelation 19:20.

His spirit is cast into the depths of Sheol and his body will have no grave, Isaiah 14:9-10.

His body is cast alive into the Lake of Fire, Revelation 19:20.

His continuous and conscious torment will go on forever, Revelation 20:10.

The major emphasis of the predictions concerning the Wilful King is on the religion of the end times. The book of Daniel is a polemic against the Babylonian mystery religion. After this prince gains power, he will turn against this mystery religion, which helped him rise to power, in accord with God's sovereign plans and purposes.

> The beast and the ten horns you saw will hate the prostitute. They
> will bring her to ruin and leave her naked; they will eat her flesh and
> burn her with fire. For God has put it into their hearts to accomplish
> his purpose by agreeing to give the beast their power to rule, until
> God's words are fulfilled (Revelation 17:16-17).

At that time, the Wilful King's prerogative, pride and profanity will be
exposed. "He will exalt and magnify himself above every god and will
say unheard-of-things."

Through the Wilful King, Satan will attempt to have the world worship
him. It has been Satan's goal from the beginning to exalt himself above
God.

> How you have fallen from heaven, O morning star, son of the dawn!
> You have been cast down to the earth, you who once laid low the
> nations! You said in your heart, "I will ascend to heaven; I will raise
> my throne above the stars of God; I will sit enthroned on the mount
> of assembly, on the utmost heights of the sacred mountain. I will
> ascend above the tops of the clouds; I will make myself like the Most
> High" (Isaiah 14:12-14).

> He will show no regard for the gods of his fathers or for the one
> desired by women, nor will he regard any god, but will exalt himself
> above them all. Instead of them, he will honor a god of fortresses; a
> god unknown to his fathers he will honor with gold and silver, with
> precious stones and costly gifts. He will attack the mightiest
> fortresses with the help of a foreign god and will greatly honor those
> who acknowledge him. He will make them rulers over many people
> and will distribute the land at a price (Daniel 11:37-39).

"The gods of his fathers" is associated with the Babylonian mystery
religion since it will be revived along with the Roman Empire
(Revelation 17). In the ancient Greek and Roman religions, the chief
deities of the pantheons were the god Jupiter, in Rome, and the god Zeus,
in Greece. This chief god was regarded as the sender of thunder and
lightning, rain and winds, and his traditional weapon was the

thunderbolt. He was called the father (that is, the ruler and protector) of both gods and men.

Jupiter and Zeus were counterparts to Babylon's Marduk. The Babylonian religion had merged into the successive empires of Medo-Persia, Greece and Rome. Therefore, Christ is able to destroy and scatter all four to the wind at the time of His second advent (Daniel 2:34-35).

The absorption of religion from one empire to the next sheds light on the phrase "the one desired by women." In the Ancient Near East, the one desired by women was known by the names of Tammuz, Bacchus, Horus, Osiris, Adonis, and Cupid. This god was the Lamented One, who supposedly had been slain by a boar and had risen from the dead after forty days of weeping and sorrow by women. Even the Israelite women desired Tammuz at the time of the Babylonian captivity.

> Then he brought me to the entrance to the north gate of the house of the LORD, and I saw women sitting there, mourning for Tammuz (Ezekiel 8:14).

The Wilful King's god is not identified, but he attributes his success to him. We know from Scripture that Satan empowers the Antichrist. This unknown god will not be one out of the past. So will Satan be worshiped openly in the end times?

Note that the Wilful King cannot be Antiochus IV Epiphanes since his god was Zeus and he erected an image of Zeus on the altar at the Temple. Therefore, this entire section of the prophecy concerns the distant future.

"He will be successful until the time of wrath is completed" refers to the Tribulation Period. During the seventieth seven, the judgments accompanying the seven seals, seven trumpets and seven bowls will bring woes upon humanity for their sins (Revelation 6-18). "Until the time of wrath is completed" by implication refers to the end of Israel's rejection of the Lamb of God. During His reign, Christ will rid the earth of all rebellion and sin (1 Corinthians 15:24-28; Ephesians 1:9-10). "What has been determined must take place."

Two Events

THE MID-TRIBULATION CRISIS (11:40-45). Attempts to tie these details to Antiochus IV Epiphanes have proven futile. "At the time of the end" places this prophecy in the Tribulation Period. This prophecy begins at the middle of the Tribulation since the Wilful King will invade the Beautiful Land (Israel) after setting up the abomination that causes desolation (Revelation 12:13-17).

If the identification of the princes is continuous from the previous prophecies in this chapter, the King of the South (Egypt) and the King of the North (Syria) will engage the Wilful King in battle. Egypt definitely loses one way or the other.

The historical boundaries of the King of the North reached as far north as Alexandria Eschata (Leninabad, Russia). It is possible that Russia and the nations surrounding the Black Sea are involved in the battle against the Antichrist.

Interestingly, Egypt and Syria proclaimed on February 1, 1958, a political union called the "United Arab Republic." It ended on September 28, 1961, when Syria declared itself independent of Egypt. Is it possible this alliance will be renewed in the end times?

History often repeats itself and it appears that "the land between" will be invaded again as the Wilful King's forces pursue the Egyptians. Amazingly, Edom, Moab and Ammon (modern Jordan) will be delivered from the hands of the Wilful King. Geographically, this land is a desirable place for the inhabitants of Israel to flee. Petra and the deep canyons of Moab and Edom are natural fortresses. They might well be the prepared desert place of Revelation 12:13-14. The fleeing Israelis will be protected for the final three and one-half years of the Tribulation. The Wilful King will invade the Holy Land after plundering Egypt.

> But reports from the east and the north will alarm him, and he will set out in a great rage to destroy and annihilate many. He will pitch his royal tents between the seas at the beautiful holy mountain. Yet he will come to his end, and no one will help him (Daniel 11:44).

The kings of the North and the kings of East may form a coalition against the Wilful King. Most likely, "reports from the east" refers to an invasion of a massive army of two hundred million soldiers from east of the Euphrates River. This army will have killed a third of mankind (Revelation 9:16-19). God is sovereign in the affairs of men; having cleared the way for their arrival, He shall gather the nations to the great Plain of Esdraelon.

> The sixth angel poured out his bowl on the great river Euphrates, and its water was dried up to prepare the way for the kings from the East (Revelation 16:12).

> Then they gathered the kings together to the place that in Hebrew is called Armageddon (Revelation 16:16).

The Plain of Esdraelon is famous for two great victories, that of Barak over the Canaanites, and of Gideon over the Midianites; and for two great disasters, the deaths of Saul and Josiah. In Revelation, it is a place of great slaughter, the scene of a terrible retribution inflicted upon the wicked. It is popularly known as the Battle of Armageddon.

Armageddon is a transliteration of the Greek αρμαγεδδον (ar-mag-ed-dohn'). In Hebrew, *Har-Magedon* means the mountain of Megiddo ("a place of crowd"). In Bible times, the city of Megiddo commanded the entrances to the Coastal Plain, the Plain of Acco, and the Valley of Jezreel.

An Egyptian account of Pharaoh Thutmose III's campaign through Palestine boasted that "taking Megiddo is like taking a thousand cities" (*ANET*, 237). Megiddo is one of the more strategic military places in Palestine, and many crucial battles have taken place in its immediate vicinity. The Battle of Armageddon is foreshadowed in Judges 5:19:

> Kings came, they fought; the kings of Canaan fought at Taanach by the waters of Megiddo, but they carried off no silver, no plunder.

In the ninth century B.C., Yahweh predicted through the prophet Joel the place the final battle would take place, as well as its outcome.

I will gather all nations and bring them down to the Valley of Jehoshaphat. There I will enter into judgment against them concerning my inheritance, my people Israel, for they scattered my people among the nations and divided up my land (Joel 3:2).

"Let the nations be roused; let them advance into the Valley of Jehoshaphat, for there I will sit to judge all the nations on every side. Swing the sickle, for the harvest is ripe. Come, trample the grapes, for the winepress is full and the vats overflow—so great is their wickedness!" Multitudes, multitudes in the valley of decision! For the day of the LORD is near in the valley of decision" (Joel 3:12-14).

The site where the Battle of Armageddon will take place is called the Valley of Jehoshaphat because it was there that God destroyed Israel's enemies (2 Chronicles 20:20-26). Jehoshaphat (יהושפט) means "Yahweh has judged." Ironically, the Wilful King will set out in a great rage to destroy and annihilate many, but his army will be struck down by a sharp sword out of the mouth of the rider on the white horse, who is called Faithful and True (Revelation 19:11-16). This is the harvest of the earth.

I looked, and there before me was a white cloud, and seated on the cloud was one "like a son of man" with a crown of gold on his head and a sharp sickle in his hand. Then another angel came out of the temple and called in a loud voice to him who was sitting on the cloud, "Take your sickle and reap, because the time to reap has come, for the harvest of the earth is ripe." So he who was seated on the cloud swung his sickle over the earth, and the earth was harvested.

Another angel came out of the temple in heaven, and he too had a sharp sickle. Still another angel, who had charge of the fire, came from the altar and called in a loud voice to him who had the sharp sickle, "Take your sharp sickle and gather the clusters of grapes from the earth's vine, because its grapes are ripe." The angel swung his sickle on the earth, gathered its grapes and threw them into the great winepress of God's wrath. They were trampled in the winepress outside the city, and blood flowed out of the press, rising as high as the horses' bridles for a distance of 1,600 stadia (Revelation 14:14-20).

Sixteen hundred stadia (about 180 miles) is the distance from Dan to Beersheba. The height of the initial flow of blood will be astonishing. Most likely, the flow of blood will taper down as it flows from the Valley of Jezreel (Jehoshaphat, Decision, and Megiddo), into the rift of the Jordan Valley, and onward to the Dead Sea. Scavengers will be invited to clean up the flesh of the slain.

> And I saw an angel standing in the sun, who cried in a loud voice to all the birds flying in mid-air, "Come, gather together for the great supper of God, so that you may eat the flesh of kings, generals, and mighty men, of horses and their riders, and the flesh of all people, free and slave, small and great" (Revelation 19:17-18).

The Wilful King will attempt to counterfeit Christ in every way. "He will pitch his royal tents between the seas at the beautiful holy mountain. Yet he will come to his end, and no one will help him." His goal is to set up a one-world government and one-world religion that worships Him alone. "His royal tents" refer to his palace. "Between the seas at the beautiful holy mountain" is Mount Zion/Moriah, which is Jerusalem. However, the Rock will smash his kingdom and "he will come to his end, and no one will help him."

THE FINAL DELIVERANCE OF ISRAEL (12:1-3). "At that time" refers to the "time of Jacob's trouble" (Jeremiah 30:4-11). Liberal commentators attempt to place "at that time" in the period beginning with the death of Antiochus IV Epiphanes, saying there is no jump from the contemporary scene to some distant future. As previously demonstrated, there is nothing contemporary to Antiochus in Daniel 11:36-45. Moreover, Jesus saw this time as being distant future, even from His day.

> So when you see standing in the holy place "the abomination that causes desolation", spoken of through the prophet Daniel—let the reader understand—then let those who are in Judea flee to the mountains. Let no one on the roof of his house go down to take

anything out of the house. Let no one in the field go back to get his cloak. How dreadful it will be in those days for pregnant women and nursing mothers! Pray that your flight will not take place in winter or on the Sabbath. For then there will be great distress, unequaled from the beginning of the world until now—and never to be equaled again (Matthew 24:15-21).

"At that time Michael, the great prince who protects Israel will arise." In some way, Michael provides the protection necessary for the Israelis to flee to the mountains and desert of Moab and Edom as inferred from Daniel 11:41 and Revelation 12:13-16.

Two-thirds of those in Israel will die during the second half of the seventieth seven (Zechariah 13:8). Evidently, the majority of Israelis will not flee, unlike the Christians living in Jerusalem around A.D. 70, who escaped the ravages of Titus. The surviving one-third of Israel will look on Christ, the One they have pierced, and God will pour out a spirit of grace and supplication on them, and all Israel will be saved (Zechariah 12:10-13:1; Romans 11:26).

Fittingly, Daniel's last prophetic vision jumps to the end of the Tribulation.

> But at that time your people—everyone whose name is found written in the book—will be delivered. Multitudes who sleep in the dust of the earth will awake: some to everlasting life, others to shame and everlasting contempt.

On the one hand, it is likely that Michael, the great prince and archangel, will be associated with the resurrection of the Israelites in light of Jude 9. On the other hand, the dead in Christ will be resurrected, then those who are alive in Christ will be raptured when the Lord Himself comes down from heaven, with a loud command, with the voice of the archangel and with the trumpet call of God (1 Thessalonians 4:16-17).

Do the multitudes, rising to everlasting life, include the Church, OT saints, and Tribulation saints? Yes! Both the OT and NT saints are in Christ. The whole OT Tabernacle system pointed to Christ. The OT saints are saved because their sacrifices, which were offered in faith, were completed in Christ on the Cross. In other words, God accepted, as atonement for sin, the blood of animals until Christ became the once-for-all sacrifice (Hebrews 7:27). Scripture is crystal-clear that salvation is in Christ alone.

> He is "the stone you builders rejected, which has become the capstone." Salvation is found in no one else, for there is no other name under heaven given to men by which we must be saved (Acts 4:11-12).

Thus, everyone (the saints of all ages) whose name is found written in the book, that is the Lamb's Book of Life (Revelation 3:5; 13:8; 21:27), will be מלט (*malat*, delivered, saved or preserved).

There are two resurrections according to Jesus: the *first* unto everlasting life and the *second* unto shame and everlasting contempt.

> Do not be amazed at this, for a time is coming when all who are in their graves will hear his voice and come out—those who have done good will rise to live, and those who have done evil will rise to be condemned (John 5:28-29).

The first resurrection has at least two stages: (1) Church and OT saints and (2) Tribulation saints at the end of the times of distress. The second resurrection occurs after Christ's thousand-year reign on earth, and it is unto eternal damnation (Revelation 20:4-15). Again, the name "Daniel" (God is Judge) connects with his prophecy.

> Those who are wise will shine like the brightness of the heavens, and those who lead many to righteousness, like the stars forever and ever.

Who are the wise?

> The fear of the LORD is the beginning of wisdom, and knowledge of the Holy One is understanding (Proverbs 9:10).

> The fruit of the righteous is a tree of life, and he who wins souls is wise (Proverbs 11:30).

The separate blessings of brightness and stars mentioned by Daniel indicate that the resurrected saints will be rewarded according to what they have done (cf. Romans 14:10; 1 Corinthians 3:11-14; 2 Corinthians 5:10). Daniel is like a star; he led two pagan monarchs, Nebuchadnezzar and Darius the Mede, to righteousness.

What will be Daniel's reward? His on-the-job training as Prime Minister of Babylon and Medo-Persia and his faithful service to God suggests that he might be the Prime Minister of the everlasting kingdom. He is the most qualified! In the end, the saints of Israel will be delivered and rewarded. All's well that ends well!

Applications of Chapter Eleven

Amillennialists and liberals attempt to spiritualize verses 36-45, limiting the battle to between good and evil in this world. Such hermeneutics, in light of the literal fulfillment of the previous thirty-five verses, cannot be justified.

As with all unfulfilled prophecy, filling in the details of its fulfillment is speculative. The overall message is obvious to those with spiritual discernment, however.

Some people worship the gods of sex, pleasure, money, power, and prestige. The Antichrist's god is himself. Actually, he is the ultimate manifestation of man, who rebels against God to worship and serve self. Sadly, people continue to believe the lie that Satan told Eve in the Garden in order to do what they want to do.

> "You will not surely die," the serpent said to the woman. "For God knows that when you eat of it your eyes will be opened, and you will be like God, knowing good and evil" (Genesis 3:4-5).

The people of today's world are like the nation of Israel in the times of the Judges.

> In those days Israel had no king; everyone did as he saw fit" (Judges 21:25).

Unless a person repents (turns from self to God), the same destiny awaits the unsaved as the Wilful King's—the Lake of Fire (Revelation 20:10-15). God is Judge (Daniel) of the one "who will do as he pleases" and "who exalts and magnifies himself above every god."

In the end, God's veracity, His covenants and His sovereign power will keep Israel from being wiped from the face of the earth.

The purpose of the time of distress is Israel's chastisement, purification, and salvation. It will be the catalyst that will bring the nation back into the bond of the Abrahamic Covenant (Romans 11:22-32). God will keep His promise to restore and rule Israel.

> As surely as I live, declares the Sovereign LORD, I will rule over you with a mighty hand and an outstretched arm and with outpoured wrath. I will bring you from the nations and gather you from the countries where you have been scattered—with a mighty hand and an outstretched arm and with outpoured wrath. I will bring you into the desert of the nations and there, face to face, I will execute judgment upon you. As I judged your fathers in the desert of the land of Egypt, so I will judge you, declares the Sovereign LORD. I will take note of you as you pass under my rod, and I will bring you into the bond of the covenant. I will purge you of those who revolt and rebel against me. Although I will bring them out of the land where they are living, yet they will not enter the land of Israel. Then you will know that I am the LORD (Ezekiel 20:33-38).

God will answer the prophet Habakkuk's prayer at the end of the time of distress: "In wrath remember mercy" (Habakkuk 3:2).

Instructions and Inquiries Concerning the Prophecy
(Daniel 12:4-13)

Outline of Chapter Twelve

The Instruction and Prediction, 4
The Conversation and Inquiry, 5-7
The Incomprehension and Inquiry, 8
The Answer and Comprehension, 9-13

Instructions Concerning the Prophecy

THE INSTRUCTION AND PREDICTION (12:4). The preincarnate Christ conveys final instructions for the prophet.

> But you, Daniel, close up and seal the words of the scroll until the time of the end. Many will go here and there to increase knowledge (Daniel 12:4).

Since throughout the book, portions of dreams, visions and prophecies concern the time of the end, "the words of the scroll" appears to indicate the entire prophecy (Daniel 2:28-29, 43-45; 7:17-27; 8:17; 9:27; 10:14; 11:35, 45). The double reference predictions, with both near and distant fulfillments, would have the distant predictions sealed up until the end. The narrative section (chapters 1-6) is typical, foreshadowing future events in the life of Christ, the Antichrist and Israel. Certainly, the typical sections are closed up and sealed until history unfolds their meaning. There are several ways to understand the instruction to "close up and seal the words of the scroll until the time of the end."

1. "Close up and seal" might mean until the prophecy is fulfilled or until history unfolds the prophecy, which is especially true of types.

2. "Close up and seal" might indicate the prophecy is completed. There is nothing more for Daniel to write.

3. "Close up and seal" might indicate that the predictions are not to occur until the time of the end. In Revelation 5-6, the Lamb (Christ) alone is found worthy to look in the scroll and open its seven seals. When the Lamb opens the first seal of the scroll (the title deed to the earth), the rider on a white horse inaugurates the Tribulation Period.

4. "Close up and seal" might refer to its safekeeping, especially from tampering. "Close up" would indicate that the text is unchangeable and "Seal" would indicate that it is an official text.

In contrast, the apostle John was told to do the opposite with the Apocalypse of Jesus Christ.

Then he told me, "Do not seal up the words of the prophecy of this book, because the time is near" (Revelation 22:10).

Since the book of Revelation fills in many details of Daniel's wide-ranging outline of God's plan for the end times, are the prophecies in Daniel now open and unsealed? If so, in what sense is it open and unsealed? Certainly, the book has been preserved, even though it has suffered much criticism.

The Lord gives what appears to be a time marker that must occur before the unsealing of the prophecies.

Many will go here and there [run to and fro] to increase knowledge (Daniel 12:4).

There are several ways to understand this time marker.

1. Does "run to and fro" refer to the fulfillment of the prophecy? That would be the case with all the prophecies that have been literally fulfilled from Daniel to Christ as people "run to and fro" completing the predictions.

2. Does "run to and fro" refer to a time when many travel back and forth and have increased knowledge? (Such as archeologists who travel the world to discover and understand the past).

3. Does "run to and fro" refer to searching?

The prophets Amos and Jeremiah use the phrase in the latter sense.

> And they shall wander from sea to sea, and from the north even to the east, they shall run to and fro to seek the word of the LORD, and shall not find it (Amos 8:12, KJV).

> Run ye to and fro through the streets of Jerusalem, and see now, and know, and seek in the broad places thereof, if ye can find a man, if there be any that executeth judgment, that seeketh the truth; and I will pardon it (Jeremiah 5:1, KJV).

From the time of Daniel to the destruction of the Temple in A.D. 70, Bible knowledge had greatly increased. Think of all the prophecies in chapter eleven of Daniel that had been revealed and fulfilled. Since the time of Jerome in A.D. 400, there has been a corresponding increase in knowledge, due to the rise in archaeological discoveries of ancient inscriptions and literature, accompanied by the study of linguistics. Add to all of these discoveries, Israel's nationhood in 1948; the daily flow of Jews from all over the world to the Holy Land; and the birth of the European Union accompanied by a great falling away from Christianity in Europe. As we study Daniel, time passes and knowledge of the Word of God increases.

We understand the scroll better than the prophet Daniel did! Even so, the fullest understanding of Daniel will not come until the last half of the Tribulation. Leon Wood offers a helpful paraphrase of this difficult verse.

> Many shall run to and fro in their desire for knowledge of the last things, and, finding it in Daniel's book, because it will have been preserved to this end, their knowledge shall be increased (*A Commentary on Daniel*, 321).

During the Tribulation Period, Daniel will become an open book. Its predictions will be unsealed because of their fulfillment. The prophecies will become clearest to those living through the events.

Inquiries Concerning the Prophecy

THE CONVERSATION AND INQUIRY (12:5-7). Daniel saw in his vision three men, one is clothed in linen and standing above the waters of the Tigris; the other two are on the opposite bank. Two of the three men are most likely angels. The third, dressed in white linen, is Christ. This brings to mind the LORD appearing with two angels before Abraham prior to the destruction of Sodom and Gomorrah (cf. Genesis 18:1-2; 19:1) and the two men dressed in white at the ascension of Christ (Acts 1:10-11).

In the NT, we are told, "even angels long to look into these things" (1 Peter 1:12). Thus, we should not be surprised when one of the two angels asks, "How long will it be before these astonishing things are fulfilled?" This inquiry is more than a casual one of interest since angels are involved in the great conflict. Perhaps they are weary of fighting demons and desire a quick fulfillment of the predictions.

> The man clothed in linen, who was above the waters of the river, lifted his right hand and his left hand towards heaven, and I heard him swear by him who lives forever, saying, "It will be for a time, times and half a time. When the power of the holy people has been finally broken, all these things will be completed."

What astonishing things will last for "a time, times and half a time?" The Antichrist's terror will occur from the middle of the Tribulation to its end, a period of three and one-half years. One purpose of the Tribulation is to devastate Israel—to break the power of the people God has set aside for Himself. Until the Jews become a broken people, they will not repent and turn to Christ. When all Israel is saved, all these things have been completed. When the Jews have a beatitude attitude, the promise of the kingdom of heaven is theirs (Matthew 5:3-12).

Those who believe prophecy that refers to the Church, when it speaks of Israel, should consider this prediction. Is it God's purpose to break the power of Christ's bride? It is wayward Israel that needs to become broken and return to God, which is superbly foreshadowed in the prophet Hosea's reconciliation with his adulteress wife, Gomer, after the power of her prostitution is broken.

> The LORD said to me, "Go, show your love to your wife again, though she is loved by another and is an adulteress. Love her as the LORD loves the Israelites, though they turn to other gods and love the sacred raisin cakes." So I bought her for fifteen shekels of silver and about a homer and a lethek of barley. Then I told her, "You are to live with me for many days; you must not be a prostitute or be intimate with any man, and I will live with you." For the Israelites will live for many days without king or prince, without sacrifice or sacred stones, without ephod or idol. Afterwards the Israelites will return and seek the LORD their God and David their king. They will come trembling to the LORD and to his blessings in the last days (Hosea 3:1-5).

The second half of the Tribulation Period will break the power of Israel and drive the holy (set apart) people to the Word of God to seek the answers as to what is taking place. In the Scriptures (especially Daniel), the Jews will find the answers; but best of all they will find Christ!

THE INCOMPREHENSION AND INQUIRY (12:8). Daniel addresses the man in fine white linen as אֲדֹנִי (*'adoni*, my Lord). Daniel did not comprehend what he heard, so he asked, "My lord, what will the outcome of all this be?"

We know the outcome of many of the predictions in the prophet's book; Daniel did not! The blank spaces between the lines were yet to be filled in by later prophets and writers of Scripture as well as history. Yet, much remains to be decoded, for many events and people are still future.

THE ANSWER AND COMPREHENSION (12:9-13). The Lord's reply to Daniel's question begins as a sharp rebuke; then He decides to bestow additional information to help Daniel comprehend the outcome.

> Go your way, Daniel, because the words are closed up and sealed until the time of the end. Many will be purified, made spotless and refined, but the wicked will continue to be wicked. None of the wicked will understand, but those who are wise will understand.

The Scriptures reveal all that we are to know about the future. The Word of God is of the Holy Spirit and it is not comprehended by the unsaved. In fact, "the message of the cross is foolishness to those who are perishing, but to us who are being saved it is the power of God" (1 Corinthians 1:18). Again, Proverbs 9:10 is a key that unlocks the Bible:

> The fear of the LORD is the beginning of wisdom, and knowledge of the Holy One is understanding.

Daniel said, "I heard, but I did not understand." His problem does not reside in the fear of the LORD; it is God's limitation on what He will allow to be understood at this particular time in history.

The Lord encourages Daniel by telling him that the purpose of the time of distress is to purify many and to make them spotless and refined. The greatest harvest of souls will occur during this seven-year period (Revelation 7:9-17). There will be no middle road for the atheists and agnostics in this period. One will receive the mark of the beast and worship his image or turn to Christ and face the possibility of being martyred.

The final prediction given to Daniel foretells the chronology of the time of distress.

> From the time that the daily sacrifice is abolished and the abomination that causes desolation is set up, there will be 1,290 days. Blessed is the one who waits for and reaches the end of the 1,335 days (Daniel 12:11-12).

The date on which the Antichrist confirms the covenant marks the beginning of the Tribulation Period and the middle of the Tribulation will be marked by the abomination that causes desolation. Those living on earth at that time, with Bible in hand, will need no fancy calculation to figure out the time of Christ's second coming.

The "sixty-nine sevens" reveals the exact date for Christ's presentation of Himself as Israel's King and Passover Lamb. The exact date of His second coming as KING OF KINGS AND LORD OF LORDS is recorded here. This time, the wise should not miss it!

The following chart shows the specific periods, which will be measurable in the end times.

The Tribulation Saints Can Know the Day

From the Abomination that Causes Desolation, there will be associated with the Return of Christ:

3 1/2 years (Daniel 9:27; 12:7; Revelation 12:4)
42 months (Revelation 13:5)
1,260 days (Revelation 12:6)
1,290 days (Daniel 12:11)
1,335 days (Daniel 12:12)

The day that "the abomination that causes desolation" is set up, the entire world will be commanded to worship the image. Israel will flee into the desert to a place prepared for her by God, where she might be taken care of for 1,260 days. At this point, everyone can begin counting the years, months, and days to the Second Advent of Christ.

Christ will return to earth on day 1,260. What will happen on days 1,290 and 1,335? Scripture does not spell it out. An educated guess is that after Christ returns, it will take 30 days to gather the survivors (the nations) to Jerusalem, and another 45 days for the separation of the sheep and goats.

All the nations will be gathered before him, and he will separate the people one from another as a shepherd separates the sheep from the goats. He will put the sheep on his right and the goats on his left. Then the King will say to those on his right, "Come, you who are blessed by my Father; take your inheritance, the kingdom prepared for you since the creation of the world" (Matthew 25:32-34).

Accordingly, day 1,335 commences the Millennial Kingdom and the blessed ones (the sheep) enter it on this day. Furthermore, these extra days allow for the purification of the Temple and the assembling of God's people for its dedication (cf. Ezekiel 43:1-12; 45:18-20). Typical prophecy of Daniel 8:14 requires that the Temple be reconsecrated as it had been on December 25, 165 B.C. It is noteworthy that Hezekiah postponed Passover for one month (thirty days) in order to allow time for enough priests to consecrate themselves and for the people to assemble at the Temple (2 Chronicles 30:2-4).

The final part of this vision began "many will go here and there to increase knowledge." It will be impossible to miss the beginning date of the last three and one-half years of the Tribulation according to Jesus.

> So when you see standing in the holy place "the abomination that causes desolation", spoken of through the prophet Daniel—let the reader understand—then let those who are in Judea flee to the mountains (Matthew 24:15-16).

When the image of the beast is erected, the wise will have increased in knowledge, thereby, being able to count down the arrival of Christ from that day.

If this is so, what are we to make of passages like "therefore keep watch, because you do not know the day or the hour" (Matthew 25:13)? In short, Scripture presents a *known day* and an *unknown day*. Since the Bible never contradicts itself, there must be two days. Christ comes, not once, but twice—once in the air for His Church and once to the earth as the Rock, who smashes the nations in order to establish the everlasting kingdom and His thousand-year reign.

True to the pattern of Scripture, the Lord's parting words to Daniel promise comfort and hope.

> As for you, go your way till the end. You will rest, and then at the end of the days you will rise to receive your allotted inheritance (Daniel 12:13).

God's faithful servant is numbered with the wise! What words of assurance: Go, rest, rise! "Go your way to the end" speaks of the prophet's spirit and soul going to Sheol, the place of the departed dead. Jesus described this place as Abraham's side (Luke 16:22) and called it Paradise (Luke 23:43). Daniel's body would return to dust and rest in the ground until the end. Afterward his body would be resurrected and he would stand before His Lord and receive his allotted inheritance.

Interestingly, Daniel was told that he was highly esteemed three times (Daniel 9:25; 10:4, 19). He was a prime minister in the empires of Babylon and Medo-Persia. His allotted inheritance just might be as prime minister of a third kingdom—Christ's.

Daniel is on the winning side of the great conflict! Nothing can separate him from his allotted inheritance in the kingdom of God. It is based on the promise of Christ! It is written in the Book of Truth! It is not hard to imagine Daniel going away from this vision giving thanks to the Most High God. Daniel is not unique; all born-again believers have this hope and praise of gratitude in their hearts.

> For I am convinced that neither death nor life, neither angels nor demons, neither the present nor the future, nor any powers, neither height nor depth, nor anything else in all creation, will be able to separate us from the love of God that is in Christ Jesus our Lord (Romans 8:38-39).

With the Apostle Paul, we can give thanks to the Father, who has qualified believers to share in the inheritance of the saints in the kingdom of light (Colossians 1:12). As for you, is this your hope?

Applications of Chapter Twelve

History is God's story! His prophets have written it down in the Holy Scriptures, the Bible. The wise, who diligently search the Scriptures, will understand what He has revealed about the future. Therefore,

> Do your best to present yourself to God as one approved, a workman who does not need to be ashamed and who correctly handles the word of truth (2 Timothy 2:15).

Do not miss what the Bible says about the coming of Christ. Jesus chastised the Jews of His day for not understanding and believing what the OT foretold about Him.

> And the Father who sent me has himself testified concerning me.

You have never heard his voice nor seen his form, nor does his word dwell in you, for you do not believe the one he sent. You diligently study the Scriptures because you think that by them you possess eternal life. These are the Scriptures that testify about me, yet you refuse to come to me to have life (John 5:37-40).

The book of Daniel predicts the two advents of Christ. It predicted that God's people would not receive Him the first time. All Israel, however, will be saved before He comes the second time to reign as KING OF KINGS AND LORD OF LORDS.

Like Daniel, we will not understand everything! Nevertheless, we should have the same burning desire to know and understand more about God's plans for the future. Ask questions as you read the Word of God. There is a wealth of knowledge in the Scriptures for our digging out and decoding. What we do understand will build our faith in God, our hope of eternity, and our love for the Anointed One, who was cut off and had nothing so we might have everything—our allotted inheritance in His kingdom.

Daniel was God's man for his times for many reasons; several reasons stand out:

1. His faithfulness to God and His Word while in a pagan world
2. His persistence in prayer
3. His testimony of the Most High God before peers and superiors
4. His desire to know and understand the things of God

DARE TO BE A DANIEL!

BIBLIOGRAPHY

Anderson, Robert. THE COMING PRINCE.
Grand Rapids: Kregel Publications, 1984.

Archer, Gleason L. IN THE EXPOSITOR'S BIBLE COMMENTARY: DANIEL.
Volume 7. Grand Rapids: Zondervan Publishing House, 1985.

Blair, J. Allen. DANIEL: DEVOTIONAL STUDIES ON LIVING COURAGEOUSLY.
Neptune, New Jersey: Loizeaux Brothers, 1971.

Boutflower, Charles. IN AND AROUND THE BOOK OF DANIEL.
London , New York, Toronto: The MacMillan Co., 1923.

Bullock, C. Hassell. AN INTRODUCTION TO THE OLD TESTAMENT PROPHETIC
BOOKS. Chicago: Moody Press, 1986.

Campbell, Donald K. DANIEL: DECODER OF DREAMS.
Wheaton: Victor Books, 1977.

Clarke, Adam. COMMENTARY ON THE BIBLE.
Published in 1832: Online Bible Electronic Texts by Sulu D. Kelley, 1997.

Collins, John J. A COMMENTARY ON THE BOOK OF DANIEL.
Minneapolis: Fortress Press, 1993.

Dake, Finis Jennings. DAKE'S ANNOTATED REFERENCE BIBLE.
Lawrenceville, Georgia: Dake Bible Sales, Inc. 1963.

DeHaan, M. R. DANIEL THE PROPHET: 35 SIMPLE STUDIES IN THE BOOK OF
DANIEL.
Grand Rapids: Zondervan Publishing House, 1947.

Durant, Will. THE STORY OF CIVILIZATION: OUR ORIENTAL HERITAGE.
Volume 1. New York: Simon and Schuster, 1954.

Freeman, Hobart. E. AN INTRODUCTION TO THE OLD TESTAMENT PROPHETS.
Chicago: Moody Press, 1968.

Gammie, John G. DANIEL.
Atlanta: John Knox Press, 1983.

Glubb, Sir John. THE FATE OF EMPIRES AND SEARCH FOR SURVIVAL.
Edinburgh, Scotland: William Blackwood and Sons, Ltd, 1981.

Gonzalez, Jorge. DANIEL: A TRACT FOR TROUBLED TIMES.
New York: The United Methodist Church, 1985.

Greene, Oliver B. DANIEL: VERSE BY VERSE STUDY.
Greenville, South Carolina: The Gospel Hour, Inc., 1964.

Hoehner, Harold W. CHRONOLOGICAL ASPECTS OF THE LIFE OF CHRIST.
Grand Rapids: Zondervan Publishing House, 1977.

Hummel, Horace D. THE WORD BECOMING FLESH: AN INTRODUCTION OF
THE ORIGIN, PURPOSE, AND MEANING OF THE OLD TESTAMENT.
St. Louis: Concordia Publishing House, 1979.

Jeffery, Arthur and Kennedy, Gerald. THE BOOK OF DANIEL. In The Interpreters
Bible, Volume 6. New York: Abingdon Press, 1956.

Keil, C. F. COMMENTARY ON THE OLD TESTAMENT: EZEKIEL, DANIEL.
Volume 9. Grand Rapids: William B. Eerdmans Publishing Co.

Kent, Homer A. Jr. DANIEL XI—THE PROPHECY CONCERNING THE NATIONS
(11:2-35). Winona Lake, Indiana: Unpublished class notes from Grace Theological
Seminary, 1986.

Larkin, Clarence. THE BOOK OF DANIEL.
Philadelphia: Rev Clarence Larkin Estate, 1929.

Laure, Gerald A. BABYLON AND THE BIBLE.
Grand Rapids: Baker Book House, 1969.

Harrison, Ronald K. INTRODUCTION TO THE OLD TESTAMENT.
Grand Rapids: William B. Eredmans Publishing Company, 1969.

MacArthur, John, Jr. AN UNCOMPROMISING LIFE.
Panorama City, California: Word of Grace Communications, 1983.

MacArthur, John, Jr. THE COMING KING.
Panorama City, California: Word of Grace Communications, 1983.

MacArthur, John, Jr. THE FUTURE OF ISRAEL.
Panorama City, California: Word of Grace Communications, 1985.

MacArthur, John, Jr. THE RISE AND FALL OF THE WORLD.
Panorama City, California: Word of Grace Communications, 1984.

McClain, Alva J. DANIEL'S PROPHECY OF THE 70 WEEKS.
Grand Rapids: Zondervan Publishing House, 1940.

Payne, J. Barton. ENCYCLOPEDIA OF BIBLICAL PROPHECY.
Grand Rapids; Baker Book House, 1973.

Pentecost, J. Dwight. DANIEL. The Bible Knowledge Commentary: Old Testament,
Wheaton: Victor Books, 1985.

Pettingill, William L. SIMPLE STUDIES IN DANIEL.
Wilmington: Just A Word Incorporated, 1933.

Porteous, Norman W. DANIEL: A COMMENTARY.
Philadelphia: The Westminster Press, 1965.

Pritchard, J. B., editor. ANET
Princeton: Princeton University Press, 1969.

Rawlinson, H. HISTORICAL EVIDENCES OF THE TRUTH OF THE SCRIPTURAL
RECORDS, 1859.

Rox, George. ANCIENT IRAQ.
Middlesex, England: Penguin Books, 1964.

Saunders, Lowell. DANIEL SPEAKS TO TEENS.
Denver: Baptist Publication, 1971.

Showers, Renald E. THE MOST HIGH GOD: A COMMENTARY ON THE BOOK OF
DANIEL. Bellmawr, New Jersey: The Friends of Israel Gospel Ministry, Inc. 1982.

Spence, H. D. M. and Exell, Joseph S. THE PULPIT COMMENTARY: DANIEL,
HOSEA & JOEL. Volume 13. Grand Rapids: Wm. B. Eerdmans Publishing Co.,
reprinted 1983.

Strauss, Lehman. THE PROPHECIES OF DANIEL.
Neptune, New Jersey; Loizeaux Brothers, 1969.

Thomas, D. Winton, Editor. DOCUMENTS FROM OLD TESTAMENT TIMES.
New York: Harpers & Row Publishers, 1958.

Unger, Merrill F. ARCHAEOLOGY AND THE OLD TESTAMENT.
Grand Rapids: Zondervan Publishing House, 1954.

Unger, Merrill F. UNGER'S COMMENTARY ON THE OLD TESTAMENT:
ISAIAH-MALACHI. Volume 2. Chicago: Moody Press, 1981.

Walvoord, John F. MAJOR BIBLE PROPHECIES: 37 CRUCIAL PROPHECIES THAT AFFECT YOU TODAY. Grand Rapids: Zondervan Publishing House, 1991.

Walvoord, John F. DANIEL: KEY TO PROPHETIC REVELATION Chicago: Moody Press, 1971.

Walvoord, John F. THE PROPHECY KNOWLEDGE HANDBOOK. Wheaton: Victor Books, 1990.

Wesley, John. JOHN WESLEY'S NOTES ON THE NEW TESTAMENT. Published in 1767: Online Bible Electronic Texts 1997 by Sulu D. Kelley.

Wetzel, R. C. A Chronology of Biblical Christianity. Albany, Oregon: AGES Software, 1997.

Whitcomb, John C. DANIEL. Chicago: Moody Press, 1985.

Willett, Herbert L. DANIEL. In the Abingdon Bible Commentary. New York: Abingdon-Cokesbury Press, 1929.

Wilson, Robert Dick. STUDIES IN THE BOOK OF DANIEL. Grand Rapids: Baker Book House, 1917.

Whiston, William, Translator. THE WORKS OF JOSEPHUS. Peabody, Massachusetts: Hendrickson Publishers, 1985.

Wood, Leon. A COMMENTARY ON DANIEL. Grand Rapids: Zondervan Publishing House, 1973.

Encyclopedias, Dictionaries, Lexicons

A Concise Hebrew and Aramaic Lexicon of the Old Testament, William L. Holiday, Editor

Cyclopedia of Biblical, Theological, and Ecclesiastical Literature by John McClintock and James Strong.

Encyclopedia Britannica, 1949 and 1999.

Hastings Dictionary of the Bible.

Old Testament Word Studies by William Wilson.

Strong's Exhaustive Concordance.

The Analytical Hebrew and Chaldee Lexicon by Benjamin Davidson.

The International Standard Bible Encyclopedia, James Orr, General Editor.

The New Brown, Driver, and Briggs Hebrew and English Lexicon
    of the Old Testament.

The Revell Bible Dictionary.

The Zondervan Pictorial Encyclopedia, Merrill C. Tenney, General Editor.

Theological Wordbook of the Old Testament, R. Larid Harris, Editor.

Unger's Bible Dictionary.

Vine's Expository Dictionary of Biblical Words.

ABOUT THE AUTHOR

Robert P. Conway holds a Master of Divinity Degree from Grace Theological Seminary, Winona Lake, Indiana. He has studied on four occasions with Jerusalem University College in the land of Israel and he is a graduate of the York Bible Training Institute.

Bob is an ordained minister in the Church of the United Brethren in Christ. He retired as a senior pastor in 2004.

Before entering into the pastoral ministry for seventeen years, Bob was a vice president in the senior management of a bank's trust division. He graduated from American Institute of Banking, National Graduate Trust School of Northwestern University and was a Certified Financial Services Counselor of the American Bankers Association.

He has been teaching Bible, Theology and Biblical Hebrew for the past eight years at Regent College of the Caribbean, Mandeville, Jamaica WI.

Bob has taught many courses for continuing education credits for pastors, spoken at conferences and taught at various Bible institutes.

Bob and his wife Lois will celebrate their fiftieth wedding anniversary in 2014. They have worked side by side in various ministries, especially enjoying the pastorate along with teaching at youth and children's camps for some forty years.

Bob has been an avid student of the Bible, which he has been teaching for almost fifty years. He has self-published thirty books. Eight of his books can be read online at www.decodingdaniel.com.

Made in the USA
Lexington, KY
11 August 2014